Hannah Arendt and Education

Hannah Arendt
and
Education

Renewing Our Common World

MORDECHAI GORDON

Westview PRESS
A Member of the Perseus Books Group

Copyright © 2001 by Westview Press, A Member of the Perseus Books Group

Published in 2001 in the United States of America by Westview Press, 5500 Central Avenue, Boulder, Colorado 80301-2877, and in the United Kingdom by Westview Press, 12 Hid's Copse Road, Cumnor Hill, Oxford OX2 9JJ

Find us on the World Wide Web at www.westviewpress.com

Library of Congress Cataloging-in-Publication Data

Hannah Arendt and education : renewing our common world / edited by Mordechai Gordon.
    p.   cm.
  Includes bibliographical references and index.
  ISBN 0-8133-6632-1 — ISBN 0-8133-3964-2 (pbk.)
  1. Arendt, Hannah—Views on education. 2. Education—Philosophy. I. Gordon, Mordechai

 LB880.A652 H36   2001
 370'.1—dc21

  The paper used in this publication meets the requirements of the American National Standard for Permanence of Paper for Printed Library Materials Z39.48-1984.

10   9   8   7   6   5   4   3   2   1

For my daughter
JULIA,

and for

GABRIELA,
*who has helped me renew
a common world.*

Contents

Foreword

MAXINE GREENE

Since I began teaching educational philosophy, Hannah Arendt's work has given rise to what I conceive to be the most significant themes in my professional life. They have been interwoven, it is true, with some of John Dewey's ideas and certain fundamental existential preoccupations, particularly those of Maurice Merleau-Ponty. But Arendt's notions of thought and thoughtlessness, her emphasis on the necessity to "stop and think" at moments of decision, and her linking of human freedom to action in a public space have opened (and continue to open) for me a great range of perspectives on the "common world" and on the education that might bring it into existence and keep it alive. Because of all that, I welcome this rich and many-faceted book. As its editor makes clear, the connections between education and politics are explored as never before in this field. So are the relations between Arendt's notions of natality, tradition, and authority and what happens in colleges and universities.

Reading these thoughtful and often critical essays, I cannot but recall the class I once took with Hannah Arendt on "History of the Will." I remember her free associations as she wrote a quotation from Cicero on the blackboard, followed by one from Dostoyevsky and another from Faulkner. We were often present to a demonstration of what Dr. Gordon so well describes as tradition viewed as "a series of innovations, itself full of breaks and fissures and the kinds of reinventions that the young can make." Pondering this notion of tradition and its implications for education, I have continually returned to Arendt's conclusion in her chapter on education in *Between Past and Future:*

> Education is the point at which we decide whether we love the world enough to assume responsibility for it and by the same token save it from the ruin which, except for renewal, except for the coming of the new and young, would be inevitable. And education, too, is where we decide whether we love our children enough not to expel them from our world and leave them to their own devices, nor to strike from their hands their chance of undertaking something new, something unforeseen by us, but to prepare them in advance for the task of renewing a common world.

This book seems to me to be among the first to explore the multiple meanings suggested here. The writers, even in the course of their explorations, make explicit the criticisms from the "critical" side and from the conservative side; and the reader may well find herself/himself with a clearer vision of the tensions and anticipations within education today, "dark times" or no.

Gateways of many kinds are opened by this book. Mordechai Gordon and his fellow explorers bring important new voices to the conversation about what it means to teach and what it means to learn.

—Maxine Greene

Acknowledgments

First of all, I would like to thank Sarah Warner, Catherine Murphy, and Katharine Chandler, my editors at Westview Press, who showed patience, gave invaluable insights, and provided me with great support throughout the work on this project. I am also grateful to all of the contributors to this collection: Kim Curtis, Eduardo Duarte, Peter Euben, Maxine Greene, Jerome Kohn, Ann Lane, Natasha Levinson, Aaron Schutz, Stacy Smith, and Elisabeth Young-Bruehl. This book would not have been possible without their dedication and efforts to bring it to fruition. Finally, I wish to thank Joe Kincheloe and Shirley Steinberg, great friends and series editors, who believed in this project from the very outset and gave me constant support and feedback.

Introduction

MORDECHAI GORDON

In recent years, there has been a renewed interest in the life and works of Hannah Arendt. Just in the past few years, the publication of three volumes of Arendt's correspondence with Karl Jaspers, Martin Heidegger, and Mary McCarthy has enriched our understanding of her life as well as of her development as a thinker. Moreover, a number of stimulating collections of essays devoted to Arendt's contributions to fields such as political theory, ethics, and feminism have been published recently. With all of this renewed interest in Arendt, a discussion of the significance of her insights for educational theory and practice is notably missing. A review of the literature indicates that very little has been written on the educational implications of Arendt's ideas. *Hannah Arendt and Education: Renewing Our Common World* is intended as an initial response to this lack.

One of the main themes recurring throughout this volume is the need to take Arendt's ideas on education seriously and to engage them critically. For example, many of the contributors to this collection challenge Arendt's view that politics and education are two very different realms that should be kept separate. Yet, although these authors maintain that Arendt's distinction between the political and educational realms is highly controversial, they also acknowledge that this distinction is important because it provokes us to reexamine the manifold relationships of education and politics. In this sense, the authors of this book are following the lead of Seyla Benhabib, who proposes to "think with Arendt against Arendt."[1] Particularly for scholars, educators, and administrators who are inter-

ested in topics such as "democratic education," "engaged pedagogy," "multicultural education," and "ideology and the curriculum," the essays in this collection provide great insights into the
lively debates being waged.

Most scholars who have attempted to analyze the connections between politics and education approach this issue from a "critical-
revolutionary" perspective. Thus, critical theorists, feminists, radical
educators, minority intellectuals, and others have not only uncov-
ered the ways in which the political, economic, and cultural powers
in the United States impact the education system on all levels; they
have also proposed alternative approaches to educating, ranging
from more representative curricula and new teaching methods to
radically different ways of establishing and running schools. What
unites these scholars is the conviction that the education systems in
this country perpetuate and reinforce gender, racial, class, and other
injustices. They argue that only a radical change in the way we think
about and practice education can begin to correct these huge injustices and "savage inequalities."

Although the essays in this volume are generally very sympathetic
to the critical-revolutionary tradition, many of the authors maintain
that the perspective from which to interrogate the relationships between politics and education needs to be expanded. Another central
thread that connects all of the essays in this collection is, therefore,
the conviction that Hannah Arendt offers a unique voice that can
enhance the critical tradition's call for transforming education so
that it can foster the values of democratic citizenship and social justice. Arendt provides us with a way of conceptualizing the educators' relationship to the past and tradition that is different from that
of both mainstream conservatives and critical theorists. Mainstream
conservatives view the past and tradition uncritically and regard the
ideas and values of Western culture as a continuous source of knowledge that can be used to alleviate our present predicaments. Conservatives believe that education should be aimed at instilling these
ideas and values in our students so that they will embrace and even
emulate them.[2]

Radical theorists and educators have all too often taken the opposite position by associating the past and tradition with the logic of

domination. In this view, the Western canon serves the interests of the dominant groups in our society, since it has been continuously used to legitimize their own values as well as to marginalize and disconfirm the knowledge and experience of subordinate groups. This position is based on the assumption that schools function primarily as agencies of reproduction and domination. From this perspective, tradition and the past are regarded as negative and oppressive forces that have no emancipatory value.[3]

As opposed to mainstream conservatives, Arendt does not view tradition as a seam that connects one generation to the next and endows human civilization with unity and significance. Neither does she take the radical approach of associating the past and tradition with the logic of domination. For Arendt, tradition should be conceived as a series of innovations, itself full of breaks and fissures and the kinds of reinventions that the young can make. In her view, the task is not to revitalize our ties with tradition and the past. It is rather to discover those ideas and values that, though they have undergone change, have survived in a different form and can be used to interrupt, critique, and transform the present. Unlike mainstream conservatives who want to use these ideas and values to bridge the gap between the past and the present, Arendt wants to use them for the sake of creating a new beginning. Moreover, as opposed to many radical theorists who primarily view this tradition critically and negatively, she believes that it can be used to foster a liberating pedagogy that empowers students to make changes and create something new. Thus, the authors of this collection believe that Arendt's unique way of conceptualizing the past and tradition has serious implications for education in a democratic society that need to be taken seriously. Many of these implications are explored in the essays that follow.

The third, and most important, unifying theme of this book is the focus on civic or democratic education. All of the essays in this volume are concerned with civic issues, such as the aims of a democratic education, the significance of multiculturalism, overcoming racial conflicts and tensions, and how to foster a critical and active citizenry. Two underlying assumptions held by many of the authors are that the present apathetic state of public affairs in the United States is intolerable and that education has a crucial role to play in transforming this state of affairs. Specifically, the contributors to this volume share the conviction that there is something wrong with a democratic society in which less than half of the eligible citizens vote in the national elections and few are involved in public affairs, in which there is a huge disparity between rich and poor, and which has a growing culture of violence but no culture of public discourse and civic action. It is a society, to borrow a phrase from Joe Kincheloe, "that consistently rewards the privileged for their privilege and that punishes the marginalized for their marginalization."[4] The contributors to this volume believe that Hannah Arendt's insights presented here can greatly contribute to the current debate on civic education and on the role of education in a democratic society.

Interestingly, although Arendt was not an educator and wrote very little on educational issues, her writings address a wide array of political concepts—such as natality, action, freedom, equality, public space, and plurality—that are particularly relevant for democratic societies. Indeed, the first four chapters of this book focus on four different Arendtian concepts that have serious implications for a number of the debates being waged regarding education in a democratic society. In the first chapter, Natasha Levinson explores the challenges posed by the condition of "natality" to the ways in which those of us engaged in multicultural and antiracist education prepare ourselves and our students for the inevitable and necessary frustrations we are likely to encounter when we attempt to engage in dialogues across racial differences. Natality, or the capacity to initiate the unexpected in a world that is increasingly skeptical of the possibility that newness can enter its domain, is central to Arendt's conception of political action. Levinson's chapter, titled "The Paradox of Natality: Teaching in the Midst of Belatedness," highlights the paradox of natality that threads through Arendt's essay "The Crisis in Education," as well as her larger inquiry into the conditions that make political action possible in *The Human Condition*. Levinson's chapter also considers the conditions of belatedness and plurality that work against natality and mitigate against the likelihood of social transformation. She shows that the concept of natality helps us better understand the many frustrations that attend efforts to dialogue across racial differences. Her hope is that this understanding will give us insight into the ways in which those encounters that often seem to accomplish so little might instead be a sign of the potential for newness to enter the world.

My own chapter, "Hannah Arendt on Authority: Conservatism in Education Reconsidered," follows and begins with the assumption that most conservative approaches to education emphasize the need to teach worthy subjects and fundamental moral values to the young. One rarely encounters a conservative educator who believes in providing students with opportunities for change and innovation. In contrast, I present Hannah Arendt's conservatism as an exception to this trend and argue that her insights on authority need to be taken seriously by democratic educators. Although Arendt favors maintaining a traditional notion of authority in education, she also insists that teachers should foster the revolutionary and the innovative in children. In effect, she helps us bridge the gap between the old (tradition) and the new (change), a problem that has troubled educators for centuries. I also argue that, unlike the views of mainstream conservatives, Arendt's conception of pedagogical authority has a number of important implications for democratic education. As such, her approach to education is not only much more convincing than mainstream conservative arguments, but it also constitutes a genuine contribution to the debate over the aims of schooling in a democratic society.

In Chapter 3, "Education for Judgment: An Arendtian Oxymoron?" Stacy Smith analyzes the tensions and possibilities of the project of "education for judgment" within Arendt's political philosophy. Smith argues that Arendt's views on judgment and politics suggest a pivotal role for democratic education in cultivating the faculty of judgment in future citizens. Moving from Kant's claim that judgment is "a peculiar talent which can be practiced only and cannot be taught," she elaborates a conception of practice as preparation that complicates Arendt's strict distinction between the domain of politics and the domain of education. In Smith's view, education for judgment is fundamental to Arendt's self-proclaimed project of preparing young people for "the task of renewing a common world."

Aaron Schutz, in "Contesting Utopianism: Hannah Arendt and the Tensions of Democratic Education," shows that there is a kind of utopian impulse informing the writings of many educational scholars on the idea of educational democracy. Schutz focuses on the vision of democracy most indebted to the work of John Dewey and draws on Arendt's writings on "public space" as a counter to this impulse. In contrast to many recent scholars, Arendt concentrates on fundamental and sometimes tragic limitations inherent in participation in an egalitarian collaborative community. After laying out Arendt's vision, Schutz explores an actual example of an effort to initiate students into a practice of democratic action, indicating some of the possibilities and limitations of her vision in particular contexts. He concludes by suggesting that we need multiple and sometimes conflicting models of democracy and democratic education if we hope to capture the promise of democratic action in the often contradictory flux of real educational settings.

The next two chapters in this volume address the question of whether Hannah Arendt's ideas have any significance for the advocates of multicultural education. In Chapter 5, Kimberley Curtis answers this question—with qualifications—affirmatively, for she believes that Arendt's educational conservatism both illuminates and underscores multiculturalism's deepest impulse. Curtis reminds us in "Multicultural Education and Arendtian Conservatism: On Memory, Historical Injury, and Our Sense of the Common" that advocates of multicultural education are not only partisans of identity groups; they are partisans of the world in an Arendtian sense. They seek to broaden and make more plural the experiences and perspectives—the in-between of the world—through which our sense of who "we" are is born. What drives them back in time to unearth and reinterpret the historical record are injuries and deprivations, forms of oblivion and exclusion suffered by groups that deform and make less common our common world. In this respect, far from inviting the dangers of fragmentation and enclave politics, multicultural education at its best makes our world more vividly, more actively held in common. Curtis's analysis draws on examples of Chicano/Chicana scholarship and makes the case that multicultural pedagogy must be informed by a probing understanding of both the entwinements and the tensions between politics and education. She suggests that Arendtian conservatism is a rich resource for rethinking multicultural pedagogy toward these ends.

Ann Lane's chapter, "Is Hannah Arendt a Multiculturalist?" continues the discussion on the relevance of Arendt's ideas for multicultural education. Lane illustrates how Arendt's depiction of Jewish pariahs, her arguments about the dangers of refounding community on the basis of suffering, her analysis of the development of totalitarianism, and her contentions about the co-responsibility of "victims" are all significant for her students. She points out that whereas the new wave of literature on Arendt engages her thought in refreshingly sophisticated ways, many of these commentaries view Arendt against a backdrop of philosophical debates or in the context of an abstract struggle of ideas about political life. For Lane's students, however, Arendt's troubling assertions about assimilation, chauvinism, and imperialism—along with her distinctions between the social and the political, between making and doing—seem to speak directly to their lives and struggles. She finds that there is not only an Arendt to remind us of "lost" political moments, but also an Arendt to warn those engaged in political movement about the dangers of losing what they have initiated.

Chapters 7 and 8 deal with Arendt's contribution to two current debates in education. In "Hannah Arendt on Politicizing the University and Other Clichés," Peter Euben makes Arendt an interlocutor in the contemporary "culture wars." Euben suggests that understanding these battles in terms of Arendt's writings on Socrates and Adolf Eichmann, as well as on education, enables us to differentiate the significant issues at stake from the self-serving hyperbole that distracts us from them. He also indicates how her work provides the conceptual basis for a distinction between a politicized education, which threatens higher education, and a political one, which is a vital dimension of it. Finally, Euben's essay employs Arendt's Hellenism as she did: to revive a notion of politics and freedom that, along with political education, she might endorse.

In "The Eclipse of Thinking: An Arendtian Critique of Cooperative Learning," Eduardo Duarte uses Arendt's "purely" philosophical depiction of thinking as a framework from which to critique pedagogical models that seek to create communities of learning based on peer-mediated, group learning processes. These pedagogical models are captured under the category of "cooperative learning." Duarte's critique is aimed at one of the fundamental assumptions of cooperative learning: that learning is best achieved in the company of others. This assumption, itself based upon a social constructivist epistemology, has led to the implementation of pedagogical models that suppress what Arendt calls the "urgent need to think" contemplatively. Because cooperative learning is structurally incompatible with the event of "withdrawal" from the company of others, upon which contemplation is based, the result is the eclipse of thinking. In sum, Duarte argues that cooperative learning models may be creating conditions of "nonthinking."

The final chapter of this book is an epistolary exchange between two former students of Hannah Arendt. In "What and How We Learned from Hannah Arendt: An Exchange of Letters," Elisabeth Young-Bruehl and Jerome Kohn not only bring to life the "pleasure of having studied with Arendt," they also enlighten us on her views about the kind of education that is particularly suited to prepare people for understanding politics. Kohn emphasizes that Arendt's basic teaching and the source of everything that followed was the unprecedented event of totalitarianism: "What I want to stress is that Arendt tried to make clear to her students . . . that totalitarianism occurred right in the heart of Western civilization, that it was not imported into it from the outside, 'not from the moon,' as she used to say, or from anywhere else." Young-Bruehl agrees with Kohn and argues that the consequence of the appearance of totalitarianism in the twentieth century for thinking is that people must now envision and make an effort to live in "a decent world." This world, Young-Bruehl writes, is "not a utopia, not a palace of ideology, not an arena for heroics, not a moral dictation, but a decent world. In Hannah Arendt's terms, I think this meant a world in which totalitarianism is not possible." Kohn, continuing this train of thought, summarizes Arendt's basic contribution as an educator. Arendt, he writes:

> introduced us into the world by teaching us, largely by her own example, to retrieve its past. The point of that was, I think, to develop in us an ability to respond without prejudice to the great plurality of men and

women who share the world, thereby helping to sustain the common world that totalitarianism sought to destroy. Such responsibility, although not a matter of knowledge, requires thought. Arendt did not stuff our heads with knowledge but taught us to "think"; and in her sense of the word, that was practical insofar as the habit of thinking is, as she said, "among the conditions that make men abstain from evil-doing."

The outline of the essays in this collection illustrates that Hannah Arendt's legacy of political concepts as well as many of the questions and issues she raised have numerous implications for education in a democratic society. Today, when the interrelations of politics and education are becoming increasingly manifest, we can no longer afford to ignore the educational lessons that can be gleaned from one of the twentieth century's leading political theorists. Yet Arendt is not simply a major contemporary political theorist whose contribution to issues of education has largely been ignored. She is also a unique and original thinker who does not fit neatly into any of the current political or educational discourses. Whether one is discussing political, moral, philosophical, or social issues, one cannot accurately identify Arendt's views with mainstream conservatives, liberals, or radicals. The fact that Arendt does not fit into any of the existing camps is an advantage in the sense that her views can help us bridge the gap and make connections among historically opposing conceptions of education. She brings a fresh perspective from which contemporary scholars and educators can analyze various political and educational issues, as well as the interconnections of these two fields.

Notes

1. Seyla Benhabib, "Judgment and the Moral Foundation of Politics in Arendt's Thought," *Political Theory,* vol. 16, no. 1 (February 1988): 31.

2. For a detailed description of the mainstream conservative position on authority in education, see my essay (Chapter 2) in this volume.

3. See, for instance, Stanley Aronowitz and Henry A. Giroux, *Education Still Under Siege,* 2nd ed. (Westport, CT: Bergin & Garvey, 1993), pp. 135–158.

4. See his essay "The Foundations of a Democratic Educational Psychology," in *Rethinking Intelligence: Confronting Psychological Assumptions About Teaching and Learning,* ed. Joe L. Kincheloe, Shirley R. Steinberg, and Leila E. Villaverde (New York: Routledge, 1999), p. 3.

1

The Paradox of Natality: Teaching in the Midst of Belatedness

NATASHA LEVINSON

That there be a beginning, man was created before whom there was nobody" said Augustine in his political philosophy. This beginning is not the same as the beginning of the world; it is not the beginning of something but of somebody, who is a beginner himself.

—Hannah Arendt, *The Human Condition*[1]

All I wanted was to be a man among other men. I wanted to come lithe and young into a world that was ours and to help build it together.

You come too late, much too late, there will always be a world—a white world—between you and us.

—Frantz Fanon, *Black Skin, White Masks*

The Paradox of Natality

In the preface to her latest anthology of writings by and about women of color, Gloria Anzaldúa shares the frustrations that emerged when her students confronted one another directly about racism and the politics of racial identity in a course she teaches on women of color in the United States.[2] This was no abstract, depersonalized discussion; Anzaldúa writes about her students of color "holding whites accountable" for racism and about her white women students, in turn, "begging" students of color to "teach them" about racism and to tell them what they wanted whites to do about it. Describing the resistance of her students of color to the white students' efforts to position them as the political conscience of the class, Anzaldúa attributes their refusal to become engaged in "time-consuming dialogues" with white women to "their hundred years' weariness of trying to teach whites about Racism."[3]

This poignant expression, the "hundred years' weariness," with which Anzaldúa aligns herself was somewhat more prosaically echoed recently by a graduating senior in my curriculum theory class, one of two African American students in a largely white class. Exasperated with the seeming lack of change in the racial dynamics and racial awareness on campus that he saw reenacted in our class discussions, he expressed frustrations similar to those of the women of color in Anzaldúa's class: "Every year we have a bunch of forums to discuss racism, and yet we never seem to make any progress in race relations on this campus. Every time the subject of racism comes up in class, I have to listen to the same white voices protesting their innocence. I'm sick of it."

I must confess to some ambivalence about this frustration. On the one hand, many students of color are justifiably tired of being put in the position of teaching whites about racism. Feminists of color have argued for some time that white feminists need to take responsibility for learning about racism, and they are absolutely right to point out that those of us who have one foot in the dominant culture—be it by virtue of our racial, gender, sexual, or class identity—must stop expecting those who are marginalized to act as our conscience, prodding us at every turn to be more aware of the ways in which particular aspects of our identity enable us to take things for granted.[4] And yet, although it is certainly not fair to expect students of color to assume responsibility for teaching their peers about race, something is missed when we take these seemingly endless repetitions as a sign of some sort of moral or political failure rather than as a signal that a necessary educational encounter is under way. Tiresome as these kinds of encounters might be for students (and teachers) who have experienced many such engagements, it is important to remember that they are not actually repetitions: They are always both familiar and new. In this sense, these encounters epitomize the practice of teaching: Both are steeped in what I will call the "paradox of natality." The paradox of natality alerts us to the many frustrations inherent in these efforts to navigate the racial divide. Coming to grips with the paradox of natality reconfigures these supposed "failures" in ways that draw attention to the fitful and decidedly nonlinear nature of educational progress.

"Natality" is Hannah Arendt's term for the human capacity for renewal. Since the desire to contribute to the re-creation of the world is what motivates political action, natality is one of the conditions of political action. At the most fundamental level, natality refers to the fact that people are constantly born into the world and are continually in need of introduction to that world and to one another. This is why Arendt writes that natality is the "essence of education."[5] Because all newcomers bring with them the possibility that the world might be reinvigorated, natality is a source of social hope.[6] However, the continual influx of newcomers means that any attempt to rejuvenate the world is likely to be interrupted and set off course.[7] Herein lies the promise and the pathos of the new: Natality is both what motivates political action and what mitigates against our actions having the intended effect.

The possibility that we might bring about something new in relation to the world is tempered by two features of natality that will be central to this essay. First, there is the simple and yet disconcerting fact that the world does not simply *precede* us, but effectively *constitutes* us as particular kinds of people. This puts us in the difficult position of being simultaneously heirs to a particular history and new to it, with the peculiar result that we experience ourselves as "be-

lated" even though we are newcomers.[8] This experience of belatedness alerts us to the increasing complexity of ontological questions
in the condition of postmodernity. If the modern can be characterized by a broad cultural desire to "put the past behind us," the postmodern might be understood as a facing up to the impossibility—
and the ethical undesirability—of this desire.[9] In Faulkner's words,
"the past is never dead, it is not even past."[10] However, if our resulting sense of belatedness is not countered by natality—our capacity
for action—it is potentially paralyzing.

The second feature of natality that has the paradoxical effect of
acting against the new is the fact that our efforts to initiate the new
take place always in the midst of other acting beings whose very
presence mitigates against our actions coming to fruition (*HC*,
221–236). Arendt refers to this as the "condition of plurality," and it
is what makes encounters across difference so wearisome: They appear to "go nowhere," and in the grand scheme of things, they seem
to accomplish so little. The apparent futility of efforts to engage in
dialogues across difference is reminiscent of Arendt's perplexing
contention that political action is possibly the most futile of human
activities, not in the sense that it accomplishes nothing, but because
it rarely accomplishes what it sets out to achieve (*HC*, 184, 197).

By grounding natality in a biological inevitability—the fact that
humans are constantly born into the world—natality is a site of potential provocation. But this biological fact does not ensure that
newness will manifest itself in the world. As Arendt puts it, "the
chances that tomorrow will be like yesterday are always overwhelming."[11] Yet this is what makes human initiative—which is, after all,
what natality signifies—all the more significant. It is the reason that
educators need to be especially attentive to the conditions that foster
natality, and it is why teachers play such a central and complex role
in relation to natality. Teachers are positioned very oddly in relation
to the new, since we are asked to facilitate its emergence at the same
time as Arendt reminds us that we can neither predict nor control
the forms this newness will take. Our task is rather, in Arendt's curious formulation, to "preserve newness" (*CE*, 193). This is no easy
task, as I will show. The difficulties that attend the task of "preserving newness" are twofold. In part, they are an inherent feature of

newness itself, a result of the paradox of natality described above; and in part, they stem from the repetitive nature of teaching itself— the sense in which we are always beginning again and the resulting impression that little progress has been made in matters of race.

The first set of challenges to our efforts to preserve newness arises out of the structure of social positioning itself. As students become aware of the ways in which their social positioning attaches to them regardless of how they might wish to be seen, they begin to feel the weight of history on their shoulders. They become increasingly aware of their representative status. This is what happens when, for example, minority students sense that their successes or failures in school reflect on their racial or ethnic group as a whole. The result is a potentially overwhelming sense of belatedness in the face of a history that bears down on them from all sides. Increasingly, however, this sense of belatedness is beginning to apply to students from dominant social groups as well. White students are similarly starting to experience themselves as particular *kinds* of people rather than as unique and unprecedented *individuals*. This is what happened to the white students in Anzaldúa's class. Finding themselves held directly accountable for racism, they, too, began to feel the weight of the past.

Belatedness poses a problem when students feel so weighted down by their social positioning that they see no point in attempting to transform the meanings and implications that attach to their positioning. But equally problematic is the opposite problem of students who refuse to see the ways in which they are belated and thus insist on their status as newcomers. This naïveté echoes Frantz Fanon's more knowing expression of his own desire to have come "lithe and young" into a welcoming world, to be a person pure and simple rather than a black or a white person. At times, these are wistful longings, a nostalgic yearning that is caught between the recognition that there is no going back and an inability to move forward. At other times, the insistence on one's status as a newcomer is an untenable invocation of innocence, a refusal to face up to connections between the present and the past. "After all," these students protest, "we were not there, we are not directly responsible, our whiteness [or maleness] is an accident of history." What is lost in this longing for innocence is an understanding that belatedness does not simply position us as individuals in relation to a past; it also positions us in relation to others in the present. Perhaps most disturbing for many students is the realization that we are held accountable, not for deliberate wrongdoings, but for "collective trespasses" that "arise as we live our locations."[12] This is what makes belatedness so crucial to our social understandings. At the same time, the weight of the past may be too heavy a burden for the newcomers to assume. A pedagogy that aims to "preserve newness" is one that can absorb the impact of "the shock of the old" in ways that foster rather than stifle the promise of natality.

Teaching to "preserve newness" is made more difficult by the repetitive structure of teaching itself. Year after year, we encounter the weariness or pessimism that some students bring to these meetings and the bewilderment of others as the certainty of their place in the world is shaken up or as their efforts to make connections with their fellow students are rebuffed. The déjà vu quality of these encounters reminds us that teaching is a matter of continual beginnings. In the sections that follow, I put this twofold structural difficulty—the fact of belatedness and the repetitive nature of education—into play in order to draw attention to the pivotal and yet precarious role of the teacher in preserving newness. Given these very real hazards of teaching, it is worthwhile to pause and consider the ways in which education can facilitate or smother natality and to reflect on the difficult mix of passion, patience, responsibility, and detachment that is essential to the important but difficult undertaking of teaching in the midst of the paradox of natality.

Teaching to "Preserve Newness"

Arendt describes the ability to act as the capacity to begin something anew (*HC*, 9). Natality is grounded in the biological fact that individuals are constantly born into the world. However, since individuals have no control over the circumstances and conditions of their initial biological birth, Arendt likens natality to a "second birth," an act of self-creation in relation to the world that preceded and surrounds us (*HC*, 9, 176–177). She writes that "the new beginning inherent in birth can make itself felt in the world only because the newcomer possesses the capacity of beginning something new, that is, of acting" (*HC*, 9). Natality signals our transformation from being passive vectors of social processes to becoming social actors—which is to say, potential deflectors of these forces. Natality is manifest in the world whenever individuals and groups act in relation to the world in ways that suggest that seemingly intransigent social processes can be changed.[13]

This conception of natality as *re*action, response, *re*configuration, aligns Arendt's work with poststructuralist reconceptualizations of the "new."[14] As Judith Butler has pointed out, "the pursuit of the 'new' is the preoccupation of high modernism; if anything, the postmodern casts doubt upon the possibility of a 'new' that is not in some way already implicated in the 'old.'"[15] Arendt's understanding of natality similarly reconceptualizes what is meant by the new. Natality does not refer to events and initiatives that are original in the sense that they have never been seen before. The new as Arendt understands it does not refer only to the few unprecedented and thus momentous events. It refers also to the more quotidian but nonetheless surprising moments in which individuals initiate relationships and thereby attempt to forge new social realities. Indeed, precisely because we live in an overdetermined world, in which so many social processes appear to take place above the level of human intervention and so much of our social behavior seems deeply ingrained and resistant to change, there is something miraculous about even the effort to unsettle, interrupt, or deflect social processes that seem inevitable and inescapable.[16]

These everyday miracles occur whenever human beings take initiative in relation to the world that precedes and constitutes them. Historical processes, Arendt reminds us, "are created and constantly interrupted by human initiative, by the *initium* man is insofar as he is an acting being."[17] This is certainly true of the major initiatives with which Arendt was concerned: the French and American Revolutions and the many instances of civil disobedience that shaped the civil rights era. But it is equally true of the small and yet profound acts of heroism undertaken by those who resist regimes that set out to dehumanize others and that, in the process, dehumanize those whose silence is a form of acquiescence.[18] These are the small acts of heroism that, however tentatively, illuminate "dark times."[19] They are manifest in forbidden friendships, expressions of solidarity with others, and—perhaps most difficult of all—in efforts to forgive those who seek to rectify wrongdoings.

What is important about each of these initiatives—and, therefore, what makes Arendt so interesting for the politics of difference—is that rather than evading political differences, these relationships resist and reconfigure the meanings that attach to differences. To have said, as Arendt did in her address to the city of Hamburg on the occasion of receiving the Lessing Prize, that it might be possible to be "a German and a Jew and friends" is one way of initiating the unexpected. Arendt's careful choice of words shows that she was not suggesting that the differences between being a German and a Jew in postwar Germany were not significant. But she added to this the unexpected phrase "and friends," which holds out the promise that Germans and Jews could reconfigure their relationship with each other even in the wake of the cataclysmic events of the Holocaust.[20]

Natality suggests the possibility that the world can be renewed, but this promise is not guaranteed. Our capacity for action must be nurtured. Precisely because the link between natality and action is not assured, education plays a crucial role in Arendt's political philosophy. Education can foster students' capacity for action or it can foreclose it. When Arendt identifies natality as the "essence of education," she alerts us to two dimensions of the relationship between education and natality (CE, 174). We educate in order to introduce the continual stream of newcomers into the world, but we have to take care to do so in a way that protects natality by preserving our students' capacities to act in ways that might renew the world. In other words, education must create the conditions for what Arendt calls the "setting-right" of the world (CE, 192).

This is not an easy task for teachers, who are placed in a particularly awkward position. We are asked to take responsibility for introducing students to the world "as it is" and not as we might wish it were (CE, 189). At the same time, we are reminded that the purpose of this introduction to the world is to prepare our students not simply to make their way in the world, but to remake the world. Further, we are admonished not to attempt to dictate the terms of this transformation. This last point is particularly important for Arendt. She explains: "Our hope always hangs on the new which every generation brings; but precisely because we can base our hope only on this, we destroy everything if we so try to control the new that we, the old, can dictate how it will look. Exactly for the sake of what is new and revolutionary in every child, education must be conservative" (CE, 192–193).

Arendt's educational conservatism warrants careful reflection. It is quite unlike the conservatism of those who turn to the past in order to resist the incursion of the new. For these conservatives, the purpose of education is to preserve the status quo or to return to a previous way of life. Arendt's conservatism, by contrast, springs from what she calls a "conservationist attitude" that strives to protect "the child against the world, the world against the child, the new against the old, the old against the new" (CE, 192). In other words, the aim of education is not to preserve the old unthinkingly (as though nothing warrants transformation), nor is it to value the new for its own sake (as though nothing that currently exists is worth preserving). To preserve newness is to teach in such a way that students acquire an understanding of themselves in relation to the world without regarding either the world or their positioning in it as fixed, determined, and unchangeable (CE, 193).

To this end, Arendt insists that students must be introduced to the world "as it is," in all its potential and with all its flaws. Only in relation to this world will students come to an understanding of what needs to be challenged and reconfigured. Arendt is particularly critical of those educators who teach as though the world were already other than it is. Her concern is twofold. First, teachers who teach as though the world has already changed—or who place great faith in a notion of progress that happens of its own accord, seemingly without human intervention—send the message to students that the world is not in need of transformation. It has already been transformed. Her second worry follows from this sense that students will become accustomed to having the world changed for them, apparently on their behalf. Both of these approaches deny students "their own future role in the body politic" (CE, 177). To teach in these ways is "to strike from the newcomer's hands their own chance at the new" (CE, 177). The predicament of the teacher in the paradox of natality becomes clear: We are asked to teach about the world as it is in such a way that we neither endorse it nor seek to direct the course of its transformation.

By reminding teachers that our responsibility is to present the world as it is to our students, Arendt is reminding us that there is more to "the world" than the teacher's perception of it. To orient students to the world is thus not to impose a singular reading of this world on them. Rather, it is to expose them to a representative sample of the many and varied ways in which the world is experienced and interpreted by its inhabitants past and present.[21] The point of this exposure to the world as it is is not to fix the world, but to motivate our students to imagine new possibilities for the future.

This takes us to the heart of the controversy over the purpose and goals of pedagogies of difference. Many educators fear that focusing on group differences risks reifying certain identities: reducing students to their social positioning, fixing them within it, and rendering them unable to move beyond it. These are valid concerns. The trouble is that in their efforts to avoid the problem of stasis, which often becomes the basis for confrontations in the classroom, these teachers teach as though group differences no longer matter. What begins as a fear of fixing students in the past or in the present ends up prematurely foreclosing opportunities for students to reconfigure their relations to their social positioning and to one another.[22] In other words, in our haste to overcome social divisions, we teach as though these divisions are just holdovers from the past. We teach as if we have already entered or are on the threshold of an era in which group differences no longer matter.

The trouble with this wishful thinking, as cultural critic Homi Bhabha reminds us, is that racism is not simply a holdover from the past; it is part of the contemporary social fabric. In a phrase that aptly captures the ways in which racial meanings are reproduced, Bhabha refers to the "enunciative present" of racial discourses, within which the possibility of their transformation has to be negotiated (*LC*, 242). This succinct formulation draws our attention to the ways in which racial ideologies continue to circulate as systems of meanings, behaviors, fears, and desires that attach to our very bodies and inhere (to greater and lesser extents) in our self-perception and social positioning. These categories are constitutive of what we are, positioning us in relation to history, one another, and the future in ways that few of us would have chosen and many of us hope to transform. It is difficult to imagine how newness might emerge in the midst of this aspect of belatedness to reconfigure seemingly intractable social relations.

Identity Matters: Teaching in the Midst of Belatedness

Natality stands for the moments in our lives when we take responsibility for ourselves in relation to others. In this way, natality initiates an active relation to the world. It signifies those moments in our lives (and there are many) in which we attempt to answer the question that Arendt argues is at the basis of all action and that is posed to every newcomer to the world: "Who are you?"[23]

This is not an easy question, in part because each of us spends our whole life fashioning ourselves in answer to it, but largely because none of us answers this question on our own.[24] Who we are is as much a matter of how we appear to others as it is a matter of our own self-perception. Indeed, our self-perception is bound up in and is largely formed in response to the ways we are named and positioned by others. In this sense, the ways in which we are positioned by others—at the level of institutions, systems, social structures, and by individuals—are constitutive of what we are. They condition, although they do not determine, who we become. This distinction—between *what* someone is and *who* someone is—is crucial to Arendt (*HC*, 179–180). Our whatness refers to the characteristics we share with others but that say little about our distinctive capacities. Who we are, by contrast, is what distinguishes us from others, and it is largely in order to disclose and discover who we are as "unique and distinct" individuals that we act. Our capacity to act emerges always in relation to the ways in which we are positioned by others.

We experience ourselves as belated in two ways: in relation to the world as a whole and in relation to those around us. For most of us, our initial experience of belatedness with regard to the world as a whole is largely a source of wonder at all that has been built and discovered prior to our arrival. But this initial excitement rapidly dissipates as we find ourselves treated as if we have been here before. This is what happens whenever we find ourselves approached by others or whenever we approach others solely as members of a social group and not as unique and distinctive beings. Encounters like these are overlaid with a sense of the familiar. Whether in some deep place of cultural memory or in more recent encounters with people "just like them," we feel as though we have met this particular person before. Encounters like these have the ironic effect of rendering this stranger, this "other," much less other: S/he is known to us; we have had experiences with this "type" of person before. On the receiving end of this equation, we find ourselves similarly thematized—reduced to an aspect of ourselves that is familiar, even if, in the fundamental irony of identity logic, it is our very strangeness that makes us familiar. We cease to be unique and become instead a genus: a woman, a Jew, an African American.

This is what happened to Fanon when he moved beyond his Martinican community only to find himself amid whites who marked him as a particular kind of person: "Look, a Negro!"[25] In "The Fact of Blackness," Fanon explores the phenomenology of this gradual merger of self-perception into social positioning. Writing of his initial desire to be unmarked by history, unburdened by colonization, Fanon explains, "All I wanted was to be a man among other men. I wanted to come lithe and young into a world that was ours and to help build it together."[26] But, marked as a black man by the points and stares of others, Fanon realizes the impossibility of attaining the humanist ideal of generic man. As he moves through the world, he is constantly reminded that "You come too late, much too late, there will always be a world—a white world—between you and us."[27] Fanon's journey into negritude begins with his realization that to be a black man in a racist society is to be "overdetermined from without."[28] It is to feel oneself perpetually belated, an heir to preexisting meanings rather than one who makes meaning for oneself.[29]

As Bhabha rightly notes, Fanon has some ambivalence about what blackness signifies. At times, belatedness is located specifically in the experience of being black—a condition that is very much a political construction and has meaning only in the context of the normative whiteness that undergirds the colonial encounter. This is why Fanon marks the world between "you and us" as a white world. Indeed, it is only in a racist society that blackness serves to mark one as a particular kind of person and becomes simultaneously a condition one might desire to escape and an inescapable condition. Bhabha points out, however, that at other moments the specificity of Fanon's "sense of the *belatedness of the black man*" gives way to the fact of belatedness in general, a broader social phenomenon that emerges out of the modern production of racial identities and serves to unmask "the *historicity* of [modernity's] most universal symbol—Man." Fanon notes that in these moments, "the Black man is not. Any more than the white man" (in *LC*, 236–237). And yet, as Fanon's experience testifies, to say that blackness or whiteness is not meaningful in any essential way does not mean that these aspects of social identity do not continue to signify.

The fact of belatedness as a general condition of postmodernity is increasingly becoming apparent as those in dominant social groups find themselves called to accountability as whites or as men for their positions of privilege. Until recently, whites and men had no desire to escape a situation that guaranteed them privileged access to public space, education, employment, and property. The fact that they, too, were latecomers was a source of gratitude, for they had inherited the earth. Now that their future roles are less and less assured, however, they, too, feel weighted down by belatedness. As whites and men are called to account for their positions of privilege in what continues to be a racial and gender hierarchy, what becomes clear is that they are less able to shirk the weight of history. Each time any of us seek to soar above the identities that attach to us by virtue of our appearance, we are brought back down to earth. Our efforts to deny our embeddedness in history are resisted by those "others" who remind us of the ways in which we continue to benefit from racism.

What educators are now confronted with is, therefore, not the belatedness of blackness, but the fact of belatedness, which is no longer restricted to social groups with a history and a cultural memory of subjugation. This is not to suggest that belatedness has the same impact on the privileged, who are now having to relinquish guarantees and assurances once taken for granted. But the psychological impact is similar. No matter what our social positioning, it seems that no sooner have we arrived than we are told that the world is tired of us; it has seen the likes of us before. In response, many of us become weary and may grow resentful, and we witness similar reactions in our students. Whether this resentment manifests itself as despondence or as self-righteous anger, it is unlikely to lend itself to the task of creating the conditions of possibility for new kinds of relations to emerge amid the politics of difference. Given the intractability of belatedness, as well as the impossibility of transcending our racial identities, what are the possibilities for transforming the meanings that attach to our social positioning, for interrupting the cycles of resentment in which so many of us and our students are liable to become knotted?[30]

Teachers are faced with two difficulties. On the one hand, students may feel "fated" by their social positioning. If students feel trapped by their social positioning, they are unlikely to take on the difficult task of social transformation. On the other hand, efforts to escape the "fatefulness" of social positioning by attempting to ignore it, downplay it, erase it, or refuse it are doomed to fail because identity is not just a matter of self-perception.[31] We constantly bump up against social structures and individuals who refuse these efforts to transcend our social positioning and persist in marking us in particular ways. But even more worrying is the increasing likelihood that prematurely foreclosing the possibilities of reconfiguring the social meanings that attach to particular identities will foster resentment. Resentment is a response to feeling trapped under "the weight of the past and the apparent foreclosing of futures" (FTPF, 344). Depending on the social positioning of the student, this resentment may manifest itself as anger at being forced into the category of oppressor or as anger that results from a history of subjugation that is simultaneously denied and reinforced by the broader culture. As Melissa Orlie points out, the problem with both of these positions is that "contestants locked in a battle of escalating recriminations, far from releasing or redeeming the past, repeat and increase its weight" (FTPF, 345).

Arendt warns against two prevalent responses to the problem of belatedness. An overwhelming sense of belatedness risks churning out "social pariahs" who feel fated by their identity—so fixed by the world that preceded them that there is no possibility of unsettling this world and of bringing something new into it. Social pariahs accept their social positioning as a given (FTPF, 345–346). They make no effort to challenge the ways in which they are reduced to their social positioning, which becomes central to their identity. Social pariahs define themselves almost entirely in terms of how they are perceived and positioned by others. In other words, "the *social pariah* embraces what-ness as given and unalterable" (FTPF, 345). The problem with social pariahs is a political one: They make no effort to transform the political status or the political meanings that attach to their social position. In short, they embrace their abject position without mounting a significant political challenge to the grounds of their exclusion.

The relation of "parvenus" to their social positioning is the complete opposite. They refuse to accept their social positioning. The trouble with parvenus is that they have no sense of history; they feel too new. As the discussion of belatedness has shown, however, we cannot avoid being positioned by others. When parvenus find themselves in this situation, they are at a loss, bewildered by this unfamiliar sense of belatedness, and they attempt to transcend it in some way, most often by claiming their common status as human beings and refusing those who position them as particular kinds of people. The problem is that the parvenu's desire to transcend his or her social positioning is destined to fail.

In the end, the parvenu comes to share the social pariah's sense of identity as fixed, determined, and inescapable (FTPF, 345). Both are likely to feel resentful as a result of their shared perception that one cannot escape one's whatness. But whereas social pariahs tend to resign themselves to their social positioning, parvenus remain disgruntled and are likely to blame others for their positioning without seeking to transform the social implications of what they are. Avoiding this entails facing up to what they are in a way that resists feeling either too late or too new to the world.

The challenge for teachers consists of creating spaces in which students can confront their sense of belatedness without feeling immobilized by it. Ideally, such spaces enable students to live out the wonder of being a newcomer to the earth, not by attempting to soar above their social positioning, but by reconfiguring it in a meaningful way.

But here teachers encounter the other aspect of the temporality of natality: that students become aware of their belatedness at different stages of their lives. Although many students—particularly minority students and women—are aware of their social positioning, and have been for a long time, other students are not used to thinking of themselves as white or as men or as heterosexual. Indeed, for many, the classroom will be the first time they are confronted with the ways in which they are belated. This sets up an asymmetry in the classroom as students confront one another and themselves not only from different social positions, but also from different time frames. The problem of asymmetry is exacerbated by the depth of anger and discomfort, outrage and resistance, that comes to the fore in discussions of identity. These are necessary difficulties, for the politics of identity cuts into the quick of what it means to live in a world one shares with others, raising hard questions about responsibility and freedom. But these are also frustrating encounters, since accusation and recrimination are often allowed to take the place of thinking productively about what it means to share a world with others.

One of the problems with Anzaldúa's framing of the classroom encounter is that she recognizes what is old and familiar about these confrontations without acknowledging that what is happening is simultaneously—and paradoxically—recognizably familiar and startlingly new. Anzaldúa's positioning of the class as a "classic example," her frustration with what appears to be (and in some senses is) white students' *persistent* insistence that others do the work of drawing attention to racism, and her own allegiance with the "hundred years' weariness" her students of color express focus on what is all too familiar about encounters across the racial divide: Once again, white women have to be challenged by women of color to recognize their position of white privilege. And once again, Anzaldúa finds herself witnessing white women responding defensively, evasively, or naively to the challenge.

In an important way, these feelings of frustration and expressions of exhaustion are educative: They draw attention to the tremendous discomfort that attends efforts to directly address racism. They also point to the repetitive quality of these discussions, which begin to seem so similar to seasoned participants that both what is said and who says what become predictable. But if, following Arendt, one takes natality as the essence of education, what is educative about this despair is also deeply disturbing. What is lost is some sense of the potential for newness that manifests itself in the face of belatedness. If the purpose of education were simply to instill in students a sense of belatedness, teaching would be a depressing endeavor indeed. The possibility that these students might reconfigure the meaning of the social positionings with which they are confronted in the classroom—forging unexpected social relations and unsettling deeply entrenched social forces in the process—is what redeems teaching, offering the possibility of hope.

What seems like old hat to the teacher may well be quite new to some of the participants, particularly those who have never before discussed racism in a mixed-race group. Such students are unlikely to have been held accountable for issues of race and racism in such a direct way before—and certainly not by these particular classmates. Even if these encounters are familiar to some students—and thus reinforce rather than ameliorate their sense of belatedness—it is important to bear in mind the asymmetrical way in which students become aware of their belatedness.

This is Fanon's point about blackness, which marks the colonized as "other" at a young age. Whereas white Americans are, at a young age, aware of the ways in which race attaches to others and marks the other as different, they do not become aware of the ways in which whiteness attaches to them until much later. Thus, white students are less likely to be "weary" of their whiteness than students of color are of their color. For many, this class may be the first time they have been called into their whiteness. As Anzaldúa's description of the reaction of her Jewish students indicates, this positioning is deeply unsettling for many students.[32] This asymmetrical reaction to belatedness, and the correspondingly unequal distribution of weariness, indicates how discussions like this are saturated in natality. The reason why these kinds of confrontations seem never to make progress is a direct result of this asymmetry that characterizes encounters across cultural difference: Newcomers are constantly being born and are continually in the process of being introduced to one another and to the world. Natality lends encounters across difference their paradoxical quality of feeling familiar and yet being new. Each confrontation feels like we are beginning again. In many ways, this is precisely what we are doing.

Of course, not all whites are new to these kinds of encounters. Many of us are equally used to these encounters, and I dare say, many of us are equally weary and frustrated at having to "prove" our race consciousness in each new encounter. However, rather than regarding the weariness as a sign of disappointment in a social process gone awry—in this case, the process is the struggle against racism—weariness ought to be taken as a sign that an ethical encounter is under way. The weariness expressed by students of color testifies to the ways in which we simultaneously are and are not new to one another. Reduced to our social positioning, we are perceived as being interchangeable with others who are "just like us." This is what lends encounters across difference their repetitive quality, as well as the frustrating sense that, in these encounters, we are always starting from scratch.

Conversely, the fact that we still undertake these encounters indicates that, on some level, we are aware that these are necessary repetitions, that each of us simultaneously is and is not new to the other. In this sense, the weariness that attends these encounters is not a mark of failure. Instead, it is a sign that to encounter an(other) ethically is an exhausting process. The process of recognizing what is new about the other and becoming aware of what is novel about each particular encounter does not eliminate what is tiring about these encounters. But it does reconfigure the weariness as an ongoing and unavoidable aspect of encounters across difference.

The problem, as I see it, is more accurately located in the governing expectation that conversations and confrontations like this will get us to a predetermined somewhere—a utopian "postdifference" space where there will no longer be a need for encounters across difference. Arendt's conception of natality as the essence of education challenges this utopian thinking by reminding us of the constant influx of newcomers who are introduced to the world at different moments and who make their way in relation to this world and one another in different time frames. Natality poses a challenge to the way we conceive of progress, reconfiguring what is usually thought of as a steady forward motion into a more apt characterization that Bhabha calls "time-lag" (*LC*, 238). The idea of a time-lag draws attention to the pauses that punctuate progress, constraining and limiting the traditional conception of a continual stream of time. It is not that Bhabha reads time as "endless slippage" and thus disparages the very idea of social progress. Rather, he wants to develop a more suitable metaphor for progress, one that attends to the ways in which the past works to slow down modernity's drive toward the future. In this view, time moves forward less steadily and social progress is never assured. The idea of the time-lag highlights the fact that belatedness always threatens to overrun the possibility of the new. It also reminds us of the constant stream of newcomers who not only make it necessary for us to begin again, but who then undertake their own new beginnings.

Bhabha is writing about the form newness takes in a postcolonial framework, in which possibilities for the new are limited by the racial configurations of a colonial past that haunts the future. He is writing also in the midst of a latent pessimism within the postmodern paradigm that suggests that all future possibilities are already worn out. However, instead of giving in to the social paralysis of these two positions, Bhabha imagines a "third-space" in which neither the past nor possibilities for agency and for bringing newness into the world are erased (*LC*, 218).

This third-space resonates with what Arendt calls "the gap between past and future."[33] Both open spaces of possibility in relation to the past. Bhabha labels it "a projective past, a form of the future anterior." In such a space, the past conditions but does not determine the future, while the present looks at the past not only in terms of what is or has been, but also in terms of what might have been (*LC*, 251–253). This third-space is the gap in which students encounter themselves as belated; but they also need to be oriented to the future in a way that is neither forgetful of nor fated by the past.

Here we come to the central role of the teacher whose task it is to preserve natality, thereby ensuring that the gap between past and future remains a space of freedom and possibility.

Teaching in the "Gap Between Past and Future"

Arendt is frequently taken to task for her insistence that politics and education not be conflated. And, indeed, her effort to distinguish the two may strike advocates of difference pedagogy as an impossible demand given the ways in which all levels of education are infused with politics (CE, 177). But Arendt is not attempting to separate politics and education into distinct spheres. She is, rather, attempting to distinguish the kinds of responsibilities and qualities demanded of us when we teach from those required of us in politics.

In Arendt's view of politics, to engage politically is to act freely among equals who are equally capable of free action. It is to assume "equal responsibility for the course of the world" (CE, 190). Because the teacher's concern is not only with the course of the world, but with the development of the student in relation to this world as well, educators must assume more responsibility than students. Further, this responsibility is of a different sort than that we assume as political activists (CE, 189–190). This is because teaching positions us in a particular relation to natality, preparing students to take their place as political actors in a weary world that is constantly in need of rejuvenation, of being "set right" in such a way that we do not dictate the terms of the transformation (CE, 192–193). Introducing newcomers into a weary world while preserving the possibility that students might undertake something new in relation to this world requires that teachers meet students in the "gap between past and future."

This gap symbolizes not an escape from history but a fissure within time. It signifies the break in tradition that characterizes modern life. Arendt points out that this break in tradition is not without its dangers—most notably, that we risk forgetting the past, which in turn means that we will have lost our guide to understanding the present.[34] Nowhere is this forgetfulness more apparent than in contemporary efforts to think us into a postracist, postsexist space without attending to the rearticulations of racist and sexist discourses and practices in the United States.

But at the same time, Arendt is optimistic about the break in tradition, which helps loosen the "chain fettering each successive generation to a predetermined aspect of the past."[35] In the process, it opens up a space of freedom that enables us to resist the notion that we are fully determined and fated by history.[36] It offers each new being an opportunity to see how they have been made what they are and provides an incentive for them to reconfigure themselves in response to this history. To teach in this gap is to commit ourselves to teaching about the past—for understanding and for guidance, and for the preservation of the memory that underlies both—and to motivate students to try to set things right. Concurrently, we have to resist the temptation of attempting to determine and control our students' futures.

This is no simple matter. It requires that teachers be aware of the difference certain social identities make and alert to the differential degrees of investment students have in their identities. It also entails recognizing the ways in which some students may be new to these issues while also attending to the ways in which others find them tiresome or exhausting. Here the teacher's role is central, since it is difficult to expect the very students who are experiencing the fraught dynamics of a direct confrontation to step back and recognize that the encounter with another is always in some sense a new beginning, even if it is saturated with deeply sedimented cultural memories. By the same token, what is difficult for other students is the realization of the ways in which they are belated and seem only too recognizable to their peers. To teach in the gap between past and future is not to neutralize either the frustration or the bewilderment, but nor should we allow these reactions to mire students in despair. Both responses would be problematic: the first because it tries to erase a genuine problem and the second because it is an evasion of the teacher's responsibility to inspire students to try to risk initiating the new.

A better strategy would be for the teacher to draw attention to the disjunctures experienced by the students and to make these the focus of attention: How is it that some of us experience our social positions as universal while others are put in Fanon's position and marked out as a particular kind of person? How do these different degrees of awareness of our social positioning shape the way we relate to the world and to one another? What kinds of responsibilities do we bear by virtue of our social positioning? And what kinds of freedoms do we have in relation to this social positioning?[37] Questions like these encourage students to think about the ways in which those who are different from them experience the world and about the ways in which their social positioning shapes that of others. In this way, the relational aspects of social positioning are brought to the fore. The possibility of bringing about new relations and new social realities begins with these kinds of realizations and recognitions.

Like other aspects of teaching, assuming this degree of responsibility requires tremendous patience on the part of the teacher, for these encounters are incessant; as long as new generations are born, they will be necessary. The precise categories of difference may change and their social effects may be greater or less, but we will always be caught in what Arendt describes as the "small non-time-space in the very heart of time, [which] unlike the world and culture into which we are born, can only be indicated, but cannot be inherited and handed down from the past; each new generation, indeed, every new human being as he inserts himself between an infinite past and an infinite future, must discover and ploddingly pave it anew."[38]

Unlike other kinds of teaching that have more concrete measures of success, this patience is not concretely rewarded. Herein lies what Arendt calls "the pathos of the new": The results of our efforts are always uncertain. This means, among other things, that we need a different conception of progress and social renewal, one that attends to the snail's pace of change. The idea that social progress proceeds seamlessly toward a utopian future in which these kinds of encounters will steadily become obsolete is in many ways an evasion of the responsibility that attends our being with others in the world. This is why Arendt takes issue with the Enlightenment view of moral progress, of the "indefinite perfectibility" of human beings.[39] She does so not just because it was shown in the twentieth century to be a tragic illusion, but because it fails to take into account "the human conditions" of natality and plurality.

The Enlightenment dream of perfection eludes us because of the peculiar quality of human affairs—which always take place in relation to what Arendt calls a "web of human relationships"—and the peculiar quality of time, which is not linear but is itself webbed. The mere fact that humans are constantly being born into the world and inserting themselves into the "web" of the world means that what is new will never proceed in a straightforward fashion toward a recognizable end point.

This means that teaching for social transformation itself requires a constantly renewed effort on the part of teachers. We need to be aware that, since newcomers are constantly born and in need of introduction to the world, our work as teachers reflects, and indeed is paradigmatic of, Bhabha's conception of the time-lag. As teachers, it is we who exist in the gap of time between past and future, and it is within this "small non-time-space in the very heart of time" that we are asked again and again to undertake the task of "preserving the new"[40] with each generation and with every child in each generation.

Notes

This essay first appeared in *Educational Theory,* vol. 47, no. 4 (Fall 1997). I'd like to thank Nicholas Burbules and Melissa Orlie for suggesting that I pursue this project and for their careful, challenging, and encouraging comments on multiple drafts of this essay. I'd also like to thank Mordechai Gordon for his helpful editorial advice and for conceiving that the time was right for a volume of essays on Arendt and education.

1. In keeping with my argument about what it means to learn to live in "the gap between past and future," I have decided not to alter Arendt's use of the generic male (although my need to draw attention to this decision underscores a certain discomfort). My concern is not merely with the integrity of her text, but with my reluctance to rewrite the past in the image of the present. Eliminating language that makes us uncomfortable does little to help us understand the exclusions and erasures of the past. As a consequence, our motivation to transform contemporary exclusionary practices becomes less and less clear.

2. Gloria Anzaldúa, "Hacienda Caras, una entrada," in *Making Face, Making Soul / Hacienda Caras,* ed. Gloria Anzaldúa (San Francisco: Aunt Lute Books, 1990), p. xix.

3. Ibid., p. xx.

4. See, for example, Merle Woo's "Letter to Ma," in *This Bridge Called My Back,* ed. Cherrie Moraga and Gloria Anzaldúa (New York: Kitchen Table Press, 1981), p. 146.

5. Hannah Arendt, "The Crisis in Education," in *Between Past and Future* (New York: Penguin Books, 1977), p. 174. This essay will be cited as CE in the text for all subsequent references.

6. I borrow the term "social hope" from Patricia White's *Civic Virtues and Public Schooling: Educating Citizens for a Democratic Society* (New York: Teachers College Press, 1996), pp. 8–12.

7. Arendt's analysis of this emerges most clearly in the section on action in *The Human Condition* (Chicago: University of Chicago Press, 1958; hereafter cited as *HC* in the text), but it is also central to her inquiry into freedom and her assessment of "The Crisis in Education" in *Between Past and Future*.

8. Homi Bhabha, *The Location of Culture* (London: Routledge, 1994), pp. 236–237. This book will be cited as *LC* in the text for all subsequent references.

9. Jean-François Lyotard, "Notes on the Meaning of 'Post-,'" in *The Postmodern Explained: Correspondence, 1982–1985* (Minneapolis: University of Minnesota Press, 1992).

10. Quoted by Arendt, "Preface: The Gap Between Past and Future," in *Between Past and Future*, p. 10.

11. Arendt, "What Is Freedom?" in *Between Past and Future*, p. 170.

12. See Melissa Orlie's "Forgiving Trespasses, Promising Futures," in *Feminist Interpretations of Hannah Arendt*, ed. Bonnie Honig (University Park: Pennsylvania State University Press, 1994), p. 341. This work will be cited as FTPF in the text for all subsequent references.

13. Arendt explores this notion of humans as spatiotemporal creatures whose insertion into the world breaks up not only the flow of time, but the supposed flow of social forces in her meticulous explication of Franz Kafka's parable "He." Arendt takes Kafka's "he" as a metaphor for the way in which each of us is engaged in a constant battle to stave off the "force" of the past, the forward march of which threatens to trample any possibility for human freedom. The image of "he" doing battle with the antagonist of the past while trying to open the blocked road ahead is Arendt's metaphor for the gap between past and future. See her "Preface," pp. 7–13.

14. Edward Said's *Beginnings: Intention and Method* (New York: Basic Books, 1975) undertakes such an inquiry in relation to the work of novelists and literary critics. Said replaces the romantic notion of originality with the more weighty problem of "beginnings," which always start from somewhere, even if the initiating moments are hidden from view in the text itself.

15. Judith Butler, "Contingent Foundations: Feminism and the Question of Postmodernism," in *Feminist Contentions*, ed. Seyla Benhabib, Judith Butler, Drucilla Cornell, and Nancy Fraser (New York: Routledge, 1995), p. 39.

16. Arendt, "What Is Freedom?" Arendt writes that "it is not in the least superstitious, it is even a counsel of realism, to look for the unforeseeable and unpredictable, to be prepared for and to expect 'miracles' in the political realm. And the more heavily the scales are weighted in favor of disaster, the more miraculous will the deed done in freedom appear; for it is disaster, not salvation, which always happens automatically and therefore always must appear to be irresistible" (p. 170).

17. Arendt, ibid.

18. These major and most public initiatives are explored by Arendt in *On Revolution* (New York: Penguin Books, 1963) and *Crises of the Republic* (New York:

Harvest/HBJ Books, 1972). The less momentous but equally profound moments that Arendt wishes to bring more fully into public light—by way of illuminating what is so often dimmed—are explored in *Men in Dark Times* (New York: Harvest/HBJ Books, 1968).

19. Arendt, *Men in Dark Times.*

20. Arendt raises this issue most pointedly in "On Humanity in Dark Times: Thoughts About Lessing," the title of the speech given in Hamburg on the occasion of receiving the Lessing Prize; reprinted in *Men in Dark Times,* pp. 17–23.

21. This insistence on a plurality of perspectives is by no means an escape from the need to make judgments about the ambivalent legacy that is our world. Plurality is not a form of cultural relativism. On the contrary, for Arendt, the ability to think from the perspectives of others and the need to engage with others are prerequisites for being able to make sound judgments. Arendt's views on the relationship between the ability to judge and the exposure to multiple points of view are scattered throughout her writings, especially in her later work. The most concise formulations of these views are found in "The Crisis in Culture," in *Between Past and Future,* and in "Thinking and Moral Considerations," *Social Research,* vol. 38, no. 3 (Autumn 1971).

22. Orlie points out the problems with foreclosing identities in "Forgiving Trespasses, Promising Futures," p. 344. The discussion of resentment (and its connections to the problem of foreclosure and fixity) that threads through my argument is also indebted to Orlie's essay.

23. Arendt, *The Human Condition,* p. 178. The language here is significant. Arendtian actors want to show who and not merely what they are. In other words, this is an individuating language.

24. In *The Human Condition,* Arendt writes that "it is more than likely that the 'who,' which appears so clearly and unmistakably to others, remains hidden from the person himself, like the *daimon* in Greek religion which accompanies each man throughout his life, always looking over his shoulder from behind and thus visible only to those he encounters" (pp. 179–180). It follows from this that the actor is not the best teller of the story of his or her life. Arendt's emphasis on the other's perception of who one is heightens the intersubjective dimension of her conception of political action.

25. Frantz Fanon, "The Fact of Blackness," *Black Skin, White Masks* (New York: Grove Press, 1967), pp. 109–114.

26. Ibid., p. 112.

27. Ibid., p. 122.

28. Ibid., p. 116.

29. Ibid., p. 134.

30. I am indebted to Melissa Orlie for this idea of "interrupting" cycles of resentment by taking responsibility for "how we display the effects of what we appear to be." She explains: "We cannot altogether change what we are, nor the fact that in the course of living we trespass against others. But we can change the meaning and significance of what we are when we transmute its effects by challenging the patterns of social rule that multiply our trespasses. . . . When we become responsive to others' claims about our effects and when we show a willingness to transpose them, we may disrupt what are predicted to be and redirect the social necessities that flow

from our inherited subject positions" (see "Forgiving Trespasses, Promising Futures," p. 348).

31. I derive this term from Orlie's discussion of the relationship between foreclosing identity and resentment (see "Forgiving Trespasses, Promising Futures," p. 344).

32. Anzaldúa, "Hacienda Caras," p. xx.

33. See Arendt's "Preface," pp. 10–14 in particular.

34. Ibid., p. 13.

35. Arendt, "What Is Authority?" in *Between Past and Future*, p. 94.

36. Ibid.

37. Orlie, "Forgiving Trespasses, Promising Futures," pp. 343–345.

38. Arendt, "Preface," p. 13.

39. Arendt, "The Crisis in Education," pp. 176–178.

40. Arendt, "Preface," p. 13.

2

Hannah Arendt on Authority: Conservatism in Education Reconsidered

MORDECHAI GORDON

Most conservative approaches to education emphasize the need to teach worthy subjects and fundamental moral values to the young. For educators like Edward Wynne, the main mission of schools is to indoctrinate the young in the moral values of the great tradition.[1] One rarely encounters a conservative educator who believes in providing students with opportunities for change and innovation. Since they disregard issues such as plurality, individual creativity, and critical citizenry, these educators, as Barbara Finkelstein and others have shown, cannot contribute much to the current debate on democratic education.[2]

This chapter presents Hannah Arendt's conservatism as a unique approach that resists the reactionary tendencies of many conservative arguments. In what follows, I first show that Arendt's conception of authority shares a number of fundamental assumptions with the mainstream conservative view of authority. However, the political philosophy that Arendt developed is far from being "conservative" since it is heavily influenced by her existentialist convictions. This unusual blend of a traditional view of authority with an existentialist approach to politics shapes her ideas on education, which I discuss in the second part. One cannot fully grasp her views on education without seeing them as emerging out of these two elements. I compare Arendt's view on authority in education to mainstream conservative approaches and argue that her view constitutes a genuine alternative to these approaches, one that throws fresh light on the meaning of conservatism in education. The final part of this essay explores the implications of Arendt's insights on authority for the debate on democratic education. I show that, unlike the views of two mainstream conservatives, Arendt's conception of pedagogical authority has a number of important implications for democratic education.

Authority and Political Existence

A Conservative Historical Conception of Authority

Before discussing the similarities between Arendt's conception of authority and that of mainstream conservatives, I want to briefly indicate what is meant here by the term "conservative." Although there are significant differences between conservative thinkers, it is possible to delineate a number of central convictions that most of them share. By "conservatism," I mean an attitude that seeks to preserve the customs, values, and institutions that have been successfully established in the past. Most conservative thinkers "have agreed that virtue, stability, and civilization depend on the continuity of long-established institutions. Political stability is founded on state, church, and family, while moral stability rests upon a strong sense of duty, preferably buttressed by religious belief."[3] Conservatives are usually suspicious of, and even hostile to, radical social transformation, particularly change that is instituted by governments to advance the underprivileged sectors of society. Even when they call for change and reform, their intention is usually to restore some of the values and practices of tradition to their former influence.

Given this general definition of conservatism, it is possible to identify at least four basic assumptions about authority that Arendt shares with mainstream conservatives. Yves Simon, for example, argues that the need for authority is not derived from a lack of agreement about truth claims or from the privation of justice. Rather, authority has an essential, constructive function:

> Given a community on its way to its common good, and given, on the part of this community, the degree of excellence which entails the possibility of attaining the good in a diversity of ways, authority has an indispensable role to play, and this role originates entirely in plenitude and accomplishment. . . . An ideally enlightened and virtuous community needs authority to unify its action. By accident, it may need it less than a community which, as a result of ignorance, is often confronted with illusory needs. But by essence it is more powerful than any community afflicted with vice and ignorance, and as a result of its greater power it controls choices involving new problems of unity which cannot be solved by way of unanimity but only by way of authority.[4]

One assumption held by many conservatives, then, is that in the life of a community, authority has an inherently positive role to play. Whereas conservatives like Simon recognize that authority may also have some negative functions, as when opinions are disputed by appeals to authority rather than reason, they insist that its central role is constructive.

The notion that authority's role is essentially constructive is at the basis of Arendt's interpretation of the Roman origin of the word and concept: "The word *auctoritas* derives from the verb *augere*, 'augment,' and what authority or those in authority constantly augment is the foundation. Those endowed with authority were the elders, the Senate or the *patres,* who had obtained it by descent or by transmission (tradition) from those who had laid the foundations for all things to come, the ancestors, whom the Romans therefore called the *maiores* [the great ones]."[5] In Arendt's view, the meaning of "authority" is closely connected to the words "augment" and "foundation," both of which have positive connotations. "Foundation," in this context, refers to the original establishment of the city of Rome with its institutions, laws, and values, whereas "to augment" means to add to and enhance the original foundation. Thus, like mainstream conservatives, Arendt believes that the role of authority is essentially positive and constructive rather than negative and limiting.

Another assumption that Arendt shares with conservative thinkers is that authority is intimately connected to both tradition and religion. Authority, tradition, and religion are all regarded by conservatives as the foundations for the ways in which we act and think in the present. The three are considered indispensable because they provide stability, meaning, and virtue to our lives. For conservatives, moreover, the surge of problems like violence and teenage pregnancy is closely related to our break with the trinity of authority, tradition, and religion. Though Arendt does not share mainstream conservatives' uncritical reverence for this trinity, she does agree that, historically speaking, the three were connected. Indeed, she argues that whenever one of the elements of the trinity was challenged, the other two were no longer secure. The decline of political authority in the modern age, for instance, has proved to be such a significant loss because it was also a loss of tradition and religion: "For to live in a political realm with neither authority nor the concomitant awareness that the source of authority transcends power and those who are in power, means to be confronted anew, without the religious trust in a sacred beginning and without the protection of traditional and therefore self-evident standards of behavior, by the elementary problems of human living-together" (WA, 141).

A third belief that Arendt shares with mainstream conservatives has to do with the issue of the purpose of authority in the life of a community. Many conservative thinkers contend that authority is needed in a community in order to unify the action of the individual members. Simon argues that since "a community comprises a number of individuals, the unity of its action cannot be taken for granted: it has to be caused. Further, if the community is to endure, the cause of its united action must be firm and stable."[6] Because a community is made up of individuals who are different from one another, a principle is needed to guarantee that each one will follow the same procedures and norms. Conservatives believe that authority is perhaps the only principle that can bring about this unity of judgment and action. To be sure, Arendt does not go this far, and her concept of action (discussed below) illustrates the importance of public debates and deliberation in the life of a democracy. Yet, like mainstream conservatives, Arendt maintains that, historically, authority is the principle that "had endowed political structures with durability, continuity and permanence" (WA, 127). It is this same principle, she believes, that previously unified human action and gave meaning and coherence to human existence.

Finally, Arendt shares the conviction of many conservatives that authority does not rest on persuasion and rational debate. She thinks that the two are fundamentally different because, unlike authority, persuasion presupposes a relationship of equality and works through a process of argumentation: "Where arguments are used, authority is left in abeyance. Against the egalitarian order of persuasion stands the authoritarian order which is always hierarchical" (WA, 93). This means that conservatives reject the claim voiced by many liberals that the obedience inherent in the authority relation rests on rational discussion and persuasion. They point out that the authority of the expert is based on the subjects' trust in the expert's superior knowledge and moral integrity. Consequently, this authority is almost always accepted without argument and cannot be questioned or doubted. Alven Michael Neiman explains this point with the example of teachers and students: "Students of mathematics come to believe in the correctness of certain formulae for dividing fractions simply on the basis of what a teacher says. They come to accept and depict certain conceptions of how a poem is to be interpreted for similar reasons. In each case the students implicitly trust that their acceptance, without discussion or argument, is correct."[7] Conservatives like Neiman and Simon share Arendt's view that the authority relation between bearer and subject is based on a hierarchical order "whose rightness and legitimacy both recognize and where both have their predetermined stable place" (WA, 93).

An Existentialist View of Political Existence

Thus far, I have argued that Arendt's conception of authority has several underlying assumptions in common with the mainstream conservative view of authority. Yet, as we shall soon see, this "conservative" conception does not fully account for her views on authority in education. In order to get a firm grasp on the latter, I need to also explain her notions of action and natality, since they are central to understanding Arendt's approach to political existence.

In *The Human Condition,* Arendt discusses political existence from the vantage point of the agent who acts in history and tries to create a new beginning. Political action, according to Arendt, is connected to the human condition of "natality," to the fact that we come into the world through birth and that each birth is an entirely new beginning:

> The new beginning inherent in birth can make itself felt in the world only because the newcomer possesses the capacity to begin something anew, that is, of acting. In this sense of initiative, an element of action, and therefore of natality, is inherent in all human activities. Moreover, since action is the political activity par excellence, natality, and not mortality, may be the central category of political, as distinguished from metaphysical, thought.[8]

Arendt explains that to act is to insert ourselves into the world with words and deeds. Yet this insertion is neither moved by necessity, like labor, nor prompted by utility, like work. Action, she holds, is often aroused by the presence of others whose company we may wish to join, but it is never conditioned by them. The impulse to act springs from the beginning that came into the world when we were born and to which we respond by beginning something new on our own initiative.

Her point is twofold: First, she thinks that action's worth is in the activity itself, unlike work and labor, which are instrumental activities, being merely means to achieve higher ends.[9] Action should be viewed outside of the means/ends category precisely because it has no end. The strength of the action process can never be reduced to a single deed with a definite outcome but, on the contrary, can grow while its consequences multiply. Second is the fact that human action, unlike animal behavior, can never be completely conditioned or controlled. In other words, action, like birth, contains an element of surprise since its outcome can never be fully predicted in advance. This is because it comes about through the joint efforts of beings who are beginnings (unique) and beginners (who initiate) in this world and, therefore, have the capacity to make the unexpected happen. One can never anticipate all the possible consequences of a public debate or a workers' strike, let alone a revolution. In short, action is the actualization of the human condition of freedom; it is the realization of our capacity to initiate something altogether new.

Yet Arendt teaches us more about political existence than the fact that action is a kind of activity that transcends the means/ends framework and that this activity is the same as the experience of being free. No less important is her insight that action saves human deeds from the doom of history and from the fatality of historical processes. If left to themselves, human affairs must follow the law of mortality, which is the inevitable outcome of every individual life. Action is the activity that interrupts the irreversible and unpredictable course of human life in order to begin something new. The point is that action, as the ability to interrupt and begin again, bestows meaning on human existence, which would otherwise resemble such other natural processes as the life of a volcano.

To combat the irreversibility and unpredictability of human deeds, action does not need to enlist a higher faculty, since the remedy for this predicament is one of the potentialities of action itself. The remedy for not being able to reverse what one has done is the act of forgiving, whereas the remedy for the uncertainty of the future is contained in the act of making and keeping promises. Without being forgiven, we could never be released from the harmful consequences of our actions, thereby greatly limiting our capacity to act anew. And without being bound to keep our promises, we would never be able to master the chaotic future that is simultaneously shaped by human freedom and plurality. Taking into account the power to initiate, to forgive, and to make promises, action seems like a miracle. This miracle not only bestows on human affairs faith and hope, but it also ensures that greatness (great words and deeds) will always be a part of the political realm: "The miracle that saves the world, the realm of human affairs, from its normal, 'natural' ruin is ultimately the fact of natality, in which the faculty of action is ontologically rooted. It is, in other words, the birth of new men and the new beginning, the action they are capable of by virtue of being born."[10]

This brief account illustrates that although Arendt derives many of her political notions from the ancient Greek and Roman experience and philosophy, there is a strong existentialist component in her thinking. She stresses, more than most political philosophers, the human capacity to act and to begin something new in the face of powerful historical processes and long-lasting oppressive institutions (for instance, the modern revolutions). And she insists that no democratic country can be deemed egalitarian and just unless the ordinary citizens have an opportunity to gather, deliberate, and decide on issues of public concern. In such a society, the positive freedom of individuals, the freedom to collaborate with others on political projects, is guaranteed. Such freedom, Arendt believes, carries with it the burden of responsibility for the decisions that we make. For to give the citizens freedom to decide on public issues makes no sense if they are not simultaneously required to assume responsibility for these decisions. As we shall soon see, these existentialist convictions had a profound effect on Arendt's views on education.

Rethinking Conservatism in Education

Authority in Education

In "The Crisis in Education," Arendt argues against those who view the crisis in educational authority of the late 1950s—a crisis lasting, I believe, up to the present time—as nothing more than a local phenomenon, peculiar to U.S. society and unconnected to the larger issues of the twentieth century. If this were the case, the crisis in U.S. schools would not have become a political problem and educators would have been able to deal with it in time. Much more is involved here, she felt, than the decline of elementary standards throughout the American school system. Rather, the problem is that the widespread erosion of authority in the Western world has infiltrated the U.S. school system and education in general. Therefore, she believes that the crisis in education that is still being felt strongly in the United States could easily become a reality in other countries in the foreseeable future.

But what is the nature of the particular authority that is being eroded in the American educational system? For Arendt, authority in education is intimately connected to assuming responsibility for the world. She explains:

> The educators here stand in relation to the young as representatives of a world for which they must assume responsibility although they themselves did not make it, and even though they may, secretly or openly, wish it were other than it is. This responsibility is not arbitrarily imposed upon educators; it is implicit in the fact that the young are introduced by adults into a continuously changing world. . . . In education this responsibility for the world takes the form of authority. The authority of the educator and the qualifications of the teacher are not the same thing. Although a measure of qualification is indispensable for authority, the highest possible qualification can never by itself beget authority. The teacher's qualification consists in knowing the world and being able to instruct others about it, but his authority rests on his assumption of responsibility for that world. Vis-à-vis the child it is as though he were a representative of all adult inhabitants, pointing out the details and saying to the child: This is our world.[11]

I have quoted this passage at length not only because it reveals Arendt's view on the nature of authority in education, but also because it points to the connection between this kind of authority and political authority. Further, it shows how her existentialist beliefs influenced her ideas on education. For the ancient Romans, but also for many of the succeeding generations, including the founders of the U.S. republic, true authority was always joined with responsibility for the course of events in the world. Those in authority knew that they had to assume responsibility for themselves and their property and for everyone and everything else under their jurisdiction. Similarly, in education, Arendt holds that to be in authority requires parents and teachers to take responsibility for preparing the young to take part in the common world. Hence, her conception of authority in education is based on her understanding of the ancient Roman experience of political authority.

However, Arendt's insistence that the teachers' authority rests on their assumption of responsibility for the world illustrates how her views on education were also shaped by her existentialist beliefs. To demand of parents and teachers to assume responsibility for the world into which they introduce the young, as she does, presupposes that responsibility and freedom are fundamental possibilities of the human condition. In fact, she believes that the current loss of authority in education was partly brought about by parents and teachers who refused to assume this responsibility. Arendt argues that in this realm, adults and children cannot equally share in the responsibility for the education of the latter. "Children cannot throw off educational authority, as though they were in a position of oppression by an adult majority" (CE, 190).[12] Rather, she thinks that authority has been discarded by the adults, which means that adults are increasingly refusing to assume responsibility for the world into which they have brought the children. To illustrate this point, we just need to think of the number of cases in the United States in which parents who themselves abuse drugs and alcohol bring children into the world for whom they can take little or no responsibility.

Thus, Arendt's existential convictions infiltrate her traditional conception of authority and create an unusual conservative approach to education. As she describes it, "To avoid misunderstanding: it seems to me that conservatism in the sense of conservation, is of the essence of the educational activity, whose task is always to cherish and protect something—the child against the world, the world against the child, the new against the old, the old against the new. Even the comprehensive responsibility for the world that is thereby assumed implies, of course, a conservative attitude" (CE, 192). It implies, in other words, the need to preserve the world from the hands of the young, who might destroy parts of it if left to their own devices. Arendt means that since the world is constantly made and remade by mortals, it runs the risk of becoming as mortal and temporary as they are. She is referring here primarily to the world that humans have created—that is, to the totality of human culture.

To preserve this human world against the mortality of its creators means to constantly renew it so that it can provide a permanent home for succeeding generations that will inhabit it. This point is reminiscent of the mainstream conservative argument that holds that society and tradition are to be preserved by imparting to the young the worthy values and great ideas of the past.

Yet Arendt also presents a stronger argument: that conservatism in education implies a willingness on the part of adults to protect the young from a world (e.g., from social conventions) that seeks to suppress the new and revolutionary in every child. Unlike mainstream conservative approaches that, at best, ignore the fresh possibilities the newborn brings into the world, Arendt's approach insists that educators must cherish and foster such possibilities. For Arendt, perhaps the most important and difficult problem in education is how to preserve the new and revolutionary in the child while simultaneously conserving the world as a permanent home for human beings. The question is, then: How do we protect the world from the actions of the young while not squashing their chance to be creative and original? In short, the problem in education is one of bridging the gap between the old (the past and tradition) and the new (change and creativity). In Arendt's view, as we shall soon see, the only way to solve this problem is by adopting a conservative attitude.

The conservative attitude that provides, according to Arendt, the answer to the central dilemma facing education today should be distinguished from mainstream conservative approaches. On the one hand, she agrees with mainstream conservatives like Edward Wynne and Allan Bloom who claim that the task of educators is to mediate between the old and the new. This means that their very profession requires of them an attitude of reverence toward the past. Wynne, for instance, thinks that educators need to be sensitive to the implications of our break with the great tradition: the deliberate transmission of moral values to students. He insists that "to understand the significance of the great tradition, we must engage in a form of consciousness-raising by enriching our understanding of the past and by understanding the misperceptions that pervade contemporary education."[13]

On the other hand, Arendt suggests that these conservatives ignore the fact that the crisis in authority is closely connected to the crisis of tradition. She points out that, together with authority, the value and relevance of Western tradition have been called into question in modern times and that we can no longer take for granted the Roman attitude of respect toward the past. This view is strengthened by contemporary liberal and radical thinkers who argue that educators need to critically engage the works of tradition because of their limited scope and oppressive elements. Unlike most conservatives, Arendt acknowledges the assertion that the educator's attitude toward the past and tradition has become problematized.

Moreover, Arendt criticizes mainstream conservatives for attempting to return to an old-fashioned political existence in which tradition and authority played such important roles. Such a position seems absurd to her because

> wherever the crisis has occurred in the modern world, one cannot simply go on nor yet simply turn back. Such a reversal will never bring us anywhere except to the same situation out of which the crisis has just arisen. . . . On the other hand, simple, unreflective perseverance, whether it be pressing forward in the crisis or adhering to the routine that blandly believes that the crisis will not engulf its particular sphere of life, can only, because it surrenders to the course of time, lead to ruin. (CE, 194)

This quote points to a fundamental distinction between Arendt and other conservative thinkers regarding the educator's attitude toward the past. What I am suggesting is that Arendt's way of conceptualizing tradition is very different from that of conservatives like Bloom and Wynne. This difference is expressed most clearly in the essay she wrote on the German literary critic Walter Benjamin. Arendt notes that Benjamin was well aware that the crisis in authority and the break with tradition were irreversible and that he therefore attempted to find new ways of dealing with the past. This he achieved through "the destructive power of quotations" and by "thinking poetically." Arendt writes that this kind of thinking is fed by the present and "works with the 'thought fragments' it can wrest from the past and gather about itself. Like a pearl diver who descends to the bottom of the sea, not to excavate the bottom and bring it to light but to pry loose the rich and the strange, the pearls and the coral in the depths and to carry them to the surface, this thinking delves into the depths of the past—but not in order to resuscitate it the way it was and to contribute to the renewal of extinct ages."[14]

Unlike the pearl diver, conservatives like Bloom and Wynne respond to what they perceive as the nihilism of our time by attempting to resuscitate the past and renew the values and practices of tradition. Bloom and Wynne believe that if the great works and deeds of the past can be brought to light and appreciated, authority and tradition can be saved from decay and revitalized. Underlying this conviction is the notion that tradition is like a seam, the function of which is to connect the present with the past and provide a sense of unity to the different periods of human civilization. The educator's task is, therefore, to repair and nourish this seam or to "protect and cultivate the delicate tendrils"[15] so that the past can continue to throw light on the present and provide us with a sense of coherence and unity.

As opposed to conservatives like Bloom and Wynne, Arendt does not view tradition as a seam that connects one generation to the next and endows human civilization with unity and significance. Rather, for her, it should be conceived as a series of innovations, itself full of breaks and fissures and the kinds of reinventions Arendt wants the young to make. To clarify this idea, let us return once again to the metaphor of the pearl diver. Arendt shares Benjamin's view that although human culture is subject to the ruin of time, "the process of decay is at the same time a process of crystallization, that in the depth of the sea, into which sinks and is dissolved what once was alive, some things 'suffer a sea-change' and survive in new crystallized forms and shapes that remain immune to the elements, as though they waited only for the pearl diver who one day will come down to them and bring them up to the world of the living."[16]

From this perspective, the challenge is not to revitalize our ties with tradition and the past, as one would mend a worn-out seam. It is rather to discover those crystallized forms and shapes that have survived the forces of destruction so that we can use them to interrupt and critique the present. For Benjamin, this meant that the quotations he collected were used not to reestablish a connection to the past, but to arrest the flow of the present and introduce something new. Arendt applies this idea to the educational realm and argues that educators need to help students become "pearl divers" who can descend into the depths of the past and find the crystallized artifacts. That is, educators should expose students to those ideas and values that, though they have undergone change, have survived in a different form and can be used to interrupt, critique, and transform the present.

Unlike mainstream conservatives who want to use these ideas and values to bridge the gap between the past and the present, Arendt wants to use them for the sake of creating a new beginning. The former insist that a deep familiarity with the past means to study the works of tradition in their original context and complexity. Arendt, following Benjamin and Heidegger, thinks that it is rather the ability to find "living eyes and living bones that had sea-changed into pearls and coral, and as such could be saved and lifted into the present only by doing violence to their context in interpreting them with 'the deadly impact' of new thoughts."[17] Mainstream conservatives hold that the treasures of the past can provide our lives with continuity, unity, and meaning; in contrast, Arendt views these treasures as tools that enable us to critique problematic aspects in the present and help us to generate fresh initiatives.

Practical Implications

One of the most pressing problems confronting educators in the modern age, according to Arendt, is that, on the one hand, they cannot forgo either authority or tradition; yet, on the other, they must continue living in a world that is neither bound by authority nor held together by tradition. For her, this means that all adults, not just educators and teachers, should apply a radically different attitude toward children than the one they apply toward one another. She states that we should separate the realm of education from all others, especially the political sphere, in order to "apply to it alone a concept of authority and an attitude toward the past which are appropriate to it but have no general validity and must not claim a general validity in the world of grown-ups" (CE, 195). In saying this, Arendt is not suggesting that we should not respect children or that they should be arbitrarily subjected to our will. But she does think that, in education, grown-ups should not treat children as equal partners, since only the former are truly responsible for the well-being of the latter and the world.

The demand to separate education from all other realms in order to maintain there a traditional concept of authority has a number of practical implications. First, Arendt thinks that we should recognize that the function of the school is to teach children *about* the world and not to instruct them in the art of living. This is because authority, in the sense of assuming responsibility for the world, presupposes that one is familiar with that world and can instruct others about it. Since the world is always older than the children, learning will inevitably be aimed at the past, no matter how much they need to adjust to a changing present. In this way, both authority and tradition will always play a major role in education, even as both are losing their grasp on other aspects of our lives. The advantage of this approach to pedagogy, as Natasha Levinson noted in the previous chapter, is that "it offers each new being an opportunity to see how they have been made what they are and provides an incentive for them to reconfigure themselves in response to this history."

Second, the dividing line maintained between children and adults through authority signifies that one can neither treat children as though they were grown-ups nor educate adults. Yet Arendt quickly adds the qualification that this line should not be allowed to grow into a wall closing off all contact between children and the adult community. She thinks that we ought to relate differently to children than we do to one another, which means that we should neither allow them the same rights and freedoms that adults enjoy nor hold them responsible in the same way. However, she does not call for a complete separation between the two, one that would involve setting up an autonomous world for the young governed by its own laws.

But what does Arendt mean when she says that one cannot educate adults? To understand this statement, I think it is important to keep in mind that she is distinguishing between educating and learning. Arendt believes that adults can certainly learn by being instructed about a particular aspect of the world. Education, though, has a more specific function and aims at introducing a young person to the world as a whole. It has to do with responsibly preparing children to live in and renew the common world. Arendt insists that education involves assuming responsibility for both the world and our children in order to protect them from harm and preserve the possibility for renewal. The common world needs to be protected from the actions of human beings, and children require a safe environment to enhance their development. This conservative attitude, applied to both the world and the young, helps to bridge the gap between the old and the new in education. Since both the children and the world need to be protected, they should no longer be conceived as diametrically opposed.

From this perspective, education involves a unique triadic relationship among our educators, our world, and our children, in which it is the former's task to mediate between the latter two. Such a relationship, according to Arendt, is both difficult to maintain and undesirable in other realms, since it is based on authority and therefore fundamentally inegalitarian. But in education, it is precisely the authority relation and its corresponding conservative attitude that make room for renewal and innovation. Renewal and innovation are contingent upon the young coming to know the world; and it is only the adults, because they are already familiar with the world, who can teach children about it. Education, she argues, is worthwhile when the conservative and the revolutionary go hand in hand, when we preserve the past for the sake of the new: "Exactly for the sake of what is new and revolutionary in every child, education must be conservative; it must preserve this newness and introduce it as a new thing into an old world, which, however revolutionary its actions may be, is always, from the standpoint of the next generation, superannuated and close to destruction" (CE, 192–193).

This last point should be underlined because I believe that Arendt is one of the only modern thinkers who insists that we must be conservative in education for the sake of the new (Antonio Gramsci is another noteworthy exception). She is not arguing, as mainstream conservatives have, that children should be taught the great works of the past because of their important educational insights and relevance for our lives. Rather, she is claiming that the past and the relation of authority are essential to help children realize their possibility of creating something new. Without being taught the classic works of tradition, children would not have the basic knowledge needed to change and renew the world. And without adults assuming responsibility for the common world and guiding the young in it, they would not have the security needed to operate adequately in a rapidly changing world. In Arendt's view, the most important goal of education is to help children become familiar with the world and feel secure in it so that they may have a chance to be creative and attempt something new.

Yet what distinguishes Arendt's conception of educational authority is not merely the idea of preserving the past for the sake of the new. No less important is her emphasis on human action and the fact of natality on which action is ontologically based. For Arendt, each child has the potential to initiate something new in the world by virtue of the fact that "with each birth something uniquely new comes into the world."[18] The fact that birth constantly brings newcomers who are not only beginners but also unique into our world means that the unexpected can be expected from them. It means that the young can intervene in the ordinary course of events and initiate radical changes in society. Since Arendt strongly believes in the human capacity to act, she would reject the view of conservatives like Bloom and Wynne that a worthy education is based primarily on the transmission of the great ideas and values of the past to the young. Instead, education should be aimed at preparing the young to a life of action, to a life of involvement in and transformation of the world:

Education is the point at which we decide whether we love the world enough to assume responsibility for it and by the same token save it from the ruin which, except for renewal, except for the coming of the new and young, would be inevitable. And education, too, is where we decide whether we love our children enough not to expel them from our world and leave them to their own devices, nor to strike from their

hands their chance of undertaking something new, something unforeseen by us, but to prepare them in advance for the task of renewing a
common world. (CE, 196)

In Arendt's view, therefore, education is aimed at preparing the
young for taking responsibility for the world. Yet this responsibility
for the world does not mean clinging to traditional morals or returning to a "golden past," as many conservatives advocate. It means
rather, as I noted, preparing our students for action—that is, for in-
tervening in the world and creating a more humane society. In this
context, it is interesting to note the difference between Bloom's interpretation of the university students' protest movement and that of
Arendt's. Bloom argues that students played a marginal role in the
civil rights movement and other major historical changes in the
United States between 1950 and 1970 and that many students were
plagued by a "histrionic morality."[19] Arendt, on the other hand,
claims that students played a decisive part in bringing about these
changes and that the student movement "did not simply carry on
propaganda, but acted, *and, moreover acted almost exclusively from
moral motives.*"[20]

What is involved here is not simply two different readings of historical events, but, more significantly, divergent conceptions of the
relation of education and action. For Bloom, action, as manifest in
the student protest movement, is primarily a way of evading the true
learning that goes on in the classroom and the responsibility for
one's education as a free spirit and a lover of truth. Contrarily,
Arendt believes that education is ideally a space that can help students prepare for taking responsibility for the world by providing
them with the kind of information and skills (e.g., moral reasoning)
that they will need to act. In brief, Bloom considers action as a vain
diversion from education whereas Arendt sees action as its fulfillment.

Arendt and Democratic Education

I have argued that Arendt's conservative approach to education represents a genuine alternative to mainstream conservative arguments, one that is not only more convincing, but also empowering. Whereas mainstream conservatives disregard the creative possibilities of the young, she celebrates these possibilities and insists that educators should foster them. In the final part of this chapter, I would like to discuss the relevance of Arendt's views for the debate on democratic education. In my view, her insights on authority constitute a significant contribution to the debate on the ways to attain democratic educational aims. This view is encouraging because, as Henry Giroux and Peter McLaren have shown, the new conservative discourse strips public education of a democratic virtue by emphasizing objectives such as standardization, competency, technical expertise, and a narrow and uncritical view of culture:

> The ideological interests that inform the new conservative proposals are based on a view of morality and politics that is legitimated through an appeal to custom, national unity, and tradition. Within this discourse, democracy loses its dynamic character and is reduced to a set of inherited principles and institutional arrangements that teach students how to adapt rather than to question the basic precepts of society. What is left in the new reform proposals is a view of authority constructed around a mandate to follow and implement predetermined rules, to transmit an unquestioned cultural tradition, and to sanctify industrial discipline.[21]

Giroux and McLaren are referring to conservatives like Allan Bloom, who, troubled by the relativism and anti-intellectualism of U.S. college students, argues that the only way to combat these problems is by returning to a type of liberal education that privileges the classic books of Western culture. Bloom's conception of liberal education consists of "reading certain generally recognized classic texts, just reading them, letting them dictate what the questions are and the method of approaching them—not forcing them into categories we make up, not treating them as historical products, but trying to read them as their authors wished them to be read."22

What is troubling about Bloom's conception of liberal education is not so much his preference for a very limited notion of the Western canon as the fact that he favors a pedagogy that relies heavily on transmission and imposition. For Bloom, it is obvious that there is only one legitimate way to read the classic texts and that the lessons that can be gleaned from them are explicit and timeless. In this view, "reading critically is reduced to appropriating so-called legitimate cultural capital, decoding texts, or authorizing the voice of the 'masters.'"23

Another conservative pedagogical approach that shares some of Bloom's basic assumptions about teaching and learning is that of E. D. Hirsch. In his book *Cultural Literacy,* Hirsch addresses the problem of ignorance and lack of mature literacy among American students, as exhibited primarily in declining standardized test scores. Hirsch defines cultural literacy as

> the network of information that all competent readers possess. It is the background information, stored in their minds, that enables them to take up a newspaper and read it with an adequate level of comprehension, getting the point, grasping the implications, relating what they read to the unstated context which alone gives meaning to what they read. . . . The achievement of high universal literacy is the key to all other fundamental improvements in American education.24

In short, for Hirsch, cultural literacy is essentially the body of information or facts that enables people to understand texts, communicate effectively with one another, and compete effectively in the marketplace. This notion of literacy presupposes what Paulo Freire calls "the banking concept of education," which consists of depositing information in students' heads, information that is often meaningless to them.25 Freire shows that this approach to education fosters students who are passive, disciplined, and content rather than students who can question, doubt, and think for themselves. In Hirsch's case, what we are offered is an approach to literacy that focuses on the need to appropriate a universal cultural capital and has little to say about how to develop those skills and capabilities that students need to evaluate and critique this capital.

In contrast to both Bloom and Hirsch, Arendt's unique conservative approach to education can be used to reinforce the liberal and radical efforts to establish more democratic classrooms that develop critical and active students. To advance my argument, I would like to focus on this question: What can we learn from Arendt's conception of pedagogical authority about the conditions necessary to achieve a democratic education? I believe that a conception of authority rooted in assuming responsibility for the world suggests that democratic educators need to take into account two primary conditions in their efforts to redefine the practices of teaching and learning. First is the idea that the democratic aim of enhancing children's creativity and initiative cannot be achieved unless teachers instruct the young about the cultural traditions of the past. The reason for this is that it makes no sense to critique, change, and renew the world without being thoroughly familiar with it first. That is, Arendt rightly emphasizes the fact that a worthy and effective critique is always grounded in a profound knowledge of the past. Likewise, creativity and innovation are truly significant only in relation to the world that came before them. "Only in relation to this world will students come to an understanding of what needs to be challenged and reconfigured."[26]

The significance of Arendt's view, therefore, is in her claim that an education that rests on the responsible initiation of students to the cultural traditions of the past, far from being opposed to creativity and critical thinking, can actually foster these goals. According to this view, learning about the past and the great works of tradition should not be done, as mainstream conservatives claim, in order to glorify and imitate them. Rather, such works should be taught in order to encourage children to respond to these examples and create something new. In this case, students' creativity and initiative are not stifled by coming to know a particular aspect of one's tradition and past, but they in fact emerge as a response to it. This point is crucial not only because Arendt is going beyond mainstream conservative educators who claim that the great works of tradition should be taught because they contain invaluable insights for our lives; she is also making a stronger point than a number of progressive educators who stress that the past and tradition have to be incorporated for pragmatic reasons. John Dewey, for instance, contends that unless democratic education starts with an idea of the existing society and practices, its goals will be utopian and impracticable.[27] In short, Arendt provides democratic educators with a more convincing rationale than the existing arguments for incorporating tradition and the great works of the past into the curriculum.

Still, how would an Arendtian pedagogy bridge the gap between the need for each generation to know what has come before it and the need to renew the world? And what would an Arendtian engagement with "the canon" look like? In my view, the answer to these questions lies in Arendt's emphasis on the twofold responsibility of educators: the responsibility to preserve the totality of human culture (the world) and the responsibility to protect the young's possibility for renewal and creativity. The strength of Arendt's approach is in her insistence that these two responsibilities are mutually dependent rather than opposed. On the one hand, as I argued above, children will not be able to be revolutionary and creative unless educators first introduce them to the traditions and ideas of the past. On the other hand, the continuous creation of great works of art is contingent on the ability of the young not simply to repeat the past, but to change and renew it.

What I am suggesting, following Arendt, is that it is not the case, as feminist literary critics like Judith Fetterly would have us believe, that "to read the canon of what is currently considered classic American literature is perforce to identify as male."[28] By arguing that women are *obliged* to respond to a text in a certain way, Fetterly, in effect, takes for granted the same traditional notion of reading embraced by mainstream conservative educators. According to this notion, the author has already defined the meaning of a text and the reader's task is to try to discover this hidden meaning independently of his or her context. Today, however, it is widely recognized that the meaning of a text cannot be separated from the social and political context of its readers. Moreover, since readers bring different perspectives to the encounter with the text, its meaning arises out of multiplicity and the recognition of otherness.[29] Arendt would say that to argue that works of literature *require* readers to adopt a certain meaning disregards the capacity of humans to challenge and create something new.

Neither is it correct to suggest, as Fetterly does, that texts typically elicit a response of "identification." Rather, it is more accurate to say, as Martin Buber does, that of the many things that impress upon our character, some "exert their influence by stimulating agreement, imitation, desire, effort; others by arousing questions, doubts, dislike, resistance. Character is formed by the interpenetration of all these multifarious, opposing influences."[30] My experience of reading and discussing classic texts with hundreds of female and minority college students indicates that identification is only one of many possible responses to these texts. In fact, resistance and dislike are just as likely to occur.

The crucial question for curriculum theory and pedagogy is, therefore, How can teachers encourage students to be critical and innovative readers and learners? Like Arendt, I would argue that what is essential in education is not so much *what* the curriculum includes, but *how* any text, whether traditional or modern, feminist or minority, is read and discussed.[31] Thus it is incorrect to assert, as a number of critical educators have, that the Eurocentric curriculum is responsible for making students passive and content.[32] This curriculum, no matter how distorted, cannot by itself, without the support of teachers who subscribe to traditional pedagogical approaches, have such an effect on students. Indeed, even texts written by authors who portray the values of a slave or an elitist society can have a liberating effect. Such an effect is possible if, for example, Plato is read "not as a cultural icon whose abstractions one might reproduce on exams, but as a living force with whom one might argue, agree and disagree, embrace and reject."[33] Alternatively, one might imagine a situation in which a feminist text is read and discussed in a dogmatic and uncritical way. Following Arendt, I submit that the educator is responsible more than any other factor for empowering students to become critical and active readers and learners.

The second condition democratic educators must meet to redefine educational practices concerns the idea that, for Arendt, assuming responsibility for the world implies not only preserving the great works of the past while protecting the young's possibility for renewal, but also preserving and renewing our common habitation so that it can provide a secure home for succeeding generations. "Because the world is made by mortals it wears out; and because it continuously changes its inhabitants it runs the risk of becoming as mortal as they are. To preserve the world against the mortality of its creators and inhabitants it must be constantly set right anew" (CE, 192). This "setting right anew" suggests that Arendt believes that educators should confront rather than avoid the problems that threaten to destroy our common world.

Responsibility for the common world is more crucial today than ever before, when millions are dying of hunger, the environment is being destroyed in the name of capitalism and free enterprise, and violence is rampant. These global and local catastrophes, often brought about by human actions, demonstrate that, for many people, the world can no longer provide a secure haven. Arendt suggests that educators need to make people aware of the fact that their actions may inevitably affect the lives of others who share this world now, as well as those who will be here tomorrow. She echoes the concern of many progressive educators who argue that democratic education should be aimed at developing a sense of community, solidarity, and responsibility for others.

However, Arendt diverges from liberals and radicals on the means to achieve such educational aims. Many liberal and radical educators argue that these goals can be attained primarily by encouraging students to think critically about and struggle against the oppressive institutions and inequities of their society. These educators subscribe to a pedagogy based on dialogue, equality, and the idea that teachers and students should share in the responsibility for the learning process. Giroux, for example, advocates a radical pedagogy that incorporates and analyzes the immediate experiences and cultures of the students. In addition, such radical pedagogy needs to

> critically appropriate forms of knowledge that exist outside the immediate experience of students' lives in order to broaden their sense of understanding and possibility. This means that students need to learn and appropriate other codes of experience as well as other discourses in time and place that extend their horizons while constantly pushing them to test what it means to resist oppression, work collectively, and

exercise authority from the position of an ever-developing sense of knowledge, expertise, and commitment.[34]

Contrary to these thinkers, Arendt maintains that the responsibility for the learning process cannot be shared with students and should be assumed by educators. For her, parents and teachers are the only ones responsible for helping students develop a sense of community and concern for the world, as well as for making sure that the world remains a safe place for children. As Elisabeth Young-Bruehl notes, Arendt strongly believed that adults must not "forgo their responsibility for children as children, they must not refuse to children a sheltered period of maturation, for being at home in the world."[35] Thus, she would criticize progressive educators like Giroux and McLaren for blurring the distinguishing line between children and adults. She would also chastise them for expecting children to assume responsibility for social problems like racial oppression and inequality and to become involved in political struggles.

Arendt's criticism of progressive educators is particularly relevant in light of a weighty problem in contemporary American education. This problem concerns the lack of a secure and nourishing place for teenagers in present-day U.S. society. Writing in the mid-1980s, David Elkind described this problem well:

> There is no place for teenagers in American society today—not in our homes, not in our schools, and not in society at large. This was not always the case: barely a decade ago, teenagers had a clearly defined position in the social structure. They were the "next generation," the "future leaders" of America. Their intellectual, social, and moral development was considered important, and therefore it was protected and nurtured. . . . Teenagers thus received the time needed to adapt to the remarkable transformations their bodies, minds, and emotions were undergoing. Society recognized that the transition from childhood to adulthood was difficult and that young people needed time, support, and guidance in this endeavor.[36]

The problem that Elkind points to is that many parents and teachers today are unable or unwilling to give adolescents the necessary guidance and direction they need in order to mature into healthy adults. Many parents and teachers assume that the teenager is a kind of adult and thus expect him or her to "confront life and its challenges with the maturity once expected only of the middle aged, without any time for preparation."[37]

Elkind claims that there are two detrimental results to the imposition of premature adulthood upon teenagers. First, the absence of a clearly defined transition period from childhood to adulthood impairs teenagers' ability to form a secure personal identity. Second, premature adulthood leads teenagers to undergo excessive stress, making it almost impossible for many of them to adapt to the demands of a rapidly changing society.

Elkind and others have argued that what is true for teenagers—the disappearance of adolescence as a clearly defined period—is equally true for younger children. In *The Disappearance of Childhood,* Neil Postman claims that childhood as a period of innocence has all but disappeared and that today's children are exposed to all sorts of information that was once the privilege of adults.[38] Television, for instance, has made violence and sexual information accessible even to young children, thereby robbing many of them of their innocence before they are ripe. As a result, young children, much like adolescents, are subjected to inordinate stress, which is proving to be too much for many of them to bear.

In my view, the problem of the disappearance of childhood and adolescence as clearly defined periods is related to a more general problem in educational authority. More specifically, I would argue that the crisis that many teenagers and young children are undergoing today is largely a product of the erosion of authority in education. Arendt is correct in her claim that the loss of authority in education suggests that adults are increasingly refusing "to assume responsibility for the world into which they have brought the children" (CE, 190). Put another way, pedagogical authority is at stake when educators repudiate responsibility for children and the world.

The refusal to assume this responsibility can be seen in the fact that many parents expect their children to confront difficult problems and make weighty decisions on their own, without adult guidance and support. Radical educators who expect students to struggle for social transformation and justice may be inadvertently contributing to the problem of the disappearance of childhood. At the very least, these educators need to be clearer about what kind of responsibility they think should be required of children at different ages. The crucial point for educators who believe that students should partake in the responsibility for the learning process is that they need to make sure that the students are ready and willing to assume this responsibility.

If we agree with progressive educators that democratic education should be aimed at fostering students who can think critically about oppressive social structures, then we must adopt a notion of pedagogical authority to which the responsibility of the educator is central. What is missing from the conception of democratic education of many radical pedagogues is the necessity of grounding critique and reform on a deep familiarity with the past and tradition. Yet also missing is the recognition that there are certain responsibilities regarding our common world that should not be shared even with the brightest children. These oversights can be corrected if radical pedagogues take seriously Arendt's claim that authority in education rests on the willingness of educators to assume responsibility for the welfare of both our children and the world.

The import of Arendt's approach is not merely in her emphasis on the twofold responsibility of educators; it is also in her ability to help us understand how these two responsibilities are connected: that children will not be able to be revolutionary and creative unless educators first introduce them to the values and ideas of the past. Recognizing that these two responsibilities are mutually dependent is significant because it enables us to break the impasse between the mainstream conservatives' emphasis on preserving tradition and the progressives' focus on critical citizenry and social justice.

Notes

An earlier version of this essay was published in *Educational Theory*, vol. 49, no. 2 (Spring 1999): 161–180.

1. Edward A. Wynne, "The Great Tradition in Education: Transmitting Moral Values," *Educational Leadership*, vol. 43 (December 1985/January 1986): 9. See also Edward A. Wynne and Herbert J. Walberg's "The Complementary Goals of

Character Development and Academic Excellence," in the same issue of *Educational Leadership*, pp. 15–18.

2. See Barbara Finkelstein, "Education and the Retreat from Democracy in the United States, 1979–198?," *Teachers College Record*, vol. 86 (Winter 1984); and Henry A. Giroux, "Schooling and the Politics of Ethics: Beyond Liberal and Conservative Discourses," *Journal of Education*, vol. 169, no. 2 (1987): 14–15.

3. Kenneth Minogue, "Conservatism," in *The Encyclopedia of Philosophy*, ed. Paul Edwards, vol. 1 (New York: Collier Macmillan Publishers, 1967), p. 196.

4. Yves R. Simon, *A General Theory of Authority* (Notre Dame, IN: University of Notre Dame Press, 1980), pp. 49–50.

5. Hannah Arendt, "What Is Authority?" in *Between Past and Future* (New York: Penguin Books, 1977), pp. 121–122. This essay will be cited as WA in the text for all subsequent references.

6. Simon, *A General Theory*, p. 32.

7. Alven Michael Neiman, "Education, Power, and the Authority of Knowledge," *Teachers College Record*, vol. 88 (Fall 1986): 68.

8. Hannah Arendt, *The Human Condition* (Chicago: University of Chicago Press, 1968), p. 9.

9. Related to this is her notion that political action resembles the performing arts in that both come to an end when the activity is over and leave no trace behind except the memory of what was seen or heard.

10. Arendt, *The Human Condition*, p. 247.

11. Hannah Arendt, "The Crisis in Education," in *Between Past and Future*, p. 189. This essay will be cited as CE in the text for all subsequent references.

12. This argument is especially strong today because the traditional despotic methods of pedagogy used in the past have been replaced by more liberal and democratic approaches.

13. Wynne, "The Great Tradition," p. 4.

14. Hannah Arendt, "Walter Benjamin, 1892–1940," in *Men in Dark Times* (New York: Harcourt Brace Jovanovich, 1968), p. 205.

15. Allan Bloom, *The Closing of the American Mind* (New York: Simon & Schuster, 1987), p. 380.

16. Arendt, "Walter Benjamin," p. 206.

17. Ibid., p. 201.

18. Arendt, *The Human Condition*, p. 178. Even thinkers like Nietzsche who share Arendt's concern for preserving the past for the sake of creativity and renewal do not consider the significance of action as a universal possibility of the human condition. For Nietzsche, what saves our civilization from doom is not the changes brought about by ordinary people who gather and act in the public realm, but rather the creative work of a handful of free spirits or great human beings.

19. Bloom, *The Closing of the American Mind*, pp. 333–334.

20. See Arendt's "Thoughts on Politics and Revolution," in *Crises of the Republic* (New York: Harcourt Brace Jovanovich, 1972), p. 203.

21. Henry A. Giroux and Peter McLaren, "Teacher Education and the Politics of Engagement: The Case for Democratic Schooling," *Harvard Educational Review*, vol. 56, no. 3 (August 1986).

22. Bloom, *The Closing of the American Mind*, p. 344.

23. See Henry A. Giroux's article "Curriculum Theory, Textual Authority, and the Role of Teachers as Public Intellectuals," *Journal of Curriculum and Supervision,* vol. 5, no. 4 (Summer 1990): 370–371.

24. E. D. Hirsch, *Cultural Literacy: What Every American Needs to Know* (Boston: Houghton Mifflin, 1987), p. 2.

25. For a detailed discussion of this notion, see chapter 2 of Freire's *Pedagogy of the Oppressed* (New York: Continuum Publishing, 1970).

26. This quote is from Natasha Levinson's essay in this volume (see Chapter 1).

27. John Dewey, *Democracy and Education* (New York: Free Press, 1966), p. 83.

28. Judith Fetterly, *The Resisting Reader: A Feminist Approach to American Fiction* (Bloomington: Indiana University Press, 1978), p. xii.

29. This view is discussed in Giroux's "Curriculum Theory." See also Tony Bennet's "Texts in History: The Determinations of Readings and Their Texts," in *Post-Structuralism and the Question of History,* ed. Derek Attridge, Geoff Bennington, and Robert Young (New York: Cambridge University Press, 1987).

30. Martin Buber, "The Education of Character," in *Between Man and Man* (London: Fontana Library, 1964).

31. At the same time, I believe that Arendt would be sympathetic to the claim of feminists and critical educators that we should incorporate into "the canon" the voices of women and minorities who historically have been excluded from joining it.

32. In addition to Fetterly's above-mentioned book, this view is exemplified by James Banks in his essay "A Curriculum for Empowerment, Action, and Change," in *Empowerment Through Multicultural Education,* ed. Christine E. Sleeter (Albany: State University of New York Press, 1991), p. 130.

33. Paul Lauter, "Whose Culture? Whose Literacy?" in *Canons and Contexts* (New York: Oxford University Press, 1991), pp. 268–269.

34. Henry A. Giroux, "Authority, Intellectuals, and the Politics of Practical Learning," *Teachers College Record,* vol. 88 (Fall 1986): 35–36.

35. Elisabeth Young-Bruehl, *Hannah Arendt: For Love of the World* (New Haven: Yale University Press, 1982), p. 317.

36. David Elkind, *All Grown Up and No Place to Go* (Reading, MA: Addison Wesley Publishing, 1984), p. 3.

37. Ibid.

38. Neil Postman, *The Disappearance of Childhood* (New York: Delacorte, 1982). See also the interview "On Our Changing Family Values: A Conversation with David Elkind," *Educational Leadership,* vol. 53 (April 1996).

3

Education for Judgment:
An Arendtian Oxymoron?

STACY SMITH

Toward the end of her life, Hannah Arendt's philosophical project centered on an explication of three mental faculties: thinking, willing, and judgment. Her final written work, *The Life of the Mind*, which her biographer Elisabeth Young-Bruehl refers to as a "treatise on mental good governance,"[1] was to include a section on each of the three faculties. She completed the sections on thinking and willing, but the final section on judgment was left with only the epigraph page in the typewriter on the evening that she died.[2]

Despite the fact that Arendt never finished her exploration of judgment, this mental faculty plays a crucial role in her ongoing project of struggling to reconcile politics and philosophy in the modern world. And although we lack the explanatory clarity that a third section of *The Life of the Mind* may have provided, there are other pieces of her work, as well as a body of secondary literature, from which to cull a sense of her views on judgment. Undoubtedly, these views are unresolved and even contradictory. But a prominent strand of Arendt's approach to judgment clearly classifies it as an important political ability. In this strand of her thinking, judgment describes the ability of political actors to engage in "representative thinking" or to take on an "enlarged mentality," which allows them to form opinions and decide future courses of action.[3]

On first glance, the important role played by the faculty of judgment in Arendt's vision of democratic politics would suggest an educational task. To the extent that processes of formal education in democratic societies are intended to prepare future citizens to engage in political life, the cultivation of judgment would appear an appropriate educational endeavor. But this preliminary conclusion is complicated by Arendt's suggestion that judgment is something that cannot be taught, only practiced, and by her strict distinction between the domain of education and that of politics. Based upon these claims, one might conclude that she would not view the cultivation of judgment as an appropriate task for educators.

An interpretation of Arendt's views on judgment and education that suggests that "education for judgment" is neither possible nor appropriate is troubling in light of the importance that she places on political equality. If judgment is "a specifically political ability,"[4] yet some people simply exercise good judgment and others do not, it seems less than satisfactory that adults as political equals would disparately possess a capacity so fundamental to political action. Moreover, since action is the means whereby individuals most fully reveal their humanity, lack of opportunity to develop one's faculty of judgment, which both guides and evaluates action, suggests a crucial constraint on one's development as an aesthetic, political, and moral being.[5] Insofar as judgment allows us to live in and share a common world with others, opportunity to cultivate this faculty seems vital, in Arendtian terms, to "becoming" complete human beings.

In this essay, I contend that cultivating judgment is an appropriate and necessary educational task, particularly in light of Arendt's vision of participatory democratic politics. Good judgment is vital for the sorts of civic engagement and political deliberation that Arendt viewed as integral to democratic public life. I argue against an interpretation of Arendt's views on judgment that would suggest that the cultivation of this faculty does not fall under the purview of education. First, I challenge her suggestion that judgment cannot be taught, only practiced, by elaborating a conception of "practice as preparation" that entails specific functions for formal education. Second, I extend this notion of practice as preparation to complicate Arendt's strict distinction between the domains of politics and education. On my reading, "education for judgment" is a pivotal component of Arendt's self-proclaimed educational project of preparing young people "for the task of renewing a common world."[6]

Judgment in Arendt's Thought

In this section, I outline Arendt's views on judgment as presented in two primary sources: her essay "The Crisis in Culture," which was published in the United States for the first time in 1961, and the "Lectures on Kant's Political Philosophy," which she delivered at the New School for Social Research in the fall of 1970.[7] In each of these sources, she drew upon Kant's model of "aesthetic" or "reflective judgment" as developed in his *Critique of Judgment*. Arendt claimed that Kant's unwritten political philosophy could be found in this work. According to Ronald Beiner, she first introduced this claim in 1961 in the essay "Freedom and Politics," where she contended that Kant expounded two very different political philosophies in his *Critique of Practical Reason* versus his *Critique of Judgment*. Arendt was particularly interested in the role of judgment in the latter philosophy, wherein "freedom is portrayed as a predicate of the power of imagination and not of the will, and the power of imagination is linked most closely with that wider manner of thinking which is political thinking par excellence, because it enables us to 'put ourselves in the minds of other men.'"[8] This emphasis on a "wider manner of thinking" or putting ourselves "in the minds of other men" is at the heart of Arendt's conception of political judgment.

According to Arendt's reading of Kant, judgment is the capacity to "tell right from wrong, beautiful from ugly."[9] Judgments can be reached when humans, in all of our distinctiveness and plurality, share our perspectives on a common world with one another. Ultimately, sharing perspectives allows humans to reach a fuller understanding than any one individual could reach on his/her own; such understanding is revealed from a general standpoint that allows an object or issue to be assessed from a variety of different angles. Thus, judgment depends upon connections and mediation between a given individual's perspective and the standpoints of others with whom this individual shares the world.

The role played by judgment in connecting individuals to their common world speaks to the crux of political life in Arendt's thought. In his interpretive essay on her Kant lectures, Beiner asserts that, for Arendt, "the faculty of judgment is in the service of human intelligibility . . . and conferring intelligibility is the meaning of politics."[10] To the extent that judgment encourages and relies upon an "enlarged mentality," whereby a person expands his/her unique perspective on the world and gains new insight, this mental capacity allows us to make sense of the world and to share its meaning with others. Therefore, Arendt insists that "judgment may be one of the fundamental abilities of man as a political being insofar as it enables him to orient himself in the public realm, in the common world" (CC, 221).

Each of these concepts—judgment, politics and the public realm, human plurality, and a common world—is unique and complex in Arendt's thought and, hence, requires some explanation. Arendt's insistence on the human condition of plurality is rooted in an ancient Greek notion of *doxa*. According to Arendt, the word *doxa* refers to each individual's "own opening to the world."[11] She explains:

> The assumption was that the world opens up differently to every man, according to his position in it; and that the "sameness" of the world, its commonness . . . or objectivity . . . resides in the fact that the same world opens to everyone and that despite all differences between men and their positions in the world—and consequently their *doxai* (opinions)—"both you and I are human." The word *doxa* means not only opinion but also splendor and fame. As such, it is related to the political realm, which is the public sphere in which everybody can appear and show who he himself is. To assert one's opinion belonged to being able to show oneself, to be seen and heard by others.[12]

This link between politics and public appearance that Arendt traces back to the ancient Greeks helps to explain why she insists that

Kant's notion of "aesthetic" judgment also provides a model for "political" judgment.

In her essay "The Crisis in Culture," Arendt makes the connection between art and politics by beginning with the concept of culture. She contends that although culture and art "are by no means the same . . . any discussion of culture must somehow take as its starting point the phenomena of art" (CC, 210–211). She posits the premises that "only works of art are made for the sole purpose of appearance" and "the proper criterion by which to judge appearances is beauty" (CC, 210). Finally, she makes the connection between art and politics with the claim that political activities also depend on appearance. She says, "truly political activities, . . . acting and speaking, cannot be performed at all without the presence of others, without the public, without a space constituted by the many" (CC, 217). Thus, Arendt concludes that reflective judgment applies to both aesthetics and politics because both sets of activities are situated in the realm of public appearance.

As Richard Bernstein explains, Arendt's notion of "judging, although a mental activity of the life of the mind, never leaves the world of appearances."[13] This is because she connects the process of judging artistic products (e.g., novels and paintings) with the process of judging political products (e.g., virtues and deeds, particularly speech deeds). Following Kant, she views judgment as arising from "a merely contemplative pleasure or inactive delight . . . called taste."[14] She then expands the role played by taste in the realm of aesthetics to extend Kant's concept of reflective judgment into another public realm of appearances: the political arena. According to her interpretation, "Taste judgments . . . share with political opinions that they are persuasive; the judging person—as Kant says quite beautifully—can only 'woo the consent of everyone else' in the hope of coming to an agreement eventually. This 'wooing' or persuading corresponds closely to . . . the convincing and persuading speech which [the Greeks] regarded as the typically political form of people talking with one another" (CC, 222).

Arendt's approach to judgment as the capacity to tell right from wrong and beautiful from ugly combines the realms of culture and politics insofar as both are concerned with the public spaces in which individuals form and exchange opinions, thereby expressing or revealing themselves. She explains: "Culture and politics, then, belong together because it is not knowledge or truth which is at stake, but rather judgment and decision, the judicious exchange of opinion about the sphere of public life and the common world, and the decision what manner of action is to be taken in it, as well as to how it is to look henceforth, what kind of things are to appear in it" (CC, 223).[15] Like the function of taste in the aesthetic realm, judgment as a political ability has to do with the transformation of individual idiosyncrasy and self-interest "into a more broadly shared public or common interest."[16] This requires the background of a common world—because the world provides stable and objective points of reference with which to orient oneself—as well as an enlarged perspective that includes the possible opinions and judgments of others. As Seyla Benhabib explains, "judging becomes an activity of 'enlarged mentality,' a capacity for presenting to oneself the perspectivality of the world, of taking cognizance of the many points of view through which a matter must be seen and evaluated."[17] This "enlarged mentality" is necessary for democratic politics because it allows individual citizens to make decisions from a general or impartial standpoint that reveals the collective, common interest of the public.[18]

The enlarged mentality necessary for political judgment can be achieved only through processes of critical thinking that entail exposing one's opinion to others in a public fashion whereby the opinion can be both expanded and tested through interaction with other opinions. One's opinions—one's *doxai* or openings onto the world—form through interaction with genuinely different perspectives on the world. And this plurality—or perspectivality—is at the heart of political life. As Bernstein explains:

> Opinions . . . are the very stuff of politics. Individuals do not simply "have" opinions, they *form* opinions. . . . Opinions can only be tested and enlarged when there is a genuine encounter with different opinions. There is no test for the adequacy of an opinion, no authority for judging it, other than the force of the better *public* argument. The formation of opinions, therefore, requires a political community of

equals, the imagination to represent other viewpoints, and the courage
to submit opinions to public exposure and test.[19]

Again, the relationship that Arendt draws here between individual
opinions and achieving an enlarged mentality in order to "woo the
consent of others" is firmly rooted in her conceptions of politics and
human plurality. Opinion formation parallels identity formation
within individuals, and both processes require a shared public space
wherein individuals appear to one another and engage in forms of
action, primarily the struggles of debate requiring persuasive speech,
that define democratic political life.

Arendt clearly states in the essay "Truth and Politics" that "debate
constitutes the very essence of political life."[20] And Bernstein reminds us that in Arendt's work: (a) "Debate itself is a form of action"; (b) "action" is the term that designates the distinctive and
highest form of human activity; and (c) it is through action
"whereby the distinctive humanity of men is *revealed*."[21] Thus, political judgment is not only a faculty whereby we pass judgment on
objects external to ourselves, but a process whereby we "form" and
"reveal" ourselves as distinct human beings. In Arendt's words:
"Wherever people judge things of the world that are common to
them, there is more implied in their judgments than these things. By
his manner of judging, the person discloses to an extent also himself,
what kind of person he is, and this disclosure, which is involuntary,
gains in validity to the degree that it has liberated itself from merely
individual idiosyncrasies" (CC, 223).

The disclosures that are revealed through the process of judging are
valid in direct relation to their position on a continuum between partial versus whole, or impartial, perspectives. To the extent that a person's perspective is merely "idiosyncratic," or steeped in the prejudices
of a particular tradition, it does not take into account the plethora of
other stances in relation to the world that one's fellow human beings
occupy and experience. Judgment is therefore the capacity whereby
we relate ourselves to the world vis-à-vis a fullness of perspectives that
relates as closely as possible to the world's "objective" status. Because
opinion formation is "representative thinking" par excellence, we can
attain this fullness only through interchange with others.

Arendt refers to this external orientation of the representative thinking that characterizes judgment as "communicability" or the "factor of publicity" (*KL*, 40–41). These are her terms for the criterion that establishes one's thinking as impartial and, hence, one's judgment as good. Although judgment is dependent on the communicability or publicness of one's critical thinking, actual interaction with other people is not always required in order to exercise the faculty. Arendt explains:

> The power of judgment rests on a potential agreement with others, and the thinking process which is active in judging something is not, like the thought process of pure reasoning, a dialogue between me and myself, but finds itself always and primarily, even if I am quite alone in making up my mind, in an anticipated communication with others with whom I know I must finally come to some agreement. From this potential agreement judgment derives its specific validity. (CC, 220)

So, even though it is essentially a "public" activity, judgment can be undertaken alone, in "anticipated" communication with others. The endeavor to render one's judgment is still fundamentally political in nature because it brings our private, subjective perspective on the world in line with the "'objective' world which we have in common and share with others." In this manner, "judging is one, if not the most, important activity in which this sharing-the-world-with-others comes to pass" (CC, 221).

Thus, in Arendt's thought, judgment plays a pivotal role as a form of action related to both individual identity formation, through revelation in public spaces of appearance, and opinion formation, as one's views are informed by and tested against others in public spaces of deliberation. The importance of this faculty, then, for individual development and for vibrant political life suggests a crucial challenge for education: How is such a capacity to be cultivated in young people? Now that Arendt's views on judgment have been established, it is also necessary to provide a context for her thinking on education in order to connect the two concepts in her work.

Education in Arendt's Thought

Arendt poses two sets of distinctions that problematize a straight-forward approach to a project of "education for judgment." First, following Kant, she distinguishes things that can be taught from things that can be practiced and places judgment in the latter category. Second, she distinguishes sharply between the domains of education and politics. If we read Arendt "literally" and interpret her distinctions at face value, there seems little reason to proceed with a project exploring education for judgment. The task would be simultaneously impossible, because judgment cannot be taught, and inappropriate, because judgment is a capacity that belongs within the political domain. But, if we follow Benhabib's lead in thinking "with Arendt against Arendt,"[22] we can interpret her intersecting claims in a more complex way that leads to a more fruitful relationship between education and judgment. In this section, I argue that she conceives of each of these distinctions too narrowly and offer a conception of "preparation as practice" that blurs the boundaries between each.

To begin, Arendt follows Kant in delineating between things that can be taught versus things that are simply practiced. In the post-script to her *Life of the Mind* volume titled *Thinking,* Arendt introduces her return to Kant's views on judgment, which she likely would have developed in her final section. She writes: "In Kant judgment emerges as 'a peculiar talent which can be practiced only and cannot be taught.'"[23] With this distinction, we are left wondering about the relationships that she conceives between "teaching and learning" versus "practice and learning," as well as how both sets of relationships intersect with the domain of education. If practice is distinct from teaching and learning, then cultivating the faculty of judgment may not fall under the purview of formal education. In other words, Arendt may not see any role for educators or for schools in cultivating the faculty of judgment in young people. I propose an approach to the "practice of judgment" that is not so easily separated from formal, school-based educational processes of teaching and learning.

Practicing Judgment as Preparation for Politics

Kant's notion that judgment can be practiced but not taught raises some interesting questions for a project of "education for judgment." There is a sense in which "practice" refers to the act of *doing* something—practicing law, for instance. But there is another sense in which "practice" refers to the act of *preparing* to do something—practicing notes on a musical scale or practicing your golf swing, for example. When one keeps in mind this dual sense of practice, Kant's strict distinction between what is practiced and what is taught appears less tenable.

Arendt elaborates Kant's notion of practice as distinguished from teaching and learning in the following passage: "For Kant 'the middle term' that links and provides a transition from theory to practice is judgment; he had in mind the practitioner—for example, the doctor or lawyer, who first *learns theory and then practices* medicine or law, and whose *practice consists in applying the rules he has learned to particular cases*" (*KL,* 36; emphasis added). Arendt's explication of Kant's views on judgment in this passage suggests that "theory" and "rules" are to be learned and therefore could fall within the realm of education, whereas judgment is practiced later, after one's formal education has ended. But this example that posits the doctor or lawyer as someone who learns and *then* practices overlooks important components of both learning and practice.

Think about the education of doctors. For two or three years, future doctors sit in classrooms where they "learn" medical theories and rules that they will later apply in their practice. But another crucial component of medical education is the time spent in internships and residencies. As interns and residents, future doctors are placed in hospitals and take part in the activity of making rounds to patients' rooms, where they apply the rules they've learned from medical books and classroom lectures to the particular cases posed by patients. A similar process applies to the education of future teachers. Students in programs of teacher education undertake a number of hours of classroom learning, sometimes accompanied by direct field experience, and then are expected to act as "student teachers." Yet they are neither students nor teachers in a full sense, but rather in a mediating stage where their action is that of both a learner and a practitioner.

This "in-between" stage, which mediates classroom learning and autonomous practice, is characterized by a form of practice whereby preparation constitutes a unique form of action. Practice in this sense is a preparatory form of action. And this process does not take place in isolation. Rather, this in-between stage of practice as preparation is overseen by a more knowledgeable and experienced practitioner. On this model, practice as preparation is part and parcel of the educational process; practice as preparation is part of *learning how* to practice in the sense of *doing* once one formally takes on the title of doctor, lawyer, or teacher.

The notion of practice as preparation for autonomous action challenges not only Kant's notion that judgment can be practiced but not taught, but also Arendt's notion that the domains of education and politics can or should be strictly separated. *Insofar as education prepares young people for politics, it is political in that preparation is a unique form of action.* I will elaborate this point by challenging and reconceiving Arendt's strict distinction between the two spheres.

The second distinction in Arendt's work, that drawn between education and politics, is potentially the most fatal for a project of education for judgment. In her essay "The Crisis in Education," Arendt contends that education should proceed from a conservative attitude regarding the world and the authority of educators based upon their "temporary superiority" as adults. Authority and conservation are appropriate for the educational realm because its processes must simultaneously accomplish two divergent ends: to protect the world as it exists and to preserve the newness and revolutionary potential, the natality, of every child who will enter this world and bring about change (CE, 191–193).

Because Arendt views authority and a conservative attitude as exemplary of the educational realm, she sees it as essential to separate education from the political realm, where equality and newness prevail. She argues: "We must decisively divorce the realm of education from the others, most of all from the realm of public, political life, in order to apply to it alone a concept of authority and an attitude toward the past which are appropriate to it but have no general validity and must not claim a general validity in the world of grown-ups" (CE, 195). Thus, education is a distinct process, aimed at children, that comes to an end as they enter the world of adults. In the political realm, adults interact with one another based upon relationships of equality and freedom, not authority. It is only within this context that action, which reveals individual identity and brings meaning to life, is possible.

Although Arendt claims that politics begins where education ends, her demarcation between the two domains is problematic on any number of grounds. Particularly in democratic contexts, the distinction is not so clear cut; both education and politics are dynamic and continuous, versus static and finite, processes.[24] But aside from the plethora of general arguments that might be made against her strict distinction between these domains, divorcing education from politics is particularly troubling in light of her claim that "the capacity to judge is a specifically political ability" (CC, 221). Since judgment is political, and education and politics are to remain separate, are we to think that Arendt means to confine all that goes along with the cultivation of judgment—for example, seeking an "enlarged mentality" and testing one's opinions against others—to the political domain? The question of how the political capacity of judgment is to be cultivated in future citizens is left unresolved given the implicit tensions within her work on judgment, political action, and education.

Nevertheless, shifting the focus away from Arendt's explicit demarcation between education and politics, which suggests that schools should not cultivate specifically political abilities such as judgment, to her positive agenda regarding education yields possible avenues for reconciling these tensions. Let's begin by returning to the question: For Arendt, what is the fundamental purpose of education? As I explained earlier, Arendt views the purpose of education as simultaneously preserving the world and the natality of young people who are poised to enter it. She eloquently articulates this vision at the conclusion of "The Crisis in Education":

> *Education is the point at which we decide whether we love the world enough to assume responsibility for it* and by the same token save it from that ruin which, except for renewal, except for the coming of the new and young, would be inevitable. *And education, too, is where we decide whether we love our children enough* not to expel them from

our world and leave them to their own devices, nor to strike from their hands their chance of undertaking something new, something unforeseen by us, but *to prepare them in advance for the task of renewing a common world.* (CE, 196; emphasis added)

If, as Arendt asserts in this passage, the task of education is to prepare children to renew a common world, then education is not an *apolitical* process. Even if kept distinct from the formal political domain, education is political in that it is involved with those shared public processes of creating and sustaining a common world. If young people are ultimately to share and renew a common world through participatory political action—including public judgment, speech, and deed—then education must prepare them to engage in these processes. Education must cultivate capacities with which to judge and, consequently, to speak and to act in a public manner that approximates fullness rather than partiality of perspectives.

Arendt's claim, then, that "education can play no part in politics" (CE, 177) does not mean that *preparation for* politics—in the spirit of preparing children for the task of renewing a common world—can play no part in education. In other words, her insistence that the realms of authority and equality remain separate does not prohibit educational authority from being employed to prepare young people to become political equals. Indeed, such a project is integral to the vision of responsible civic engagement and participatory politics that she endorses.

To the extent that Arendt's educational project entails preparing children to renew a common world, and to the extent that the capacity for judgment is central to human beings sharing this common world, we should consider one of the primary tasks of education to be the cultivation of a faculty of judgment in young people. In the next section, I explore the educational conditions necessary for preparing future citizens to exercise the faculty of judgment as equals within the political realm.

Education for Judgment

In order to reconcile the unresolved questions and tensions in Arendt's work into a coherent project of "education for judgment,"

I draw upon my interpretation of "practicing judgment" as a dual form of action. This sense of educational practice combines two simultaneous forms of action—doing and preparing—and reflects Arendt's idea that young people are in the midst of "becoming" fully human. She describes children as "human beings in process of becoming but not yet complete" (CE, 187). During this stage of becoming, but not yet adults or political equals, children practice judgment in a unique form: They practice judgment in the Kantian sense in that *they make determinations* regarding objects, and in so doing, *they prepare to authentically practice judgment* when they "become completely human." In this section, I argue that the process of "practice as preparation" is not only a learning process, but a process appropriate for the formal educational realm precisely because of the sorts of capacities necessary to exercise the faculty of judgment.

What are the capacities that young people need in order to exercise the faculty of judgment? What sorts of educational processes prepare young people to become human beings who publicly appear and act in concert with others in ways that both shape their own identities and renew a common world? Arendt's conception of reflective judgment suggests a twofold educational task in response to these questions. First, education must provide the conditions under which young people can learn to think representatively or achieve "enlarged mentalities." Second, education must provide young people with opportunities to practice judgment. Representative thinking allows individuals to assess issues in terms of the ideal of impartiality. Practice, in the educational sense of guided preparation through doing, allows students to hone the skills necessary for representative thinking, as well as those necessary for assessing judgments as "good" or "bad" within the particular context of action.

Conditions for Representative Thinking

Recall that judgment is the ability to tell right from wrong or beautiful from ugly. Arendt grounds this capacity in processes of opinion formation based upon Kant's aesthetic notion of "representative thinking" whereby the judging person hopes to "woo the consent of everyone else." As I explained earlier, communicability or the factor of publicity is a key feature of the sort of critical thinking that enables judgment. In order to think critically and, hence, make good judgments by imagining the perspectives necessary to woo the consent of others, young people require explicit, intentional exposure to diverging perspectives so that they *learn how* to think representatively.

In the Kant lectures, Arendt asserts that two mental operations are involved in judgment: imagination and reflection. She explains that the operation of imagination "prepares the object for 'the operation of reflection'" and that "this second operation . . . is the actual activity of judging something" (*KL*, 68). Imagination prepares the object for reflection by bringing it into full view; imagination allows one to view the object from a variety of perspectives rather than simply the narrow vantage point of one's particular location. Reflection, then, involves the act of judging what one sees, of approving or disapproving. One makes this assessment based on the criterion of communicability or publicity. In other words, the extent to which one can communicate one's opinion as a position that would be shared by others drives the validity of that judgment.

In order to fully understand this process, as well as the key role that education can play in relation to its importance, it is worthwhile to quote Arendt's views on opinion formation at length. The role of representative thinking in opinion formation encourages the expansion of the partial toward fuller, more informed standpoints on the world. As she describes:

Political thought is representative. I form an opinion by considering a given issue from different viewpoints, by making present to my mind the standpoints of those who are absent; that is, I represent them. This process of representation does not blindly adopt the actual views of those who stand somewhere else, and hence look upon the world from a different perspective; this is a question neither of empathy, as though I tried to be or to feel like somebody else, nor of counting noses and joining a majority but of being and thinking in my own identity where actually I am not. The more people's standpoints I have present in my mind while I am pondering a given issue, and the better I can imagine how I would feel and think if I were in their places, the stronger will be my capacity for representative thinking and the more valid my final conclusions, my opinion. . . . The very process of opinion formation is determined by those in whose place somebody thinks and uses his own mind, and the only condition for this exertion of the imagination is disinterestedness, the liberation from one's own private interests. Hence, even if I shun all company or am completely isolated while forming an opinion, I am not simply together only with myself in the solitude of philosophical thought; I remain in this world of universal interdependence, where I can make myself the representative of everybody else. Of course, I can refuse to do this and form an opinion that takes only my own interests into account; nothing, indeed, is more common, even among highly sophisticated people, than the blind obstinacy that becomes manifest in lack of imagination and failure to judge. But the very quality of an opinion, as of a judgment, depends upon the degree of its impartiality. (TP, 241–242)

This passage speaks to the importance of a project of education for judgment. Arendt's contention that even highly sophisticated people are often unable to be impartial highlights the need for educational processes that prepare young people to think representatively. Without capacities for imagination and reflection, young people may grow into adults who are unable to represent other people's perspectives on the world to themselves and, hence, are unable to make good judgments. Even when they are isolated from one another, adults as citizens must be able to think as if they were in the presence of others with vastly different perspectives.

This is where the ability to imagine comes into play. According to Arendt, the faculty that allows for representation and comparison, even in solitude, "is called imagination" (*KL,* 43). She explains:

Critical thinking is possible only where the standpoints of all others are open to inspection. Hence, critical thinking, while still a solitary business, does not cut itself off from "all others." To be sure, it still goes on in isolation, but by the force of imagination it makes the others present and thus moves in a space that is potentially public, open to all sides; in other words, it adopts the position of Kant's world citizen. *To think with an enlarged mentality means that one trains one's imagination to go visiting.* (*KL*, 43; emphasis added)

The sort of training described in this passage is precisely the task of a project of education for judgment. Within the confines of their idiosyncratic traditions, young people may not have any fodder to spark their imaginations. One of the primary functions of education for judgment must be to cultivate young people's capacities to imagine and to reflect so that they can make judgments based on an ideal of impartiality. Formal education is uniquely prepared to hone the operation of imagination in two ways: by training minds "to go visiting" and by exposing individuals to actual others from diverse traditions.

First, formal education encourages the mind to go visiting through disciplinary study in the fields of literature, history, and anthropology, among others. Education for judgment must provide young people with structured processes and instructional support that train the imagination to participate in the form of "representative thinking" so crucial to Kant's notion of reflective judgment. As Arendt asserts:

In matters of opinion . . . our thinking is truly discursive, running, as it were, from place to place, from one part of the world to another, through all kinds of conflicting views, until it finally ascends from these particulars to some impartial generality. [In] this process . . . a particular issue is forced into the open that it may show itself from all sides, in every possible perspective, until it is flooded and made transparent by the full light of human comprehension. (TP, 242)

When students read novels set in other cultural contexts and study the history of different peoples, for example, they need to engage in forms of academic inquiry that take the mind from place to place and encourage discursive thinking. The diversity of experiences and views transmitted within the disciplines and through interdisciplinary study must be employed to provide the light that brings subjects toward transparency and facilitates impartial understanding.

Second, formal education exposes young people to divergent perspectives through interaction with other people who occupy different standpoints on the world. A project of education for judgment must cultivate the imagination by making good use of the actual diversity of perspectives that exists within school settings. Interaction with diverse perspectives will provide young people with opportunities to form and test their own ideas according to the standard of publicity.

According to Arendt's interpretation of Kant, "the very faculty of thinking depends on its public use; without 'the test of free and open examination,' no thinking and no opinion-formation are possible. Reason is not made 'to isolate itself but to get into community with others'" (*KL,* 40). This communicability or publicness factor, however, does not necessarily entail actual dialogue with other people in order to gain access to their perspectives. Rather, Kant's ideal model of critical thinking relies on imagination to allow solitary thinking to be public thinking. Despite the fact that both Kant and Arendt insist that this sort of imagined "community with others" is possible even without actual contact with other people, I contend that individuals best learn how to examine and test their opinions through actual community with others. How are people, particularly young people who may not have many avenues for exposure to diverse points of view, to compare their judgments with possible others if they have little sense as to how someone else might view the world? How are young people to imagine, or to represent to themselves, perspectives that differ from their own vantage points if they have never been exposed to other ways of viewing the world? To the extent that comparing one's views with others is constrained by experience, time, and space, cultivation of the capacity to represent the judgments of those who are not present is a vital educational task.

This is precisely where formal education plays a pivotal role. Formal educational contexts bring individuals into contact with people whose perspectives and opinions are radically different from their own. Arendt and Kant each view the challenging of our own "idiosyncratic" perspectives as essential for critical thought and, hence, judgment. Our own private, subjective opinions, or openings to the world, are challenged by striving for an "enlarged mentality" that yields a "general standpoint" from which to view, and ultimately judge, the world.

In order to achieve this general standpoint from which to reflect upon and judge the world of human affairs, an individual must be able to apply "critical standards" to one's own perspective. Arendt explains: "To think critically applies not only to doctrines and concepts one receives from others, to the prejudices and traditions one inherits; it is precisely by applying critical standards to one's own thought that one *learns the art of critical thought*. And this application one cannot *learn* without publicity, without the testing that arises from contact with other people's thinking" (*KL*, 42; emphasis added). This testing takes place through Kant's notion of an "enlargement of the mind" whereby we "[compare] our judgment with the possible rather than the actual judgments of others, and by putting ourselves in the place of any other man" (*KL*, 43).

Here again, Kant refers to a comparison between "possible" versus "actual" judgments of others. But Kant never intended for the kind of thinking that requires solitude to be reclusive or for the conclusions drawn from such thinking to be considered definitive. Without actual interaction with other people, critical thinking would become impossible. Arendt explains: "Thinking is a 'solitary business' . . . yet, unless you can somehow communicate and expose to the test of others, either orally or in writing, whatever you may have found out when you were alone, this faculty exerted in solitude will disappear" (*KL*, 40). The realm of education constitutes an actual public space that brings together young people with partial perspectives; education for judgment emphasizes exposure to and interaction among these perspectives in order to spark imagination and critical reflection.

Thus, the domain of education is particularly well suited to play a number of roles in cultivating the representative thinking that is necessary for exercising the faculty of judgment. Education for judgment encourages the enlarged mentality required for representative thinking by bringing people into contact with individuals who have radically different perspectives on the world. Exposure to a variety of subjective positions allows students to move toward a more "general standpoint" from which to reflect on and judge objects in the

world. Education for judgment also develops the capacity to imagine, which is integral to taking others' perspectives into account even
if they are not present to represent their views. Finally, education for
judgment not only prepares young people to communicate their conclusions orally and in writing, but it also provides a variety of means
for testing the validity of these views in public contexts. In these
ways, education for judgment provides the conditions for meeting
the criterion of publicity that is necessary for representative thinking
and, in turn, the exercise of good judgment.

Opportunities for Practice

The operation that follows imagination is the operation of reflection, which entails the actual activity of judging something. Therefore, an Arendtian project of education for judgment must also provide opportunities for young people to practice making judgments.
What might such practice look like in light of Arendt's views on the
role of adult authority in educational contexts? As I outlined earlier,
Arendt emphasizes the roles of authority and a conservative attitude
in education because she views children as "unequals" vis-à-vis
adults and she sees the essence of education to be protection of the
world as it is. Moreover, education based on authority and conservation preserves "what is new and revolutionary in every child" so
that new things can be introduced into an old world (CE, 192–193).
This dual emphasis on authority and conservation may be appropriate for the early stages of a child's education. But Arendt's additional
concerns with the process of becoming completely human and with
the faculty of judgment cannot be addressed if teacher authority is to
usurp the practice of judgment throughout a child's education. If
teacher authority trumps the practice of judgment throughout
schooling, how will students make the transition from authoritarian
relationships based upon adult/child inequality to egalitarian relationships based upon political equality?

Among adults as equals, the exercise of the faculty of judgment
makes life in a common world, and hence one's humanity, possible.
Given the importance of this faculty, the stages toward the culmina-

tion of one's formal education must emphasize the cultivation of the faculty of judgment in soon-to-be adults. To the extent that formal processes of education must come to an end, as Arendt asserts, the faculty of judgment grows increasingly important as this moment of "emancipation" approaches.

Emphasizing that older students—for instance, those at the secondary level of schooling—practice judgment does not mean that educators need to abdicate their authority. Schools are distinct forms of public spaces; they are educational spaces in which the unequal relationship between adults and children is based on legitimate authority. But despite Arendt's insistence that education be divorced from politics, schools are nonetheless public spaces of appearance and action. They are, as John Dewey described them, "mini-societies" that reflect the essential features of broader democratic society. Or, in her own formulation, "school in a sense represents the world, although it is not yet actually the world" (CE, 189). In this manner, schools are part of the public world that politics negotiates, but they are distinct from other public spaces in that their purpose is not primarily political, but rather educational.

Within these public spaces that are not yet the world, students must practice judgment, even though they are not yet equal to adults as political beings. Students need practice in the types of civic engagement and collective decision-making that democratic politics requires. This practice includes judging the appropriateness of historical action, making decisions as to the rightness of future courses of action, and debating and speaking persuasively so as to form and convey such opinions. As students engage in such processes, they are not only preparing for public life in democratic contexts, they are also revealing, and thereby creating, their own identities as distinct human beings.

The sort of practice that I am advocating here goes beyond simply presenting a speech in front of class in order to be graded in rhetorical devices or making a moral decision in response to a case study as part of a classroom exercise. Schools as mini-societies, or "not yet worlds," provide a number of contexts for practicing judgment in a much deeper sense. Student government, for example, provides opportunities for students to participate in democratic decision-making regarding issues of collective concern that carry real consequences.

Although many representative forms of student government include only a handful of students in a given school, often those students most comfortable with the norms of the school culture, other models of governance encourage greater student participation. Town meetings or all-school meetings wherein timely and relevant issues are discussed and acted upon are examples of models that increase the potential for student participation and inclusion. These models encourage the entire student body of a school to engage in debate, to form and test their opinions in a public fashion, and to experience the consequences of decisions that are made within such forums. These forms of practice provide students with meaningful contexts and experiences with which to assess whether judgments are good or bad. Moreover, in these school-based public forums, students are engaging in the types of action that Arendt identifies as the highest form of human activity. It is just this sort of concrete experience that will prepare students to take on the responsibility of sharing their common world when their formal schooling comes to an end.

In addition to student participation in school governance, community service and broader political forums provide opportunities for students to practice judgment. Community service expands horizons in a manner consistent with cultivating the capacity to imagine others' perspectives while simultaneously raising moral questions about one's position within broader social structures and appropriate courses of action within specific service contexts. Student participation in activities such as voter registration, polling, protests or demonstrations, or letter-writing campaigns to media outlets or elected officials influences the political process. Although students are not yet citizens, the action that they undertake in these venues nevertheless has the potential to impact public opinion and political outcomes.

In sum, practicing judgment as preparation for citizenship simultaneously constitutes the political action of children as minors and precedes the "authentic" political action of adults as civic equals. As students practice judgment in school roles such as student governance bodies, they are both engaging in a form of political action within the school context, albeit as unequals vis-à-vis faculty, and preparing for the future practice of judgment as full citizens within broader local, state, and national contexts. The same dual aspect of practice as preparation or action is at play when students engage in community service and other forms of civic engagement.

Such an Arendtian project of education for judgment would both benefit democratic public life and provide schools with a framework for curricula that are meaningful and cohesive because they are driven by overarching moral questions and political issues. Rather than memorizing the dates of events such as World War II, for example, students might be asked to question the roles played by ordinary Jews and Germans during the Holocaust and to compare judgments of these historical behaviors to contemporary examples of ethnic cleansing in Eastern Europe. Or students might be asked to develop an opinion regarding the appropriateness of human cloning in light of Hitler's eugenics program during the war. Such questions not only require the practice of judgment, they also provide meaningful instructional contexts within which students learn relevant facts, build concrete skills, and hone critical-thinking capacities.

Conclusion

In Arendt's thought, "judging is one, if not the most, important activity in which . . . sharing-the-world-with-others comes to pass" (CC, 221). This is the case because judgment is a public faculty; its objects are in the world of appearances, and its standards are derived from the validity of enlarged versus partial perspectives. Arendt's appropriation of Kant's model of reflective judgment links the domains of aesthetics and politics in a manner that not only provides grounding for the legitimacy of political action, but also implicates the domain of education. As Arendt herself insists: "The common element connecting art and politics is that they both are phenomena of the public world. What mediates the conflict between the artist and the man of action is the *cultura animi*, that is, a mind so trained and cultivated that it can be trusted to tend and take care of the world of appearances whose criterion is beauty" (CC, 218–219).

Insofar as the mental faculty that assesses the world is that of judgment and the purpose of education is "to prepare [our children] for the task of renewing a common world" (CE, 196), the training and cultivation of judgment are not just an appropriate but a vital educational task. This task can be pursued by providing conditions for representative thinking—conditions that encourage the mental operations of imagination and reflection—and by providing age-appropriate opportunities for practice. In such contexts, young people will practice judgment in ways that simultaneously form and reveal their political opinions and their identities as human beings.

Notes

1. Elisabeth Young-Bruehl, *Hannah Arendt: For Love of the World* (New Haven: Yale University Press, 1982), p. 458.

2. This information is recounted by Mary McCarthy in the editor's postface to *The Life of the Mind* and in Ronald Beiner's interpretive essay "Hannah Arendt on Judging" in the volume that he edited on Arendt's Kant lectures. See Hannah Arendt, *The Life of the Mind,* vol. 1: *Thinking,* ed. Mary McCarthy (New York: Harcourt Brace Jovanovich, 1978), p. 218; and Ronald Beiner, ed., *Hannah Arendt: Lectures on Kant's Political Philosophy* (Chicago: University of Chicago Press, 1982), p. 89. These lectures will be cited as *KL* in the text for all subsequent references.

3. The strand of Arendt's thought that claims judgment as a political capacity situates the faculty within the *vita activa,* or the realm of action. Another prominent strand in her thinking situates judgment within the *vita contemplativa,* the realm of contemplation, and emphasizes not the actor, but the spectator. Whether these two approaches to judgment are at odds with each other is disputed among Arendt scholars. For further discussion on the development of her thinking on judgment, as well as the contradictions and tensions, see Beiner, "Hannah Arendt on Judging"; Seyla Benhabib, *Situating the Self* (New York: Routledge, 1992), chap. 4; Richard Bernstein, "Judging: The Actor and the Spectator," in *Philosophical Profiles* (Philadelphia: University of Pennsylvania Press, 1986); Maurizio Passerin d'Entreves, *The Political Philosophy of Hannah Arendt* (London: Routledge, 1994); and Albrecht Wellmer, "Hannah Arendt on Judgment: The Unwritten Doctrine of Reason," in *Hannah Arendt Twenty Years Later,* ed. Larry May and Jerome Kohn (Cambridge, MA: MIT Press, 1997).

4. Hannah Arendt, "The Crisis in Culture," in *Between Past and Future* (New York: Penguin Books, 1977), p. 221. This essay will be cited as CC in the text for all subsequent references.

5. Arendt's position on whether judgment is a moral faculty represents another point of tension in her work. For an interpretation of Arendt's thought that claims judgment as both a political and a moral faculty, see Benhabib's "Judgment and Politics in Arendt's Thought," chapter 4 in *Situating the Self.*

6. Hannah Arendt, "The Crisis in Education," in *Between Past and Future*, p. 196. This essay will be cited as CE in the text for all subsequent references.

7. Arendt, "The Crisis in Culture"; and Beiner, ed., *Hannah Arendt*. Other primary sources for her views on judgment include: "Truth and Politics," in *Between Past and Future* (hereafter cited as TP in the text); "Thinking and Moral Considerations," *Social Research*, vol. 38, no. 3 (Autumn 1971); and various references from the *Thinking* and *Willing* volumes of *Life of the Mind*.

8. Beiner, ed., *Hannah Arendt*, pp. 101–102.

9. Arendt, "Thinking and Moral Considerations," p. 8.

10. Beiner, ed., *Hannah Arendt*, p. 100.

11. Hannah Arendt, "Philosophy and Politics," *Social Research*, vol. 57, no. 1 (Spring 1990): 81.

12. Ibid., p. 80.

13. Bernstein, "Judging," p. 236.

14. Beiner, ed., *Hannah Arendt*, p. 15.

15. This move is of particular interest to democratic theorists because it provides grounding for the legitimacy of political outcomes. Deliberative democrat Seyla Benhabib, for instance, argues that "in Kant's conception of reflective judgment, restricted by Kant himself—erroneously in Arendt's eyes—to the aesthetic realm alone, Arendt discovered a procedure for ascertaining intersubjective validity in the public realm" (*Situating the Self*, p. 132). Arendt derived this validity from Kant's notion of an "enlarged mentality," which consists of being able to "think in the place of everybody else" ("The Crisis in Culture," p. 220).

16. Seyla Benhabib, *The Reluctant Modernism of Hannah Arendt* (Thousand Oaks, CA: Sage Publications, 1996), p. 42.

17. Ibid., p. 191.

18. On my reading, impartiality functions for Arendt as a regulative ideal. In other words, because each individual views the world from his/her own perspective, complete impartiality is at odds with being human. But an impartial standpoint is something to be worked toward insofar as it represents fullness of understanding rather than a narrow or idiosyncratic point of view.

19. Bernstein, "Judging," pp. 227–228.

20. Arendt, "Truth and Politics," p. 241.

21. Bernstein, "Judging," p. 222.

22. Benhabib, *Situating the Self*, p. 123, and *Reluctant Modernism*, p. 198.

23. Hannah Arendt, "Postscriptum," in *Life of the Mind*, vol. 1: *Thinking*, ed. McCarthy, p. 215.

24. I disagree with Arendt's notion that the domains of education and politics can be strictly separated given that the institution of education in our democratic society is inextricably linked to political processes and decisions. Politics is at play in the governance of educational settings, as well as in decisions that must be collectively made as to what our children should learn and how they should be taught. But, given the purpose and space constraints of this chapter, I do not address issues of governance. Instead, I confine my argument here to challenging Arendt's distinction between the two realms by explicating some important ways in which education prepares young people for the political domain and, in this manner, is political in a weaker sense.

4

Contesting Utopianism: Hannah Arendt and the Tensions of Democratic Education

AARON SCHUTZ

Throughout the twentieth century, a diverse group of educational scholars struggled against what they saw as fundamentally undemocratic schools and an only nominally democratic society. Often speaking from the margins, scholars working in this vein rejected, for example, the largely rote learning predominant in the nineteenth and early twentieth centuries and forms of education that doomed poor and minority students to the lower strata of the labor force. At the core of many of these projects was an effort to create more democratic schools that could foster citizens empowered to change society for the better.[1] Today, questions of democracy are as peripheral to the mainstream educational discourse as they have usually been in the past, taking a backseat to fears about global competitiveness, declining academic achievement, and individual morality, among other issues. Nonetheless, scholarly attempts to envision and promote more democratic schooling have continued unabated, with a large number of books and articles appearing recently. And with the resegregation of education in the cities of the United States and with the rise of efforts to "standardize" students through increasingly high-stakes, narrowly conceived, standards-based assessments, the struggle for more democratic schooling remains of crucial importance.[2] It is as a contribution to this larger effort that I discuss Hannah Arendt's distinctive model of "public space," exploring its potential role in our understanding of the relationship between democracy and education.[3] Perhaps most important, her work provides a potential counter to what I perceive to be a problematic "utopian impulse" among many current educational scholars.

But what exactly *is* democratic education? The fact is that, a vast range of different forms of community have been termed "democratic" at different times, and different scholars have drawn from very different understandings of this term.[4] A broad spectrum of different policy efforts, ranging from vouchers to home schooling to civics classes to standards development projects, have at different times been called "democratic." As Michael Apple and James Beane point out, although "the idea of democracy presumably serves as a crucial benchmark for judging events and ideas" in the United States, "central tenets and ethical anchors" of this kind "tend to be converted into rhetorical slogans and political codes to gain popular support for all manner of ideas." Thus, "we hear the democracy defense used countless times every day to justify almost anything people want to do."[5]

Despite this diversity, there is a core group of scholars in education that tends to draw a basic understanding of democracy from the most prominent writer on educational democracy: John Dewey.[6] Beginning in earnest at the turn of the twentieth century, Dewey wrote in response to the predominantly regimented schooling of his time, as well as to a society in which he felt individuals were increasingly powerless against an expanding industrialism. Dewey argued that democratic communities are those in which a collection of individuals participates together on a shared project, in which, as Dewey said, "each has to refer his own action to that of others, and to consider the action of others to give point and direction to his own."[7] In democracy, as Dewey understood it, people collaborate together to solve shared problems. Further, he argued that every human being is unique, with a unique potential all her own.[8] In schools (and society) the way it was (and still is), however, this potential rarely had an opportunity to fully manifest itself. He was convinced that it is only within the context of democratic communities that individuals are able to flourish in their distinctiveness, as each person learns to make creative contributions to shared efforts. Current scholars often add a discussion of the importance of "group" diversity to this mix. Finally, central to his model is the idea that through critical, "scientific," collaborative engagement with the world, we have at least the potential to develop increasingly democratic and egalitarian societies, eliminating the oppressions and inequalities of the present and breaking down the barriers that separate groups and classes.[9] By learning through our interactions with the environment, he believed, we could slowly develop increasing control over aspects of our world and ourselves.

Dewey understood that tremendous obstacles stood in the way of the development of a more democratic society. He was quite clear that what might constitute "democracy" as a concrete set of social practices in any particular context could never be determined ahead of time in the abstract. He did not argue that the contentiousness of democratic engagement would be overcome, nor did he believe it should be. And although those who follow or draw from him generally acknowledge that democracy is a "process" and not a clearly defined goal, that perfect democracy is an impossibility, Deweyan *criteria* of democracy are often presented as if they constitute an unproblematic good, universally relevant for all human beings. Furthermore, Dewey firmly believed that anything was at least possible for human beings and that all barriers could at least potentially be overcome through careful "scientific" inquiry.[10] Thus, there is what I would call a subtle "utopian" aspect to Dewey's democratic model and among those influenced by him: a vision, despite its abstraction, of a kind of shining city on the hill, if you will, that is always to be sought, even if it can never quite be achieved.[11]

The wide range of work in the current literature that draws upon Dewey's vision is quite diverse, each scholar arriving at her own particular interpretation and usually drawing on other sources as well. Nonetheless, versions of the basic criteria for democracy I sketched above remain prominent. Apple and Beane provide a good example.

Even though they do not focus on Dewey's work, they acknowledge that "most of the impulse toward democratic schooling rests on . . . [his] prolific work," and the model they sketch is largely compatible with the one I have just discussed (*DS,* 21). With Dewey, Apple and Beane acknowledge, "exercising democracy involves tensions and contradictions" that "point to the fact that bringing democracy to life is always a struggle." Ultimately, however, they argue that "beyond them [i.e., these tensions and contradictions] lies the possibility for professional educators and citizens to work together in creating more democratic schools that serve the common good of the whole community" (*DS,* 8). The problem for Apple and Beane, then, as for many proponents of visions of democratic education indebted to Dewey, is not with what Apple and Beane call the "'idealized' set of values" of an egalitarian democracy, which they note "we must live [by] and that must guide our life as a people" (*DS,* 7); instead, it is with the failure to fully live up to these ideals. They therefore admit "to having what Dewey and others have called the 'democratic faith,' the fundamental belief that democracy has a powerful meaning, that it can work, and that it is necessary if we are to maintain freedom and human dignity in our social affairs" (*DS,* 6).

My point is not to reject democracy, nor is it to denigrate the important work that has been done on educational democracy. Nevertheless, I worry, along with Cornel West, that Dewey and those like him have sometimes failed to understand (or at least to emphasize) that "all human struggles . . . including successful ones—against specific forms of evil produce new, though possibly lesser, forms of evil."[12] I will argue that Arendt's vision of the public is useful for education in part because it takes the inevitability of these limitations and trade-offs seriously. As she once said in an interview, "I know that one has to pay a price for freedom" even though "I cannot say that I like to pay it."[13]

Like Dewey, Arendt developed her model of the public in response to oppressions she encountered in the world—specifically, her experience and later study of Nazi Germany. Unlike Dewey, however, she learned from the Nazis the dangers of believing that "everything is possible."[14] It was because the Nazis believed this, Arendt argued, that they came to see "everything that exists . . . [as] only a temporary obstacle" to their desires (*OT,* 387). For those unethical experimentalists, those twisted pragmatists, the inconvenient facts of reality, especially its unpredictability and complexity, became unbearable constraints to their ambitions. Like Dewey, they created laboratories, but not in the spirit of democracy; instead, in search of absolute "scientific" control in their concentration camps, they conducted an "experiment with or rather against reality" on their own citizens, carrying out "the indecent experimental inquiry into what is possible" (*OT,* 392, 436). Instead of fostering individual fulfillment in the midst of community, the Nazis sought to eliminate every last vestige of individual agency, to develop a realm truly of the living dead, who, like Pavlov's dog, "all react with perfect reliability even when going to their deaths" (*OT,* 455). They attempted to create a totally malleable, fictional world, in which the totalitarian movement and its leaders, as a collective organism, achieved total domination.

Whereas Dewey believed that increasingly perfect, if always shifting, democracies could be achieved through wholly democratic methods[15]—in fact, he argued that democracy could be achieved only through democratic means—the Nazis taught Arendt that the very practice of aiming toward utopian ends, the belief that everything is possible, the refusal of human limitations, can be the first step toward totalitarianism.[16] If Dewey's vision and that of many of those who draw from him tends toward the "transcendent," then Arendt's is firmly "human" and "tragic,"[17] rooted in the mud of tenuous compromises and the necessity of loss.[18]

I begin with an overview of Arendt's model of the "public," followed by a discussion of the compromises she was convinced her model entails, illustrating its potential relevance for schools as I go. I then explore a relatively detailed example of how "public space" might actually be instantiated into an educational context. Although I discuss some key similarities and differences between Arendt and Dewey as I proceed, there is not space to do full justice to a detailed comparison of their rich visions, nor is this my goal. Ultimately, my aim is not to somehow replace Dewey's model with Arendt's or to synthesize them together. Rather, I hope that Arendt's model of the public will serve as an instructive corrective to what I see as problematic "utopian" tendencies in the current literature on democracy and education. Whereas the particular human limitations she discussed are internal to her particular conceptualization of democratic action, her work models an anti-utopian approach to democratic education that, I argue, is relevant more broadly. At the same time, I seek to provide a deeper understanding of the unique ways her theoretical perspective might illuminate possibilities for democratic action in educational settings, in conjunction, perhaps, with other visions like Dewey's.

Public Space: A First Approximation

Arendt believed that all human beings are fundamentally unique, to the point that "with respect to this somebody [i.e., everybody] who is unique, it can truly be said that nobody was there before." This uniqueness, she argued, arises largely out of each person's unrepeatable biography of experiences. In Arendt's view, it is because of each person's uniqueness that "the unexpected can be expected from him . . . [and that] he is able to perform what is infinitely improbable."[19] It is for this reason that all human beings are capable of what she called "action," the ability to start entirely new processes that could not have been predicted from what came before.

Arendt argued, however, that authentically human action is not possible without the accompaniment of speech, which discloses the actor who acts. Although a person's "deed can be perceived in its brute physical appearance without verbal accompaniment," she noted, "it becomes relevant only through the spoken word in which he identifies himself as the actor, announcing what he does, has done, and intends to do" (*HC*, 178). Without speech to disclose the actor behind an action, a "deed" becomes a mere happening, a brute event without any clear connections to the desires of an agent. Her vision of democracy, then, is very much a dialogic one.

But although *all* speech discloses one's uniqueness to one extent or another, Arendt's examination of totalitarianism taught her that there were in fact contexts in which an individual's uniqueness could be almost entirely suppressed, that people could be reduced to the level of robots. Furthermore, she worried that, in the modern world, what she called "society" or the "social" increasingly predominated, expecting "from each of its members a certain kind of behavior, imposing innumerable rules, all of which tend to 'normalize' its members, to make them behave, to exclude spontaneous action" (*HC*, 40). In fact, all around her she saw a society in which speech had increasingly lost its ability to disclose "who" individuals were in their uniqueness and in which, in ways reminiscent of the Nazi era, unpredictable, individual agency was slowly becoming simply a threat to the smooth, predictable functioning of the collective organism of the "social." In response, Arendt looked back through the record of Western history, seeking evidence of social practices that might allow individuals to respond collectively to oppression without being absorbed into a group. Drawing from an astonishingly diverse range of examples, from the ancient Greeks to the French and American Revolutions to her experience serving on a civil jury, she synthesized her model of "public space."

A public space, for her, is created when individuals come together in a particular way around an issue or object of common concern, something perhaps best understood as a "common project." Such a project acts as what she called an "in-between" or, from the Latin, "*inter-est*" that both "relates and separates men at the same time," each participant contributing her own unique interpretations of it (*HC*, 182, 54). Out of these multiple interpretations, the space itself is *constituted* as a space, as each member "appears" in a distinctive "location" with respect to their shared concern. Although in other contexts an individual might disclose something about herself by speaking, only in public can individuals achieve a coherent *position* by relating their own opinions to those expressed by others in that space. In such a space, individuals act, not as a unit, but, in Arendt's words, "in concert," each making a unique contribution to their collective effort. And because each participant is neither autonomous nor simply a cog in a collective machine, immense creative "power" for unpredictable change is generated (*HC*, 201). She contrasted this with the "strength" that comes from a collection of individuals who come together as a unit, like a mob or a cult, which, she argued, can always be overcome by the potentiality represented by power.[20] In fact, she noted that through public action, "popular revolt against materially strong rulers . . . may engender an almost irresistible power even if it forgoes the use of violence in the face of materially vastly superior forces" (*HC*, 200–201).

Public spaces do not simply allow us to act together with others, however. They also provide the only contexts in which we are able to fully experience ourselves as coherent agents. Paradoxically, in Arendt's model, we can emerge as unique actors only if we act *with* others. As Bonnie Honig notes, in Arendt's writings, "prior to or apart from action," from an appearance in a public space, a "self has no identity; it is fragmented, discontinuous, indistinct. . . . Arendt's actors do not act because of what they already are, their actions do not express a prior, stable identity; they presuppose an unstable multiple self that seeks its, at best, episodic self-realization in action and in the identity that is its reward."[21] Only in the public can individuals experience this shock of self-discovery. And when discourse in a public space ceases, when individuals cease to appear in locations with respect to one another, the space collapses and participants are returned to the evanescent realms they inhabited before they entered the public. In fact, Arendt's work implies that individuals often shift back and forth between public and nonpublic ways of being in the world. Public selfhood for Arendt, then, is extremely tenuous.

As should be clear from my introduction, this vision of the public holds many similarities to basic Deweyan democratic ideals. It is instructive to note, however, that while Dewey also stressed the importance of participation in democratic projects in fostering one's unique potential, his descriptions of the selfhood one achieves reflect little of the evanescence that is so prominent in Arendt's writings. Moreover, as I note in more detail below, Arendt's model is focused on tensions created when utterly unique individuals seek to act together without giving up their distinctiveness, an issue Dewey never really addressed in any detail. In fact, as Craig Cunningham notes, Dewey acknowledged near the end of his life, in response to the rise of the same totalitarianism that informed Arendt, "that individual initiative and choice were far more important for securing democracy than he had previously thought."[22] In some sense, then, Arendt's work explores the implications of an aspect of egalitarian democracy that remained largely submerged in Dewey's own writings, although the path she takes is surely quite different from the one Dewey might have taken.

A recent article discussing a fifth-grade elementary school class that worked together, successfully, to change the child seat-belt laws in their state provides a useful example for illuminating some of the implications of Arendt's model for actual classroom practice.[23] Because the authors do not give much detail about exactly what the students did, we are left to imagine different possibilities. Already, one could imagine ways to go about this project that would not correspond to Arendt's public model. One could imagine, for example, a process dominated by the teacher, or by a few articulate or forceful students, in which the perspectives of all would not be heard and everyone's contributions would not count equally. Other problematic approaches would assign individuals to predetermined roles and responsibilities before the activity even began. If this classroom were to engage in "public" action as Arendt defined it, not only would the perspectives of all need to be taken into account, but students would need to feel safe enough to be as honest as possible in their contributions.

Tensions in the Public

Despite the enormous creative power of public spaces, Arendt argued that they are precarious achievements. As I note in this section, they are sustained by a complex dance of engagement in which participants seek an elusive balance between conflicting ways of being and acting with others. There are, I maintain, at least three fundamentally different tensions faced by participants in a public space. First of all, if they are to avoid either splintering their space apart or collapsing it into a realm of mass society, actors must be willing to risk disclosing their unique perspectives while restraining themselves from expressing their full singularity. Second, although participants must constantly make judgments, courageously taking sometimes controversial positions, they must avoid attempts to coerce others through assertions or logical demonstrations of incontestable truth and certainty. Finally, if they are to maintain possibilities for free action, participants in a public space must establish some stability and predictability in their shared space but must reject efforts to control and dominate the future. Fundamentally, excess of all kinds is corrosive to the fragile compromise that, for the time a public space can be maintained, allows a collection of unique individuals to retain their distinctiveness while still working together as a collective. In fact, the demands of this practice are so great that even though Arendt searched for ways that more permanent public realms could be founded, in her early writings on the subject she feared that public action was something "too anarchic to be compatible with any settled political structure."[24]

Between Distinctiveness and Banality

Although Arendt believed that each individual human being is unique, and although she envisioned the public as a place where this individual distinction might "appear," she was convinced that the very structure of the public puts severe limitations on the level of distinctiveness that might be expressed there. As I noted above, public spaces cannot exist without objects of common concern that allow members to locate themselves with respect to other participants. Thus, a space survives only so long as these objects, these shared projects, can "be seen in a variety of aspects without changing their identity." In other words, when participants can no longer understand how the actions or comments of others are addressed to the *same* issue that they themselves are concerned with, the space disintegrates (*HC*, 57–58).

In public, then, only contributions that can be understood by other participants as "relevant" can be allowed. The radically unique "thoughts of the mind, the delights of the senses" must be "transformed, deprivatized, deindividualized, as it were, into a shape to fit them for public appearance" (*HC*, 50). A person who refuses to engage in such a transformation will find herself inexorably expelled from the public, as other participants increasingly cannot see her interpretations as coherent contributions to the project they share. And if large numbers of participants in a public engage in such interpretive excess, the entire space can splinter completely apart, as participants become lost in the isolated singularity of their own experience, as the *common* nature of their effort is entirely lost. Of course, this raises difficult questions about what will "count" as relevant and about potential limits on the amount of diversity such an apparently egalitarian space can actually embrace, and it implies (although Arendt did not argue this) that there will often be a multiplicity of public spaces on a single issue, multiply conceived.

Similarly, efforts by participants to see others in their complete distinctiveness, to turn public relationships into what she called "intimate" ones, also threaten the existence of the public. Love, for example, because it encompasses another person in his or her totality, "is unconcerned to the point of total unworldliness with *what* the loved person may be, with his qualities and shortcomings no less than with his achievements, failings, and transgressions, . . . destroy[s] . . . the in-between which relates us to and separates us from others" (*HC*, 242). Love, she argues, eliminates our ability to place others in relatively coherent locations with respect to a shared concern, as well as our ability to respond to others as political actors whom we judge by their actions instead of as loved ones we accept for who they are. Arendt's point here is not that we cannot create public spaces with those we love—in fact, intimate relationships with others can help us better understand the experiences that lie behind what people say in a public space.[25] Instead, to enter a public space, we must temporarily alter the way we interact with those we love. Two senators may be married, but in the Senate, they must treat each other as senators. To participate in public, love must be left at least temporarily behind, isolated away from the public and replaced with respect and regard for the political positions taken by others. Public dialogue, Arendt writes, is "not intimately personal but makes political demands and preserves reference to the world."[26]

Not only extreme uniqueness threatens the public, however; banality, shallowness, and attempts to submerge oneself into the crowd are also dangerous. As I noted above, Arendt worried constantly that public spaces were rapidly disappearing from the modern world, as individuals increasingly engaged in activities in which their unique potential was largely irrelevant. If such attitudes and ways of being invade a public space, if participants become unwilling to risk exposing their particular perspectives and understandings before others, the plurality of the space will disappear and the space will collapse into banality.

To return to our example of the elementary school classroom, Arendt's model indicates that students learning to participate in public spaces with others must learn to separate their personal friendships from their "public" relationships with often the same children. In this sense, then, initiating students into public practices requires them to distinguish between the selves they and others take on when they are and are not participating in public action. If the space is to remain vibrant, the children would need to help one another keep their comments relevant to the project under consideration. At the same time, however, they would need to listen carefully to what their classmates are saying, since many seemingly irrelevant contributions may actually represent potentially innovative ideas that require other participants to shift their understandings of the nature of their shared project in order for their relevancy to be understood. Finally, they would need to learn to constantly balance the encouragement of heartfelt participation with the danger that their space might splinter apart under the pressure of too much diversity, walking a fine line between distinctiveness and banality.

A teacher would need to artfully guide such activity, because the complexity of these ideas means that no set of predetermined rules could ever do them justice. The very idea of "relevancy," for example, would need to be grappled with constantly in the course of their collective engagements. Interestingly, under this model, an activity like brainstorming, in which there is no clear common project guiding dialogue and in which there is no pressure to be relevant, constitutes an essentially *pre*political practice. It may in fact be true, however, that the prepolitical engagements we have with others, getting to know them in their full cultural and personal individuality, are fundamental requirements for the development of public spaces in which all but the most homogeneous might join together.[27]

Between Truth and Relativism

If someone in possession of the truth were to enter a public space, there would be no reason for her to pay much attention to the opinions of others; the only goal of communication, for her, would be to coerce others through the force of her logic or rhetoric to adopt her point of view. If she were successful, however, if a consensus on the truth were actually achieved within a public, if the multiple perspectives of participants were reduced to a single identically shared perspective, the space, dependent upon disagreement for its very existence, would immediately collapse. Arendt argued, therefore, that "public debate can only deal with things which . . . we cannot figure out with any certainty."[28] In fact, however, since all individuals are fundamentally, utterly unique under this vision, it is not possible for any two people to *fully* agree, to entirely correspond in their understandings, unless one or both of them suppress aspects of their own perspectives. Whereas a particular scientific finding, for example, might not be effectively contestable by participants, the implications of this finding for the world can nonetheless remain very much an open question (*MDT*, 7).[29]

One of the best examples of Arendt's musings on how public actors should approach the issues they encounter in public arenas arises in her essay on the eighteenth-century writer Gotthold Lessing. Rejecting efforts to achieve some detached and universal objectivity on the issues of his time, Arendt noted, Lessing sought to preserve a form of freedom that was "endangered by those who wanted 'to compel faith by proofs'" (*MDT*, 7). "He not only wanted no one to coerce him, but he wanted to coerce no one, either by force or by proofs" (*MDT*, 8). In his efforts to create a world in which creative, engaged thought would be paramount, he was willing to sacrifice even "the axiom of noncontradiction, the claim to self-consistency, which we assume is mandatory to all who write and speak" (*MDT*, 7). Self-contradiction for the sake of the world was, for him, a virtue. "He was glad for the sake of the infinite number of opinions that arise when men discuss the affairs of this world," fearing that if absolute truth were actually found, this would mean "an end to discourse and thus to friendship, and thus to humanness" (*MDT,* 26).

Yet, in his rejection of truth, Lessing did not go to the opposite extreme, to a celebration of the kind of thoughtless relativity and free play visible, for example, in some of the more simplistic versions of "postmodernism" that have recently deluged cultural theory. Instead, Lessing's opinions were always responsive to the contributions of others and sensitive to what he understood as the needs of the world at the particular moment that he wrote (*MDT,* 7).[30] From Arendt's perspective, then, the opinions one presents in public cannot be simply drawn somehow from the darkness of one's inner self but must instead arise from a concerned engagement with the opinions of others and the particulars of the issue under consideration. Thus, although Lessing lived at a time in which there were few public spaces available, Arendt nonetheless saw him as a quintessential proto-public actor whose partisan opinion "has nothing whatsoever to do with [isolated] subjectivity because it is always framed not in terms of the self but in terms of the relationship of men to their world, in terms of their positions and opinions" (*MDT,* 29). It was, Arendt argued, "because Lessing was a completely political person [that] he insisted that truth can exist only where it is humanized by discourse, only where each man says not what just happens to occur to him at the moment, but what he 'deems truth'" (*MDT,* 30). Actors in Arendtian public spaces attempt to persuade others, then, but their perspectives must always remain open to being changed by the actions and statements of these others. A public opinion, reflecting neither certainty nor subjectivity, can never be more nor less than simply a considered, contingent judgment.

This tension is perhaps the most compatible with Dewey's pragmatic vision. For Dewey, as well, rejected any "quest for certainty" in the world, stressing the constant change and uncertainty human beings must always face, despite his fundamental belief that we could slowly increase our control of our environment through scientific engagement. Even so, however, he did not focus to my knowledge, in the way Arendt did, on the danger that "truth" could hold for the very existence of democracy itself.[31]

In response to this tension between truth and relativism, our elementary students would need to learn to follow Lessing's example of a complex balancing act in their engagement with the world. For the children, authentic public action would entail a constantly shifting engagement with the world and with the multiple perspectives of other participants, the unique ways of seeing of each becoming a resource for their shared effort. From a strictly Arendtian perspective, for example, the desire to find the correct answer, common in many current schooling practices, would be seen as a tool for shutting down dialogue and destroying the possibility of "concerted" as opposed to mass action. Of course, this is clearly compatible with some recent writings on constructivist teaching. Furthermore, the Lessing example emphasizes the extent to which the focus of action in a public space must be on a collective effort to "care for the world," in Arendt's terms, instead of on any child's particular interests. Personal opinion in this sense becomes not how one wishes the world to be, but what one understands the world to need in this particular moment.

Between Control and Chaos

The most difficult tension of the public arises from the fact that the very conditions that generate creative power in the public also produce instability and unpredictability, the effects of which reverberate uncontrollably into the world and constantly threaten to tear apart public spaces (and sometimes the world itself). For, *by definition,* one can never control the results of one's actions in a public space or the ways in which others interpret what one says.

"In the realm of action," Arendt noted, "isolated mastership can be achieved only if the others are no longer needed to join the enterprise of their own accord, with their own motives and aims" (*HC,* 222). In fact, "since action acts," within the public at least, "upon beings who are capable of their own actions," she argued, "reaction, apart from being a response, is always a new action that strikes out on its own and affects others." Public action is boundless, reverberating potentially forever into the future, and "the smallest act in the

most limited circumstances bears the seed of the same boundless-
ness, because one deed, and sometimes one word, suffices to change
every constellation" (*HC*, 190). Action, then, is fundamentally
tragic, because "he who acts never quite knows what he is doing, . . .
he always becomes 'guilty' of consequences he never intended or
even foresaw" (*HC*, 233). Because of this, an actor in this model appears "much more the victim and the sufferer than the author and
doer of what he had done" (*HC*, 234).

Arendt argued that this unpredictability of action led many in the
past to seek out ways to stabilize and control these processes, to escape the tragedy that almost invariably accompanies public action
and collective power. Yet the very structure of the public means that
to control the results of one's actions would be to destroy the space
itself, eliminating the creative and thus unpredictable initiative of
one's fellow actors. Even to guarantee one's own future actions
would be destructive to agency, eliminating the freedom of one's future self to respond to the contingencies of an unknown tomorrow.

Chaos, however, is just as unacceptable as total control of the future. No coherent public could hope to survive for any perceptible
period of time in the midst of chaos. It would inevitably be torn
apart by its own productivity, generating unstoppable processes and
wracking the world with storms of destructive change. Complete unpredictability would even be destructive of our own sense of coherent selfhood; for if we were unable to depend at all on who we
would be tomorrow, "we would never be able to keep our identities;
we would be condemned to wander helplessly and without direction
in the darkness of each man's lonely heart, caught in its contradictions and unequivocalities" (*HC*, 237). We must have some assurances about how others in the space with us and even how we ourselves will act, some limit on the abilities of all to act creatively.

In Arendt's view, the only solution to the twin dangers of control
and chaos is to seek an unstable and always uncertain balance between these two extremes, bringing some stability to the public and
to the world without also eliminating the very freedom that allows
the public to exist at all. This compromise involves two different aspects for Arendt: our capacity for making promises and our capacity
for forgiving others. Promises allow the collective of the public "the

sovereignty of a body of people bound and kept together, not by an identical will . . . but by an agreed purpose for which alone the promises are valid and binding"; this limited arena of certainty has an "unquestioned superiority over those who are completely free, unbound by any promises and unkept by any purpose" (*HC*, 245). It is by being "bound to the fulfillment of promises" to others that we are "able to keep our identities," holding ourselves responsible for what we have said before and making guarantees about what we will do in the future (*HC*, 237). Through such promises, free participants in public spaces "leave the unpredictability of human affairs and the unreliability of men as they are, using them merely as the medium, as it were, into which certain islands of predictability are thrown." But "the moment promises lose their character as isolated islands of certainty in an ocean of uncertainty, that is, when this faculty is misused to cover the whole ground of the future to map out a path secured in all directions, they lose their binding power and the whole enterprise becomes self-defeating" (*HC*, 244).

Promises alone are not enough to provide stability to the public, however, both because of the enormously productive reverberations that result from the chains of action and reaction and because participants are constantly in the position of failing to live up to the contracts they have made with others. "Without being forgiven, released from the consequences of what we have done," Arendt worried, "our capacity to act would, as it were, be confined to one single deed from which we could never recover; we would remain the victims of its consequences forever" (*HC*, 237). "Only through this constant mutual release from what they do," Arendt noted, "can men remain free agents, only by constant willingness to change their minds and start again can they be trusted with so great a power as to start something new" (*HC*, 240).

But this tenuous solution largely applies to reverberations *within* a public space and cannot reach particularly far beyond it. When one acts into the world, one begins processes that progress beyond the ability of anyone to predict or control. Arendt feared, for example, that by acting into nature, scientists were increasingly "unchaining . . . potentially irreversible, irremediable 'processes of no return' . . . whose outcome remains uncertain and unpredictable whether they are let loose in the human or the natural world" (*HC*, 231–232).[32] For this and other reasons, she vehemently rejected efforts to understand public "action" through the metaphor of "making," as if one could control the results of action through a kind of planned fabrication of the future.

This is where Arendt's vision diverges perhaps most fundamentally from a Deweyan one. As I have noted, Dewey saw democratic action as a process of seeking increasing control over one's environment. In Dewey's pragmatic vision, all actions are aimed toward particular, although always interim, ends in the world, ends that then become means for yet further actions. In a Deweyan world, one always acts to obtain consequences in the world, and one always judges the outcome of one's act by the consequences it produces.[33] In contrast, Arendt argued, in part because of the dangers I noted above, that actors should never treat their engagement in public as an attempt to achieve particular ends (*HC*, 229). Instead, actors and spectators should act and judge based on what she called, rather vaguely, "principles," noting that "action, to be free, must be free from motive on the one side, from its intended goal as predictable effect on the other."[34] Thus, she said, "the innermost meaning of the acted deed and the spoken word . . . must remain untouched by any eventual outcome, by their consequences for better or worse" (*HC*, 205).

Though there is more subtlety to Arendt's claim than I have done justice to here, still her stance appears to be a relatively extreme response to the problems she has raised.[35] Dewey, for example, is surely right that although we can never fully know the results of an action, we can certainly begin to notice patterns of results that occur when we act and thus begin to achieve a level of control in our environment, even if it is never perfect. However, Arendt does point us to an area that Dewey and, I am convinced, many current scholars tend to neglect. For Dewey did in fact acknowledge the limitations inherent in ever tracing the impact of one's actions into the future, noting, for example, that "no one can take into account all the consequences of the acts he performs."[36] Yet it is not Dewey but Arendt who plays out the potential implications of this limitation, who illuminates the inherent tragedies of action.

Indeed, I am convinced that her vision has special relevance for us as we enter the twenty-first century. Ulrich Beck has recently argued, for instance, that we have created with our technology and our science a "risk society," with reverberating environmental and other dangers of such scale and complexity that "the very idea of controllability, certainty or security . . . collapses."[37] Beck's comments stand in stark contrast to Dewey's hopes for an ever-increasing control of the environment through democratic "scientific" inquiry.[38] To fail to address these issues with students, or in our writings on democracy and democratic education, seems, to me at least, enormously problematic and potentially dangerous.

Despite the dangers, Arendt was not attempting to argue against public action, which she celebrated, but instead against hubris. In fact, if one tempers Arendt's statements about the relationship between public action and particular goals or aims in the world, one arrives at a vision that is very compatible with that of West, whose

> prophetic pragmatism denies [both] Sisyphean pessimism and utopian pessimism. Rather, it promotes the possibility of human progress and the human impossibility of paradise. This progress results from principled and protracted Promethean efforts, yet even such efforts are no guarantee. . . . It calls for utopian energies and tragic actions, energies and actions that yield permanent and perennial revolutionary, rebellious, and reformist strategies that oppose the status quos of our day.

West argues that "these strategies are never to become ends-in-themselves, but rather to remain means through which are channeled moral outrage and human desperation in the face of prevailing forms of evil in human societies and in human lives." It is in this way, West argues, that the inescapable fact of "tragedy can be an impetus rather than an impediment to oppositional activity."[39]

To respond to this third and final tension within the classroom, then, the teacher would need, first, to help the elementary school children learn to accept, and perhaps even value, the mistakes of others. Further, although they would need to create a collective plan for action, this plan would need to remain open to the creative actions of others, often refraining from mapping out the future in specific terms. They would need to learn to traverse the tension between agreements that mean nothing and contracts that are set in stone, unbreakable regardless of changes in the world. Finally, with respect to the world beyond their small public, helping children understand this particular tension of public spaces would almost seem to require engaging students in an activity, like an attempt to change a state's child seat-belt laws, that takes them beyond their classrooms. For it is very difficult to simulate the complex and often perverse workings of the larger society inside a school.

Certainly, students could engage with the stories of past struggles, discussing, for example, the conflicted outcomes of the effort to eliminate segregated schooling (or, actually, to achieve equal access to education) in the United States. Without denigrating what was achieved, students could learn how "success" led to thousands of African American teachers being fired, to thousands of students of color being tracked into lower-level classes in majority white schools, and to hundreds of local African American schools being dismantled.[40] Ultimately, however, only by engaging in an actual collective effort in the world beyond the school, only by leaving the safety of their relatively controlled environment, could students hope to fully experience the myriad and uncontrollable factors that arise when one acts into the world. And it is only through such rich experience that they could hope to truly learn the dilemmas that come with public engagement. Thus, within an Arendtian model, learning to accept failure and the often unpredictable outcomes that arise from action is on a par with learning to "succeed." To gloss over these complexities for students, to allow them to wear rose-colored glasses about their own projects, would be extremely detrimental to their ability to act together in public in the future.

Putting It All Together:
The Example of Public Achievement

At this point, I examine a comprehensive effort to initiate youth into a vibrant practice of citizen politics that resonates with much of Arendt's vision. I begin by emphasizing those aspects of a project named Public Achievement which map onto Arendt's model of the public, also noting areas in which she would probably have pushed the project's developers further. Although much of Public Achievement is compatible with her understanding of public action, and although some of the developers were clearly influenced by her ideas, the project nonetheless diverges from her vision in a number of significant ways, as I discuss at the end of this section.[41]

Public Achievement, originally a joint project of the mayor of St. Paul, Minnesota, and Project Public Life (now the Center for Democracy and Citizenship), based at the University of Minnesota, is "an experiment in civic education for young people."[42] It draws from a vision of democracy developed by Harry C. Boyte, co-director of Project Public Life, and his colleagues, in which "the politics of serious democracy is a give and take, messy, everyday activity in which citizens set about dealing with public problems, the issues of our common existence." Participating in such "citizen politics," the developers argue, "requires an education in political ideas and skills, and environments in which people can learn and practice political arts" ("Evaluation," 3).

As a part of the project, "teams of six to twelve young people work within their schools or other organizations, with coaches, to solve public problems that are important to them." These teams are based in "public, private, and parochial elementary and middle schools, along with a few community based organizations and high schools." The coaches are "college students, adult leaders of the youth institutions, and in some cases community leaders" who work to guide students' efforts to develop their plans and issues and who help students learn from and reflect on their experiences ("Evaluation," 4).

The manual for the effort, written and rewritten at different times by a broad collection of individuals involved with the project, describes a series of steps students can take as they move toward action. (I draw here on two different versions of this manual, titled *Making the Rules*, that include a wider range of exercises.) First, students are encouraged to tell their "story," to get in touch with the history of experiences that makes them unique. These stories, the manual tells students, help others understand each person's perspective, giving others "clues about who we are." At the same time, the manual notes, such stories "help you understand yourself, too." It argues, therefore, that "learning who you are by learning to tell your unique story is the first step toward working in the public arena." Early on, then, the project focuses on encouraging students to tease out their distinctive perspectives.[43]

The writers also argue that as a part of this process, students should come to know their "self-interest" better. Although this may initially seem quite different from Arendt's admonition to care for the world, the manual actually distinguishes between "selfishness," which is about one's private desires, and "self-interest," in which one connects one's interests with those of others in public more broadly. Through one's self-interest, one serves the world at the same time as one serves issues relevant to oneself. In fact, although the developers do not cite Arendt, they clearly draw upon her idiosyncratic definition of what she called *"inter-est"* when they note that it "comes from the Latin phrase 'to be among'" and argue, therefore, that "self-interest always has to do with what you're working for in a group of people" (*MTR*, 10).

The manual gives a range of activities for helping students get in touch with their distinctive biographies; yet it also cautions them that there are important differences between the kinds of relationships and selves they can take on in private settings among friends and family as opposed to those in public spaces amid other political actors. Not everything from their personal story can be brought into the public. Much like Arendt, the project developers argue that private life "is where you seek close relationships . . . [and] where you gain acceptance for just being yourself, and not so much what you contribute." The private is where you can bring your whole self. The public, in contrast, is "where you become aware of hopes and concerns you share with others and where you act on them. It's where you learn the value of hearing many different viewpoints. It's where you are held accountable and get recognition for what you contribute. . . . It is where your actions, commitment, and effectiveness determine how seriously people take you" (*MTR*, 20). Furthermore, like Arendt, they argue that it is in public that one achieves "a sense of self-discovery" (*MTR*, 21). Despite these similarities to Arendt's model, the manual does not emphasize one of Arendt's key issues on this point—namely, the extent to which excessive distinctiveness of each individual is a danger to the continued existence of the public—though it does discuss the broader challenges of group diversity.

Beginning with a brainstorming session, the manual guides students through a process designed to help them uncover a common problem that connects with their myriad self-interests. After they define a common problem, students are to develop a mission statement, something like the following: "We, the Public Achievement team at Hypothetical Jr. High, will no longer stand by as our school ignores the pollution we cause in our community and the world. As a first goal to reduce our negative environmental impact, we will work with the administration, staff, and students to develop a recycling program in our school" (*MTR*, 14). Such a statement clearly fulfills two of Arendt's principal requirements for a common project. First, although it represents an agreement about future actions, it leaves quite a lot of room for flexibility about what, exactly, will be done. Second, in part because of this flexibility, this mission statement is vague enough that it can be easily interpreted in a unique way from multiple perspectives. The agreement, therefore, does not collapse the plurality in the space or the unpredictable creative contributions that might be made to it.

In fact, Public Achievement even attempts to foster an understanding among students of the diverse ways in which different individuals interpret language. It includes an activity in which students take a specific political word and define it from each of their unique personal perspectives. This exercise argues against the strategy of dictionaries, which "try to give words meanings that everyone can accept, without any personal interpretations," arguing that "like politics, language belongs to those who use it—not just the 'experts'" (*MTR*, 16). In a range of different ways, then, students are encouraged to discover unique perspectives about their shared effort.

Although the manual does not speak directly of "truth," it nonetheless presents an essentially relational vision of acting with and against others in the world. Students are expected to continually adjust tactics and strategies to the shifting aspects of their environment. The project especially focuses on building skills for interviewing and active listening so that participants might continually gather data on the perspectives, ideas, and feelings of others, both within and beyond their group, on their issue.

The key aspect of Arendt's vision that is missing from the Public Achievement model, however, is the tension she saw as perhaps most important of all: that between chaos and control. Whereas Arendt's vision on this issue is rather dark, Public Achievement's is fairly upbeat. The developers have attempted to encourage students to believe that they *can* take control, that they *can* "make the rules," and, implicitly, that they can determine the results that those rules dictate. In fact, a later version of the manual, clearly drawing from Boyte's writings on democracy as participation in "work," is titled *Building Worlds, Transforming Lives, Making History*, and it explicitly states that children in Public Achievement are taught that "they can *make history* themselves, today" and that "in a very tangible sense, PA [Public Achievement] teams *make history* every year."[44] Although the developers acknowledge that students can learn a great deal from failure, there is no discussion of the often unpredictable and counterintuitive outcomes of many important struggles. Not addressed are the ways in which victories, as West notes, often generate new "evils" of their own. From an Arendtian perspective, this threatens to mislead students, failing to fully prepare them for the realities of action in a complex and conflicted world.

Despite the ways in which Public Achievement seems largely compatible with Arendt's vision, there are in fact important aspects of this project that diverge quite significantly from her ideal model. Whereas Arendt, as a political theorist, worked to develop an idealized and relatively abstract vision of collective action, looking to a broad spectrum of the Western historical experience, the developers of Public Achievement draw from a much more practical tradition of citizen organizing, focusing more on the American experience, especially that of the twentieth century, and influenced by pragmatic "grassroots" organizers like Saul Alinsky.

Again, Arendt constructed her model of the public not only as an effort to empower people, but also as a response to the submergence of individuality that she experienced in different ways in Nazi Ger-

nany, as well as in the banality of modern "society." The mainte-
nance of a certain kind of plurality within political action was of
paramount importance to her. "Truth" is so dangerous to her vision
of the public precisely because of its tendency to collapse this plural-
ty into a transparent consensus. In fact, the collective "power" pro-
luced in the public was, for her, fundamentally dependent upon this
plurality. Instead of what she disparaged as the "strength" of soli-
larity, power in the public could arise only from the unpredictable
creative energy generated only by unique actors acting "in concert."
Because of her desire to foster the distinctiveness of each human being
as much as possible given the constraints of collective action, however,
he conceptualized actors in public as essentially free-floating, without
ight connections to particular communities or contexts. Indeed, she
leveloped the public as a space in which people could *escape* from
he constraints and roles that often come with more normalizing
orms of community.

Public Achievement also acknowledges the importance of foster-
ng the distinctiveness of all participants. Nonetheless, the developers critically describe an approach to identity like Arendt's as a "suit-
ase" model, in which one's experiences and influences are viewed as
imply possessions that one carries around with oneself. In contrast,
hey recommend the idea of a "tree" as a metaphor for identity, be-
ause it is "rooted deeply in the soil"; the manual tells students that
"your identity is rooted in your past, in the lives of your family,
ommunity, and culture. These roots—this personal story—give you
he strength and the nourishment to continually grow" (*MTR*,
10–11). In Public Achievement, then, "self"-interest takes on the
additional flavor of an at least partially *collective* interest as well.
And to some extent, the activity of telling one's unique story in Pub-
ic Achievement appears designed not only to tease out students'
unique perspectives, but also to emphasize the extent to which they
are embedded in particular groups and the extent to which they are
esponsible to these communities. Boyte and his colleagues' larger
vision is one of empowered *communities* of many different kinds,
not simply empowered individuals.[45]

Although the developers of Public Achievement value the distinc-
ive contributions of individuals, their project is much less focused

than Arendt's model on maintaining a space of fully egalitarian plurality all the time. Thus, for example, the manual contains no clear
admonitions against groups coalescing strategically into relative
states of solidarity, in which they would largely act as a unit. The
"strength" of solidarity, then, is for them simply another useful political tool. From this perspective, there would be no reason to view
the relatively free participation of individuals in efforts they did not
themselves initiate as fundamentally undemocratic, depending on
the context.

Another crucial difference from Arendt arises in Public Achievement's vision of how one "emerges" into the public from private
spaces. Arendt envisioned the public as a space of full equality in
which each actor presented herself as honestly as possible, even
though one could not fully reveal oneself because of the dangers
one's uniqueness presented for the continued existence of the space.
Public Achievement, conversely, views the public (framed more
broadly than in Arendt) as an always ill-defined space of "strategic"
action in which one can never fully trust those with whom one
works. The public, for Public Achievement, is where one is
"guarded" about what one says and how one acts.[46] The public is a
place in which there is unequal power, in which others will often attempt to use your weaknesses and information they gain about you
against you.[47]

Certainly the Public Achievement model is not the only way one
might imagine developing public spaces in educational settings.
Along with my sketchy child seat-belt example, however, it does represent one path by which Arendt's relatively abstract theoretical criteria might be appropriated into an actual educational practice. And
though there is little information on what students learned during
this process, an evaluation indicated that at least some of the teams
were relatively successful. As Boyte and Nancy N. Kari note, Public
Achievement teams "have organized high school day care centers for
unwed mothers. They have created community parks in settings
where adults had initially given up, in the face of skepticism by
neighbors. They have created curricula and strategies for dealing
with issues like racial prejudice and sexual harassment."[48] Further,
although apparently conceived as an add-on to usual classroom in-

struction, in at least one school "nearly all of the students in grades four through eight . . . have participated," and some teachers are "reinforcing Public Achievement's lessons in the classroom" ("Evaluation," 10).

Conclusion

To these preoccupations and perplexities, this book does not offer an answer. Such answers are given every day, and they are matters of practical politics, subject to the agreement of many; they can never lie in theoretical considerations or the opinion of one person, as though we dealt here with problems for which only one solution is possible.

—Hannah Arendt, *The Human Condition*

Paradoxically, it is the *differences* from Arendt's abstract model that make Public Achievement a good example of a potential instantiation of her vision. For Arendt understood that one could not determine answers in the real world from the abstract perspective of a theorist. However, the very existence of Public Achievement (as evidenced in the number of books by Boyte and others that led up to its creation) required an extensive engagement with theoretical perspectives on the nature of democratic collective action of which Arendt's was only one. What Public Achievement shows is the extent to which actually using these theories in particular contexts requires that they be adapted and transformed, that they *inform* instead of *direct* one's efforts.

The developers of Public Achievement are careful to acknowledge that they don't have all the answers, noting that other approaches to citizen action are not "wrong" and that "often an institution combines two or more approaches in its practices." In fact, they introduce their manual by stating that it provides "a tool kit to aid in . . . [this] endeavor, not a step-by-step recipe for public life. There is no such recipe, and as creative citizens, you would not want one anyway. Public Achievement is an experiment in a larger civic laboratory."[49] Still, it *is* a manual, and despite this caution, it retains a sense that there is a "correct" path that should be taken to prepare students to be active citizens. This tension-filled tendency to declare that one is open to many other possibilities while simultaneously giving the impression that there is, in fact, one correct and essentially universal answer is common among theorists of democracy. In Arendt's case, despite her statement about the limits of theory in the epigraph above, she also nonetheless often presented her model of the public as if it were "the elementary grammar of political action."[50] And I have already spoken about the way that Dewey—perhaps unintentionally—tended to present his criteria of democracy as if they were universally relevant, despite his pragmatic convictions.

Examining Public Achievement through the lens of Arendt's theory illuminates potential lacks, like the project's avoidance of the tension between chaos and control. At the same time, the case of Public Achievement reveals potential limitations in Arendt's abstract theory for particular purposes. Such dialogic interactions between theory and practice, or between theories, like Arendt's and Dewey's, are, I believe, enormously productive. In the end, however, it would be impossible—and, I would argue, counterproductive in any case—to attempt to synthesize these three visions together into a single approach to the teaching of democracy. Instead, it is important to preserve a multiplicity of very different perspectives on the nature of egalitarian collective action, ensuring that a diverse range of lenses will remain available to illuminate, and be illuminated by, the events and occasions of our age.

This is not only a theoretical issue. For example, in his examination of activism in the United States, Charles C. Euchner argues that no single political practice can be viewed as superior for all activist efforts. In fact, he argues that efforts and organizations that are successful on *multiple* levels at grappling with multiple kinds of issues and contexts are those that embody an overlapping structure of different strategies.[51] It is in this spirit of plurality and dialogue that I have presented Arendt's model of the public: not only as a counter to the field's tendency toward utopian thinking, but also as yet another lens through which scholars might engage with the dilemmas of educational democracy more broadly.

Notes

1. See, for example, Herbert M. Kliebard, *The Struggle for the American Curriculum,* 2nd ed. (New York: Routledge, 1995).

2. See, for example, Elliot Eisner, "Standards for American Schools," *Phi Delta Kappa,* vol. 76, no. 10 (1995): 758–764; and Gary Orfield, Susan E. Eaton, and the Harvard Project on School Desegregation, *Dismantling Desegregation* (New York: New Press, 1996).

3. Arendt scholars will note that I gloss over the fact that Arendt herself rejected the use of the public in schools (see Hannah Arendt, "The Crisis in Education," in *Between Past and Future* [New York: Penguin Books, 1968], pp. 173–196). I address this issue elsewhere in a work in progress. In brief, Arendt essentially argues, for assorted reasons, that the practice of the public is not a "learned" practice. This is an extremely problematic idea, however, one that leads to a number of contradictions in her work. Ultimately, I argue that it is an essentially untenable position. Here I simply assume, for reasons of focus and limited space, that the public is, in fact, a practice that must be learned like any other.

4. David Held, *Models of Democracy* (Stanford: Stanford University Press, 1987).

5. Michael Apple and James Beane, "The Case for Democratic Schools," in *Democratic Schools,* ed. James Beane and Michael Apple (Alexandria, VA: ASCD, 1995), p. 5. This book will be cited as *DS* in the text for all subsequent references.

6. To name just a few, see James W. Fraser, *Reading, Writing, and Justice: School Reform as if Democracy Matters* (Albany: State University of New York Press, 1997); Walter C. Parker, "Curriculum for Democracy," in *Democracy, Education, and the Schools,* ed. Roger Soder (San Francisco: Jossey-Bass, 1996); and Douglas J. Simpson and Michael J. B. Jackson, *Educational Reform: A Deweyan Perspective* (New York: Garland Publishing, 1997).

7. John Dewey, *Democracy and Education* (New York: Free Press, 1916), p. 87.

8. See, especially, John Dewey, "Human Nature and Conduct," in *John Dewey: The Middle Works,* vol. 14, ed. Jo Ann Boydston (Carbondale: Southern Illinois University Press, 1982); and Craig Cunningham, "Unique Potential: A Metaphor for John Dewey's Later Conception of the Self," *Educational Theory,* vol. 44, no. 2 (1994): 211–224. In this very general overview, I do not address the changes in Dewey's thought over time on this issue, as noted by Cunningham.

9. I engage in a more detailed analysis of Dewey's model of democracy in Aaron Schutz, "John Dewey's Conundrum: Can Democratic Schools Empower?" *Teachers College Record* (in press).

10. See, for example, John Dewey, *The Public and Its Problems* (Athens, GA: Swallow Press, 1927), p. 185.

11. Dewey was at least theoretically open to the possibility that even the most cherished of his values might need to change in response to what he learned through events and actions in the world. Yet, at the same time, there is an underlying tension between this pragmatism and his core faith in a particular vision of democracy. Despite his rejection of abstract visions of democracy, the outlines of a model of democracy can nonetheless be discerned in his work, and it is this vision, interpreted in myriad ways, that remains influential today. I examine an aspect of Dewey's utopian impulse in more detail in Aaron Schutz, "John Dewey and the

'Paradox of Size': Some Limitations of Teaching for Local Democracy" (paper presented at a conference of the American Educational Research Association, Montreal, 1999).

12. Cornel West, *The American Evasion of Philosophy* (Madison: University of Wisconsin Press, 1989), p. 229.

13. Hannah Arendt, "'What Remains? The Language Remains': A Conversation with Günter Gaus," in Hannah Arendt, *Essays in Understanding,* ed. Jerome Kohn (New York: Harcourt Brace & Co., 1994), p. 20.

14. See, for example, Hannah Arendt, *The Origins of Totalitarianism* (New York: Harcourt Brace Jovanovich, 1967), pp. 382, 387, 427, 441, and 471. This book will be cited as *OT* in the text for all subsequent references.

15. See, for example, John Dewey, "Freedom and Culture," in *John Dewey: The Later Works,* vol. 13, ed. Jo Ann Boydston (Carbondale: Southern Illinois University Press, 1988), p. 178.

16. In fact, as I note below, Arendt at times rejected *all* means/ends thinking, fearing that we would inevitably begin to believe that the ends would justify the means.

17. Maxine Greene, in "Exclusions and Awakenings," in *Learning from Our Lives,* ed. Anna Neumann and Penelope L. Peterson (New York: Teachers College Press, 1997), p. 22, argues that Dewey never really understood tragedy.

18. Actually, Arendt argued that what she was promoting was *more* egalitarian than democracy, or majority rule, as she said the Greeks defined this word. The public was, instead, a form of what she called "isonomy," or, as she argued in *On Revolution* (London: Penguin Books, 1963), p. 30, "no rule," "whose outstanding characteristic among the forms of government, as the ancients had enumerated them, was that the notion of rule . . . was entirely absent from it." I use the term "democracy" here, nonetheless, for reasons of simplicity and familiarity.

19. Hannah Arendt, *The Human Condition* (Chicago: University of Chicago Press, 1958), p. 178. This book will be cited as *HC* in the text for all subsequent references.

20. I extrapolate somewhat here on her definition of "strength" as she defines this in *The Human Condition.* She discusses only individuals there, but clearly, a group in which individuals were merely fulfilling roles they were assigned would be acting collectively in strength and not in power. This issue is intertwined with her discussions of "violence," which I do not address here.

21. Bonnie Honig, "Toward an Agonistic Feminism: Hannah Arendt and the Politics of Identity," in *Feminist Interpretations of Hannah Arendt,* ed. Bonnie Honig (University Park: Pennsylvania University Press, 1995), pp. 140–141.

22. Cunningham, "Unique Potential," p. 220.

23. Susan Seigel and Virginia Rockwood, "Democratic Education, Student Empowerment, and Community Service: Theory and Practice," *Equity and Excellence in Education,* vol. 26, no. 2 (1993): 65–70.

24. Margaret Canovan, *Hannah Arendt: A Reinterpretation of Her Political Thought* (Cambridge: Cambridge University Press, 1992), p. 137.

25. See Eleanor Honig Skoller, *The In-Between of Writing: Experience and Experiment in Drabble, Duras, and Arendt* (Ann Arbor: University of Michigan Press, 1993).

26. Hannah Arendt, *Men in Dark Times* (New York: Harcourt Brace Jovanovich, 1968), p. 25. This book will be cited as *MDT* in the text for all subsequent references.

27. Certainly, work like that of Nel Noddings would imply this; see, for example, *Caring* (Berkeley: University of California Press, 1984).

28. Hannah Arendt, "On Hannah Arendt," p. 317.

29. Actually, Arendt's writings are contradictory in different places about whether she thought scientific "truths" were of a *fundamentally* different kind than everyday opinions.

30. Some of Arendt's commentators, like Ronald Beiner, have argued that Arendt shifted over her lifetime from perceiving "judgment" as something undertaken by actors in the midst of public action to an activity reserved for spectators who can view all sides of the fray coolly from a distance. Although this is surely true to some extent, attempts to argue that judgment could somehow be evacuated from Arendt's vision of the public reflect a fundamental misunderstanding of the nature of the public itself. Even though the actor, in the heat of engagement, has neither the time to reflect nor the broad and nuanced view of a spectator, she must nonetheless engage in a more evanescent form of judgment as she acts, taking into account the multiple opinions that surround her and the contingent characteristics of her historical moment.

31. Dewey did focus on a similar, but nonetheless distinct, issue: the problematic separation of "thinking" from "action" and the ways in which this led, in his view, to a class distinction between those who "thought" and those who "worked," the latter doing the bidding of the former (see Dewey, *Democracy and Education*, p. 255).

32. See Hanna Pitkin, *The Attack of the Blob: Hannah Arendt's Conception of the Social* (Chicago: University of Chicago Press, 1998), who grapples with whether Arendt did in fact believe in extrahuman social forces.

33. This is laid out many times in Dewey's work, for example, in *Democracy and Education*. The simplicity of my summary belies the complexity of his discussions of this issue, however.

34. Arendt, "What Is Freedom?" in *Between Past and Future*, p. 151. I do not get into the full complexities of Arendt's arguments around this issue here.

35. Space does not allow a fuller analysis of the complexity of Arendt's discussion of "making" and politics and the problems with "means/end" thinking, nor is this complexity relevant to my discussion. But I will offer a few additional points for those who are interested: Arendt drew from the ancient Greeks a Platonic conception of "work" and of "making," in which an individual creates a durable object by holding an ideal and unchanging model in her mind. According to Arendt, then, "what guides the work of fabrication is outside the fabricator" as a model "and precedes the actual work process" (*The Human Condition,* pp. 140–141). Largely because of this understanding of work, she believed that "an end, once it is attained, ceases to be an end and loses its capacity to guide and justify the choice of means, or organize and produce them" (ibid., pp. 141–142). This, therefore, is another reason why her theory of "action" avoided any effort to achieve concrete ends.

Dewey took great issue with similar ideas when he met them in his own time. He argued that one does not simply aim for a static ideal in work; instead, one reconstructs one's aims and one's means continually through interaction with one's environment. Furthermore, Dewey remained unconcerned about the achievement of ends in politics, noting that the "consummation" of a stretch of activity only leads one to see new aims one had not seen before. Thus, he would have rejected nearly everything that, for Arendt, went under the label of "work." (One wonders if Arendt ever actually built something herself.) See, for example, Dewey, *Democracy and Education,* chap. 8.

Arendt also argued that one should not use "means/ends" logic with respect to political action because "as long as we deal with ends and means in the political realm, we shall not be able to prevent anybody's using all means to pursue recognized ends" (*The Human Condition,* p. 229). Dewey would see this as an extremely problematic separation of facts from values, which, he argued convincingly, was not required by (in fact, was impossible within) means/end thinking. See, for example, Dewey's relatively succinct "Theory of Valuation," in *Later Works,* ed. Boydston.

36. Dewey, "Human Nature and Conduct," p. 181. See also Dewey, "Freedom and Culture," p. 105.

37. Ulrich Beck, *World Risk Society* (Cambridge: Polity Press, 1999), p. 2.

38. Although Beck does, in fact, recommend more local democracy as part of the solution.

39. West, *American Evasion,* pp. 229–230. An important part of West's argument arises out of his religious commitments. I am not sure these are necessary to make his argument, however.

40. See, for example, Michele Foster, *Black Teachers on Teaching* (New York: New Press, 1997).

41. See, for example, citations of Arendt in Harry C. Boyte and Nancy N. Kari, *Building America: The Democratic Promise of Public Work* (Philadelphia: Temple University Press, 1996); and Harry C. Boyte, *Commonwealth: A Return to Citizen Politics* (New York: Free Press, 1989).

42. Melissa Bass, "Towards a New Theory and Practice of Civic Education: An Evaluation of Public Achievement" (master's thesis, University of Minnesota, 1995), p. 1; available at: http://www.cpn.org/sections/topics/youth. This work will be cited as "Evaluation" in the text for all subsequent references.

43. Melissa Bass et al., *Making the Rules: A Public Achievement Guidebook* (St. Paul, MN: Project Public Life, 1994); online manual accessed December 12, 1998, at: http://www.cpn.org/sections/topics/youth/stories-studies/makingrules.1html. This guidebook will be cited as *MTR* in the text for all subsequent references.

44. Robert Hildreth et al., *Building Worlds, Transforming Lives, Making History* (Minneapolis: Center for Democracy and Citizenship, 1998), p. 18; emphasis added.

45. See Paul Lichterman, *The Search for Political Community: American Activists Reinventing Commitment* (Cambridge: Cambridge University Press, 1996).

46. Hildreth et al., *Building Worlds,* p. 102.

47. This implies that there is a multiplicity of different publics, each with different levels of safety and trust; in fact, it contests the very idea of a simple binary between public and private. For a discussion of a related issue, see Nancy Fraser, "Rethinking the Public Sphere: A Contribution to the Critique of Actually Existing Democracy," in *Habermas and the Public Sphere,* ed. Craig Calhoun (Cambridge, MA: MIT Press, 1992).

48. Boyte and Kari, *Building America,* p. 176.

49. Hildreth et al., *Building Worlds,* p. 2.

50. Arendt, *On Revolution,* p. 173. I have engaged in a more detailed discussion of this and other contradictions in Arendt's writings in Aaron Schutz, "Theory as Performative Pedagogy: Three Faces of Hannah Arendt," currently in review. Note that even the epigraph seems to implicitly assume that public action is the avenue for solving practical problems.

51. Charles C. Euchner, *Extraordinary Politics: How Protest and Dissent Are Changing American Democracy* (Boulder: Westview Press, 1996). In Aaron Schutz, "Creating Local 'Public Spaces' in Schools: Insights from Hannah Arendt and Maxine Greene," *Curriculum Inquiry,* vol. 29, no. 1 (1999): 77–98, and in Schutz, "John Dewey's Conundrum," I argue that both Arendt's and Dewey's visions of democracy are in fact designed, at least, to serve middle- to upper-class professionals and are not at all culturally neutral.

5

Multicultural Education and Arendtian Conservatism: On Memory, Historical Injury, and Our Sense of the Common

KIMBERLEY CURTIS

American history is longer, larger, more various, more beautiful and more terrible than anything anyone has ever said about it.

—James Baldwin, "A Talk to Teachers"

History, our real history, is always excessive: It is more beautiful, more terrible than we can, on most days, bear. And so we shine it up and package it up into manageable forms, the better, we think, to understand it and to transmit it—stable, reliable, and whole—to our young. Or we simply renege on the task of passing it down to our children, so confused and disoriented do we feel toward its brutalities, its beauties, and its banalities.

The first strategy, insofar as it emancipates itself from the messiness and contingency of history by making it more neat and logical than it ever can be, is an ideological response to the unmanageability of our history, and its practitioners range across the political spectrum. The second is the response of the passive, and it plays, naturally, into the hands of the ideologues. Both strategies are signs of what Hannah Arendt called "world alienation," a condition she believed was definitive of the modern age. Under conditions of world alienation, neither relatively stable things nor human ideas and practices sufficiently form the in-between of the world that not only relates us together, giving us a sense of belonging, but also separates us so that we can retain our distinctiveness.

The "world," as Arendt conceived it, comes into being between people who share a common life in an active sense. Presupposing human plurality, it arises and is sustained by the capacity to "look upon the same world from another's standpoint, to see the same in very different and frequently opposing aspects."[1] It is alone through sharing the world in this active sense that any meaningful comprehension is possible. With world alienation, we fail to exercise this capacity and we lose the worldly in-between to which it gives rise. Our world becomes either a mass society or a place of lonely isolates. In either case, we are without sufficient bearings to make good judgments, and we feel powerless and overwhelmed by forces and processes we neither started nor seem capable of changing.[2]

The upshot of this very real and quite unbearable condition of world alienation for education is, Arendt argued, crisis.[3] Parents and educators alike feel unable to bear joint responsibility for the world, and so they cede it—not alone to ideologues, but also to children, to technicians, and to a narrow-minded method of learning that privileges "doing oneself" over a wider communicative imagination as the ground for knowledge about the world. In short, accompanying the world alienation of parents and educators is a loss of authority. Attempting to capture the average parents' sensibility under conditions of world alienation, Arendt imagines them communicating to their children: "In this world even we are not very securely at home; how to move about in it, what to know, what skills to master, are mysteries to us too. You must try to make out as best you can; in any case you are not entitled to call us to account. We are innocent, we wash our hands of you."[4]

Arendt's response to this crisis as it looked to her in 1954 was to argue what today appears to be a preposterous proposition: that the realm of education must be "decisively divorced" from the realm of public, political life.[5] Today's educational principles, she argued, must respond to our condition of world alienation. Educators must be conservative: They must conserve "the world as it is," exercising a kind of authority and an attitude toward the past entirely inappropriate to the realm of politics.[6] Moreover, Arendt claimed that the divorce between education and politics was necessary so that the young, upon completing their education, would be capable of entering the political realm, where action, judgment, and changing the world comprise the raison d'être.[7] Thus, whereas contemporary radical educators argue that, for the sake of action, we must have a politically engaged pedagogy, Arendt argues that, for the sake of freedom and action, politics and education must be decisively divorced.[8]

At first glance, it is surely Arendt's thinking that is off. Consider, for example, the implicit relation between politics and education in the following facts—a few among so many I could proffer. In highly urbanized areas, 56 percent of Latinas leave high school before graduating. Girls in general are one and one-half times more likely to feel under emotional stress than boys. Among girls, Latinas feel most anxious.[9] Nonwhite high school students perform a little worse than white students in math. That white/nonwhite differential increases in English. It is the highest in history, and girls as a group report liking history less than boys.[10] How can we understand these facts without political lenses? More to the point, how can we educators address these problems—indeed, *how can we educate*—unless our pedagogy is not *divorced from,* but deeply *rooted in,* acute and untiring political analysis, analysis that illuminates the contemporary and historical relationship between, in these cases, gender identity and power, poverty and power, racism and power? Shouldn't understanding social power and the goal of empowerment in fact be central to education in a democracy?

Advocates of what I will call "political multiculturalism" have always answered this question with a resounding yes.[11] Seeking to increase the power and agency of the historically disenfranchised, they self-consciously link politics and education. Thus, they have undertaken a highly charged, rich engagement with American history. Our stories must be rewritten and corrected, they argue. Not only must the wounds inflicted by the victors and the suffering of the vanquished be brought to light, but so, too, the struggle waged by the oppressed to keep spirit and culture alive under enormous strains. Together, these stories will help to empower disempowered agents in the present and give the nation a more complex, less ideological understanding of itself.

Both liberal and conservative critics of multicultural education deplore this self-conscious "politicization." They argue that in troubling "the marvelous inheritance [of Western civilization] that history bestows upon us," advocates of political multiculturalism invite "the fragmentation of the national community into a quarrelsome spatter of enclaves, ghettoes and tribes."[12] Moreover, multiculturalists undermine the moral wealth of Western civilization, inviting nihilism and relativism—in short, bearingless confusion that is vulnerable to manipulation by the prevailing political winds.[13]

There is agreement on both sides of this polarized debate that multicultural education weds politics and education; disagreement over how to assess the marriage.[14] Arendt's insistence on the need for a divorce between politics and education seems to pit her against the pedagogical practices and affirmations of political multiculturalists. The question I pursue here is whether Arendt's "preposterous proposition" and the conservatism it commends have anything interesting to say to advocates of multicultural education whose deepest impulse with respect to history I take to be Baldwinian: to widen, to make more terrible and more beautiful the history to which we seek to belong.

I answer that question, with qualifications, affirmatively, for I believe Arendt's educational conservatism both illuminates and underscores the significance of multiculturalism's deepest impulse. Advocates of multicultural education are not only partisans of identity groups (although they are also very often this); they are partisans of the world in an Arendtian sense. They seek to broaden and make more plural the experiences and perspectives—the in-between of the world—through which our sense of who "we" are is born. What drives them back in time to unearth and reinterpret the historical record are injuries and deprivations, forms of oblivion and exclusion suffered by groups that deform and make less common our common world. In this respect, far from inviting the dangers of fragmentation and enclave politics, multicultural education at its best makes our world more vividly, more actively held in common. Its advocates seek to preserve our *common* world.

Illuminating and embracing this conservative moment of multicultural education is important for many reasons, not the least of which is that it disturbs the caricature of multiculturalism as merely another form of interest-group politics. It also helps advocates of multiculturalism identify the dangers of too single-mindedly focusing pedagogy on empowerment and agency for the oppressed. Multicultural pedagogy must be informed by a probing understanding of the entwinements but also the tensions between politics and education. Arendtian conservatism is a rich resource for rethinking multicultural pedagogy toward these ends.

In what follows, I elaborate on the distinction Arendt draws between politics and education, examining on what grounds and to what ends she thought it necessary. I develop what I believe are Arendt's best arguments and most important concerns, and then I reflect on their usefulness to contemporary debates over multicultural education, taking aspects of Chicano/Chicana scholarship as my examples. Emerging in the late 1960s, Chicano/Chicana scholarship developed out of the Chicano movement for self-determination. It is, therefore, a particularly interesting case in light of which to consider Arendtian conservatism and the tensions between politics and education. Not only was the Chicano movement begun by high school students who argued that Mexican American culture and history were not represented in the curriculum, but one of its most significant contributions to date has been curricular. In examining some of the scholarship it engendered, we can hope to identify and clarify both the problems and the promises of the marriage between politics and education in multicultural education.

Arendtian Conservatism

Hannah Arendt's political theory has inspired legions of radical democrats. She is arguably the twentieth century's most important political theorist. I begin, then, with this question: What is the essence of Arendt's thinking on the relation between education and politics? To pursue the question requires a substantial amount of interpretive work, since the sole essay in which Arendt systematically addresses the relation between politics and education, "The Crisis in Education," contains unusually opaque arguments. In what follows, I clear my way, where necessary, by placing her arguments in the broader context of her political theorizing.

I begin with the question of the *essence* of Arendt's distinction because it is difficult for radical educators in today's educational context to take her arguments seriously. And for good reason. Contemporary forms in which parents, teachers, administrators, and citizens alike cede responsibility for the world suggest that we need more rather than fewer linkages between politics and education, less rather than more authority in the classroom, and a pedagogy oriented more rather than less toward social change. I have in mind, for example, the explosion of "gifts" to school districts by for-profit corporations in exchange for massive advertising opportunities on school grounds, the resurgence of authoritarian teaching practices in the classroom, the reduction of education as preparation for testing, and the gross inequalities in financial support between poor and affluent school districts.[15] Yet, as I hope to show, the nature of Arendt's concern with authority and with respect for the past and her arguments for a separation between politics and education have their own critical merits that radical educators ignore at their peril.

The essence of education, Arendt argued, must be conservative in the sense of "conservation." Adopting a characteristically phenomenological approach, Arendt conceives the responsibility of educators by distilling the existential situation in which the need for education arises. In this light, education has always been, across time and cultures, born of the need on the part of the old to introduce the newcomers to the world *so that* it might be, as all mortal worlds must be, renewed. As a child's primary introduction to the broader world outside the family, schools are the sites where the newcomer first learns about "the world as it is."[16] Because of this, the essential responsibility of the educator is to introduce newcomers to what will always be to them an already existing, old world. The educator's responsibility is to say, "This is our world." That is to say, the educator must assume responsibility for imparting to the child a sense of belonging, a profound sense of becoming a part of the human home to which as a stranger she has been summoned. To that end, Arendt argues, the educator must have "an extraordinary respect for the past," must seek to "accept . . . the world as it is, striving only to preserve the status quo."[17] In such conserving acceptance, she argues, lies the educator's (necessary) authority.

These arguments resonate with one of the deepest aesthetic, nearly religious sensibilities of Arendt's political theorizing: gratitude for what is. To accept responsibility for the child's presence, and to respond to the demands her sheer coming makes, the educator must feel, as one commentator put it, "a kind of holy appreciation for everything that has been given."[18] Gratitude for the miracle of being must orient and inform the educator's elemental approach to the task of educating the young.

But these sensibilities are difficult. We wish the world to be otherwise, suffering its cruelties with fury, resentment, and the desire to deny and defy it. Yet it is precisely such desires the educator must resist if she is to successfully introduce the new to the old and thereby impart a sense of belonging. A certain political forbearance, we might say, is her art.

So, with words and arguments that appear to bear great affinity to familiar conservative arguments about the need for authority and about education as the transmission of gems of knowledge that comprise "the world," Arendt argues that the educator must be conservative, applying to the realm of education a "concept of authority" and an "attitude toward the past" that can have "*no general validity* and must not claim general validity in the world of grown-ups."[19] Education is a time of tutelage. The relation between young and old, teacher and pupil, is inherently one of inequality, and the principles that guide pedagogy, therefore, stand in the strictest opposition to the relations among equals that define adult life in general and political life in particular. Indeed, Arendt argues that when political relations are structured by authority and by a conserving attitude to the world, it is "the ruin of politics, [where] the world must be set right anew each day," where world-altering action is a necessity.[20] The raison d'être of politics is freedom, the freedom to act, to "change every constellation," whereas the first, most elemental goal of education is belonging, is making the world a shared place for newcomers.[21]

Thus, Arendt sets up an antinomy between education—as a domain of tutelage, inequality, authority, and conservation in the service of world-belonging, on the one hand, and public-political life—as a domain of equality, persuasion, change, and freedom, on the other. Yet, as noted above, she does not create the antinomy for traditional conservative ends. In defending her proposition that politics and education must be "decisively divorced," she argues, "exactly for the sake of what is new and revolutionary in every child, education must be conservative."[22] Exactly for the sake of their capacity to act, children must be introduced to the world "as it is."

The essence of Arendt's argument concerning the need for a divorce between education and politics lies, then, in the contention that the child-newcomer must be carefully introduced to the world to which she has been summoned. Because it is a constantly changing world, the child's appearance in it marks an "already been" and a "not yet"; and it is this "already been" world about which adults know. The child must be guided by them to acute knowledge about it: its web of understandings, its factuality, its many "different and frequently opposing aspects." Without this depth of knowledge, the child's efforts, upon maturing, to bring her unique and specific acts to bear on the world will fail, for she will have neither a starting place from which to begin something new nor the reflective distance first to question and then to act differently. Further, the political agenda formed by adults' aspirations for a different world must not determine the nature of that education. If it does, the child's own sensibilities and aspirations will be colonized by adult desires that emerge of necessity in relation to a world, already to the newcomer, grown old.[23]

The responsibility of Arendt's educator is, therefore, twofold: (1) to preserve the world against the action of the new by taking responsibility for saying, "*This* is our world"—that is, it is something specific, complex, has a depth, is recalcitrant, here are its stories, this is its shape; and (2) to protect those characteristics and talents that comprise the uniqueness of everyone born to Earth by not attempting to foreordain how they should act in the world of which they are becoming a part. The educator is conservative in both of these senses, and he assumes responsibility for the world "as it is" in order to make responsiveness possible. Ultimately, the educator's aim is to enable the young to create their own relation to the world, thereby renewing it as a place fit for human habitation. "Hope always hangs," Arendt writes, "on the new," and the problem is always how to educate so that the young are capable of the action necessary "to set the world right anew."[24]

Yet what can Arendt mean when she enjoins educators to conserve the world "as it is?" It sounds like a politically pernicious injunction to uphold prevailing hegemonic relations. It is not; but to probe the meaning of this overly vague injunction more deeply, we must place it in the context of some of Arendt's enduring concerns. First is her concern with the fragility of factual truth.[25] Contrasting it with rational and logical truths, Arendt refers to "those facts and events that are the outcome of men living and acting together."[26] Attentive to and haunted by the world ushered in by the experience of totalitarian politics, where organized lying was perfected, Arendt argued: "Today factual truth if it is opposed to a group's pleasure or profit is greeted with greater hostility than ever before."[27] She has in mind brutally elementary data that should form our common and factual reality itself, and she offers as examples the fact that Germany supported Hitler and that France collapsed before the German armies in 1940. Referring to these specific facts in particular, Arendt comments that, to the extent that they are tolerated in Germany and France respectively, they have become transformed into mere opinion, unhinging the ground of the world. And this degradation from the status of factuality into mere opinion, she believed, was a constant temptation of our post-totalitarian world more generally.

Factual truths are fragile because they depend upon our willingness to be truth-tellers: "to testify to what is and appears to [us] because it is."[28] And such willingness depends, in turn, in part upon antipolitical (in the sense of nonpartisan) capacities: upon noncommitment, upon freedom from self-interest, upon a kind of impartiality in which we sing the deeds of *both* victors and vanquished, thereby dedicating ourselves to the preservation of that which owes its existence to humans—friend or foe. Truth-tellers are, in this sense, partisans of the world.

Such truth-telling is in dramatic tension with the essential drive of the political actor, which is to change the world. Indeed, the political actor is always tempted to reject factual truth for its opposite— lies—because lies so nicely skirt the strange and blatant quality of factual truth, which can otherwise stymie the actor's hope that the world might be different. And although Arendt's political theorizing is singularly dedicated to revitalizing political life and our capacity to alter the course of events by beginning something new, she nonetheless argues that the truth-teller in its various guises is absolutely necessary to human flourishing. Without the willingness to say what is, she argues, there can be no relative permanence, no adequate starting point from which to act, no place from which to take our bearings as we make judgments about the right course of action. Politics must be limited by what we cannot change at will. It must respect its own borders. "Conceptually, we may call truth what we cannot change; metaphorically, it is the ground on which we stand and the sky that stretches above us."[29]

Thus, when Arendt writes that the educator must assume responsibility for preserving the world "as it is," the importance and fragility of this ground/sky figure and the willingness to testify to it comprise one of her fiercest concerns. Like other truth-tellers, the educator, too, must be the keeper of the often difficult majesty of factual truth.[30]

What might this mean in practice for educators? Let me take as my example the challenge of introducing the young to the U.S. institution of slavery. In assuming responsibility for the world "as it is," the educator, as a truth-teller, is implicitly enjoined by Arendt to cut through the lies and self-deceptions deployed by the slaveholders (political actors) to alter and thereby shield themselves from the "brutally elementary" factual reality of the brutality and hypocrisy of slaveholding. Thomas Jefferson makes a fascinating case study for educators.

Jefferson held the belief, common among slaveholders, that slaves were childlike in that they lacked foresight. Indeed, historians argue this belief weighed heavily in his mind as a stumbling block to emancipation.[31] One of his favorite examples of this lack of foresight concerned his own slaves. As Jefferson (apparently often) told it, "[As summer approached,] the slaves cast off their blankets without a thought as to what is to become of them, wherever they may happen to be at the time, and then not seldom lose them in the woods or the fields from mere carelessness."[32] If we examine this matter, however, we find the truth is quite different. As historian Lucia Stanton comments, no slave in the upper South took blankets lightly. Furthermore, historical records show that Jefferson's overseers did not always issue new blankets in the regular three-year intervals, as Jefferson instructed. Ironically, the slaves' actions were therefore more likely to have been an expression of calculated foresight. Counting on Jefferson's willingness to replace their loss, through these machinations the slaves could get a new blanket that could either replace a worn-out one, become an "extra," or be sold.[33]

Bearing this example in mind, to assume responsibility for the world "as it is" means the educator must teach children about the factual reality of the brutality of enslavement. Standing on the factual ground of its brutality, they can comprehend the strategies of self-deception by slaveholders such as Jefferson and the strategies for survival undertaken by the enslaved. Responsible to this factual truth, the educator can teach the child how to inhabit different perceptual worlds: those "different and frequently opposing aspects . . . of the same" that Arendt argued constitute "the world," our *common* world. How fragile such truths are is evidenced in this case by the resilience of the stereotype of the happy, childlike nature of the African slave, carrying real ideological force even into our day.

Arendt insists, then, on the existence of factual truth. Not everything can be reduced to mere opinion. This insistence is especially important in light of the second key concern lying behind her injunction that educators conserve "the world as it is": namely, that we live in a post-traditional world. Our world has become unhinged, our old ways of thinking no longer illuminate events. We stand on the other side of an unwilled but irrevocable break with a world once structured by authority and held together by tradition.[34] In *that* world, but not in ours, tradition secured memory and promised that human experience was meaningful, providing newcomers with touchstones from the past by which to make their way in a strange and novel time. It selected and named, handed down and preserved, and thereby indicated "where the treasures [were] and what their worth [was]." It secured the past by passing it through an orderly "succession of time" and gave firm shape to the present through its sheer weight.[35]

A natural fit exists between Arendt's understanding of the educator's responsibility to conserve and this tradition-bound world. But this is not *our* world, and educators must assume responsibility for facing up to this fact. How, then, we must ask in an emphatic sense, *is* our world? And what does our answer to this question mean for the educator? *Our* world is protean, plural, and perspectival. Its very worldliness comes into being through the plurality of positions and perspectives of its inhabitants.[36] Without the power of tradition to establish and secure our world, we know with certainty only that it *exists* because others in their diverse perspectives confirm it as such.[37] When this plurality of perspectives and positions is foreclosed, we cannot be said to *have* a world, to share a space in time that sufficiently relates and separates us. Indeed, our sense of a common world, radically unassured in a traditionless world, is forged, we might say, in the present: through ongoing public witnessing to factual reality and through contestation over what experiences and whose memories count as the most significant narrative constructions of our past—and why. Where relevant perspectives and positions are excluded (say, for example, knowledge about and the perspectives of the slave), our ability to know the world we share with others is diminished. Our sense of inhabiting a world in common depends, therefore, on the existence of ongoing public testimony, disputation, and conversation among diverse people in a wide variety of public arenas. It is the world as this contentious field that the educator has the responsibility to convey to the young.

From the foregoing, it should be evident that where factual truth has become fragile, where tradition no longer secures the inbetweenness of the world, and where the past has become a "pile of debris,"[38] to enjoin educators, as Arendt does, to loyalty to "the world as it is" and to "the status quo" cannot be understood in a familiar conservative fashion. It cannot be an injunction to preserve the world as a fixed and stable body of knowledge, an unambiguous heritage that can be passed down so as to reproduce the common world. Those who continue to understand the world in such traditional terms nurture essentially reactionary and romantic longings.

Against their defensive pedagogical conservatism, Arendt offers a different possibility. The educator's responsibility in saying to the child *"This* is *our* world" is a responsibility to conserve both our fragile factual reality *and* the contemporary contours of contention and debate that actively comprise our common world. Our preserving impulse must be—paradoxically—toward the plural yet also recalcitrant world our present reveals to us. Responsibility to both the objective- and subjective-in-between of the world defines the conservatism of Arendt's educator. He is a partisan of the *world.* His responsibility is to introduce the newcomers to *our* field of contention—including the multiple pathways it opens toward the past.[39] Schools are not to be sites for ongoing public-political contestation in the service of change. That is the provenance of adults. They are, rather, to be sites for introducing the newcomer to the contentious world, bounded by truth, that they must inherit. It is this "world as it is" to which they must (first) belong if they are to be capable, upon maturity, of renewing it through action.

In the assumption of responsibility for introducing the young to the world in these senses lies the educator's authority. And this is a kind of authority suited to prepare the young for political life. The educator teaches the child loyalty not to a specific political, partisan agenda, but rather to plurality and contention, bounded by truth. A partisan of the world, she teaches him "to look upon the world from another's standpoint, to see the same in many and frequently opposing aspects."

Multicultural Education:
Reflections on Chicano/Chicana Scholarship

Okay, we might conclude at this point, well and good: Arendt's is no traditional conservatism. The educator's authority lies in accepting responsibility for factual reality and for the contentious field of our world. But *how* do educators assume such responsibility? Is Arendt's distinction between education and politics a useful guide for doing so? Yes, and no, as we shall see.

To assume responsibility for the world, the educator must exercise a kind of impartiality Arendt argued could be acquired only outside the political realm. Referring in general to the truth-telling powers of the historian, Arendt takes Homer as her model, arguing that he was the first in the Western tradition to tell of both victor and vanquished without partisanship when he sang the deeds of Achilles and Hector, Greek and barbarian. In taking Homeric impartiality as her model, Arendt conjures an attitude toward the past that is responsive to the delicate tissue of factuality: to what was suffered and endured, what resisted and vanquished—in short, to a full accounting of what happened to whom that contributed to "the world as it is." And such impartiality requires a difficult love for the world, a love close to that religious feeling of gratitude I discussed earlier.

In the strictest of senses, Arendt contrasts this impartial attitude toward the past with the attitude of the political actor. Whether seeking to sustain the hegemony of one's group or seeking to overthrow hegemony in the name of greater justice, political activists turn to the past for partisan purposes. And because this is their end, they must always alter the fabric of "what is" in order to make way for their novel actions. Political partisans, therefore, cannot be depended on for singing the deeds of both victor and vanquished. Their story of the world is necessarily slanted; facts must be rearranged. And although factual reality may not necessarily be denied (though the temptation can be overwhelming), facts are often rearranged in such a way as to obscure facets of the world that the nonpartisan would illuminate. This is, arguably, as it must be in politics, but it is destructive of the Arendtian ends of education: to introduce the young to "the world as it is" so that renewal of that old world is possible.

From this angle, Arendt's conservatism appears bitterly critical of political multiculturalism—not because "politicization" assaults our proud intellectual inheritance, as traditional conservatives would have it, but because it does *injury to the world*. Rather than introducing children to the old world, it prepares them for a world that adults wish to see but that has not yet been achieved. And in so doing, its partisan purposes and viewpoints obscure the complexity of positions and perspectives that constitute the world as it is. To this complexity the young must be introduced if they are, upon maturity, to be capable not of repeating forms of domination that instantiate the old world, but of renewing the world through their own actions. Looking briefly at recent debates in Chicano historiography, the strengths of the Homeric impartiality Arendt advocates for educators as they seek to take responsibility for the world becomes clear.

The Chicano movement erupted onto the public stage in 1968. High school students took to the streets in East Los Angeles demanding an end to racism, curricular reform that would be inclusive of their culture and their history, freedom of speech, and the hiring of Mexican American teachers and administrators. For a week and a half, the students shut down the L.A. city school system. Their activism catalyzed the formation of the Chicano student movement and the larger Chicano Power Movement of which the student movement was the most important sector. The right to cultural autonomy and national self-determination, to equality with white America, in addition to the demands listed above, formed the core goals of the Chicano Power Movement.[40] It was the first effort ever to unify Mexican Americans on the basis of a nonwhite, indigenous identity and culture and the interests of the Mexican American working class,[41] and it sought power in the name of this new Chicano nationalism.[42]

Throughout the period of Chicano nationalist activism, curricular reform remained a central organizing focus, and the outcomes of these struggles were impressive. For example, all colleges and universities in California's three-tiered system of higher education adopted programs in Chicano studies as a result of the movement. At most institutions, the educational goals were self-consciously political. They aimed to broaden and deepen the university's educational and cultural mission so that it would better provide the Mexican American community with the resources necessary to address its pressing needs. Such needs ranged from sustaining self-confidence and cultural pride through knowledge and appreciation of Mexican

Americans' own cultural heritage to developing students' bilingual and bicultural abilities to enhancing their ability to serve their largely very poor communities. The goals were, in short, to use the university to cultivate an autonomous Chicano national identity as the linchpin by which to improve Chicano communities.[43]

Retelling history so that the record would include the race and class subordination experienced by Chicano people was central to these ends, and Chicanos therefore began writing serious revisionist history in the early seventies.[44] Their historiography began in 1848 with the end of the Mexican-American War, after which, their lands annexed to the United States, the Chicano people became what these scholars termed an "internal colony." This condition of being internally colonized socially, culturally, and economically, they argued, remained essentially unchanged from its inception in the mid-nineteenth century down to the present.[45]

Economic exploitation and especially racism were the central themes of the analytical framework of the internal colony. Mexican Americans were seen as victimized by a classic colonial conquest similar in nature to the subordination by Europeans of nonwhite peoples around the globe. The political answer to the condition of internal colonization was Chicano cultural nationalism. Indeed, the virtue of this historiography from the point of view of the nascent movement to enhance the social, economic, and political conditions of Chicanos was that it pointed to a clear political agenda. Superimposed on this history was the dream of repossessing the legendary homeland of the Aztecs—"Aztlan"—which extended from Mexico to most of the contemporary U.S. Southwest.

Twenty-some-odd years after these histories were written—histories that quite self-consciously served political aspirations for change—they are being subjected to rigorous critical scrutiny, in some cases by the original authors themselves.[46] Calling for a more complex account of race and class relations, the critiques center on the argument precisely that the works were born of too partisan ends. They are too ideological and, for this reason, "distort" the record in order to meet the political needs of the day. In so doing, as historian Tomas Almaguer points out in an Arendtian vein (here about his own work as well as about the work of others), key facts are ignored.

In particular, in order to heighten focus on racism and the Anglo/Mexican American conflict, revisionist Chicano historians ignored the system of racial domination already in place prior to Anglo intervention. For example, focusing on California, Almaguer points to the widespread Native American enslavement and brutal coercion of Native American laborers by the Mexican property-owning ranchero class both before and after annexation. This eclipse of the elite's complicity in racial domination ignored the internal class stratification of Mexican Americans, giving a false sense of a common Chicano history.

Native Americans were almost altogether ignored in this revisionist historiography. The relevant history included only Mexican Americans and Anglos, occluding the fact that three distinct major groups had negotiated a life of often brutal conflict in the area, with Mexican Americans occupying a subordinate position to Anglos but one above Native Americans in the social, economic, and political hierarchy.

In almost entirely ignoring other racialized and colonized minorities, these early histories provided no context for understanding the relative place in the racial and class hierarchy occupied by Mexican Americans after 1848. In particular, Mexican Americans were granted significantly higher status than other racial minorities in the Southwest. Indeed, ironically, the Treaty of Guadalupe-Hidalgo that ratified U.S. annexation of the Mexican Southwest defined Mexican Americans as a *white* population. This codification contrasts distinctly with the nonwhite status accorded blacks and Native Americans, giving Mexican Americans important legal protections—however unevenly extended in practice to the population.[47]

Such simplifications of the constellation of forces in the Southwest were common currency for young minds nourished by the early Chicano nationalist curriculum. But history germinated in such close proximity to political mobilization did an injustice to the sheer existence of those who were superfluous to, or perhaps even in the way of, Chicano partisan ends. Ironically and tragically, Chicano history enacted its own forms of oblivion, offering a false and simplified view of the class composition of Chicanos that could not, to recall and rephrase Arendt's formulation, enable Chicanos to look upon the same world from the standpoint of Native Americans. The impoverishment of the worldly in-between embedded in this historical self-understanding could not, therefore, adequately introduce the young to the contentious field of their world and thereby help them in the understanding necessary, for example, to foster solidarities across racialized minorities. In deforming the world, this history threatened Chicanos' capacity for good political judgment and for action that, instead of repeating forms of domination that reproduce the old world (e.g., racialized class relations), might inaugurate a new one.

In this light, Arendt's concern for the fragility of truth and her advocacy of impartiality for the historian whose obligation is to be a partisan of the *world* seem to be crucial antidotes. The multicultural educator must be driven by the nonpartisan questions: Who are *we*? Who must, in my account, be present? What does the world look like from where they stand? What facts, what events are left out that are crucial to comprehension, to as full an accounting as is humanly possible? The multicultural educator needs, then, Arendt's conservatism: He must divorce partisan politics from the responsibility to educate the young; he must be driven, like Homer, to victors and vanquished alike—in all their complexity.

Yet, as important as this impartiality is, it is at the same time radically insufficient, for the educator's very ability to assume the kind of responsibility for conserving the world that Arendt advocates is profoundly parasitic upon and entwined with processes of politicization. As I shall show, this entwinement makes the decisive divorce between education and politics Arendt advocated unacceptable in its unqualified form.

To develop this point, we must remind ourselves that the conditions in which the need for multicultural education arises are conditions of domination and subordination in which ideological distortions, lies, silences, and dense webs of deception dominate and structure public knowledge—including, of course, curricular materials for history courses.[48] To cut through these, the educator needs enormous critical capacities. And such capacities cannot be sufficiently cultivated if the realm of education and that of politics are divorced, or if impartiality is the primary principle guiding our efforts to take responsibility for the world.

What, then, cultivates the educator's capacity for critical thinking? One of the most crucial things is the ability to look at the world through the eyes of the subjugated. The trouble is, of course, that the condition of being subjugated *means* that the points of view of the subjugated are by no means ready at hand. Their sufferings, their victories, their take on events exist below the surface of public knowledge.

The subjugated must, therefore, be allowed to speak, and this need for their speech is precisely what has driven multicultural educators—themselves, of course, often members of subjugated groups. Yet the situation is considerably more complicated than this, for the views of the subjugated often exist in very inchoate form among the subjugated themselves—if they can be said to "exist" at all. The process of speaking entails complex explorations of political, social, and economic systems, explorations that are not in a simple way merely about uncovering a world and perspectives already there (for which the Arendtian injunction to impartiality might be sufficient), but about *giving birth* to them. And that is profoundly political. It requires an increase in political consciousness that is possible only in relation to sustained political movement that aims at changing the world, at ending subjugation.

So, for example, let us say the social studies teacher wishes to introduce his students to U.S.-Mexican relations, including the *maquiladora* system. Put in place by agreement between the Mexican and U.S. governments in 1965, the system allows foreign-owned (mostly U.S.) companies to operate assembly plants in Mexico and to count the products as Mexican exports (although virtually none of the parts are made in that country), thereby avoiding high tariffs while benefiting from cheap local labor. It is mostly young women and children working for just above starvation pay who labor in the *maquilas*. Job turnover is between 50 and 150 percent per year because the work is so quick paced and body breaking. U.S. managers cross the border by the thousands each day, returning to their homes well paid and relatively unconcerned about an increasingly desperate border culture for the millions of Mexicans who flock to these border towns.[49]

If the educator is to introduce his students to this facet of U.S.-Mexican relations, some of the issues he will need to know about to

do so responsibly include who the laborers are and under what conditions they labor. Finding that they are poor and preyed upon
silent and unorganized, he will need to know more, know why. To
that end, political and sociological facts will serve him well. But he
will also need to know what the world looks like to them, more
about *who* they are. And for this, he will need to turn to a different
engagement with history—specifically, to the work of Chicana feminist scholars who, in the effort to give birth to themselves as speaking subjects, are critically examining and appropriating historical
discourses and ideological constructions of race, gender, and ethnici-
ties that have been in place since the time of the Conquest of Mexico—discourses that were crucial to nation-building there and thus
to present-day factual conditions of the Mexicanas who labor in the
maquilas.

In particular, Chicana scholars critically reexamine the symbolic
Manichean pair of Guadalupe/Malinche that emerged at the time of
the conquest and that continues to define the alternatives for Mexicanas and Chicanas.[50] Guadalupe, the Good Woman, is a native representative of the Virgin Mary, and although she possesses transcen-
dentalizing powers, her attributes are silence and maternal sacrifice.
Malinche, by contrast, is the Evil Woman. Sold into slavery by the
Aztecs, she became Cortez's concubine and translator, as well as legendary mother of the mestizo race. She is evil because, as indigenous
translator, she dared to speak independently of her maternal role,
dared to speak for herself. Having betrayed her culture in this respect, this mother of the mestizo race is La Vendida, the sellout, La
Chingada, the fucked one (terms that continue to imprison contemporary Mexicanas and Chicanas). The mestizo/mestiza subjectivity
that Malinche symbolically births, entails from its inception, Chicana scholar Norma Alarcon argues, "the rejection and denial of the
dark Indian Mother as Indian, which has compelled women to often
collude against themselves, and to actually deny the Indian position
even as that position is visually stylized and represented in the making of the fatherland."[51]

In this scholarship, the educator can begin to grasp the multiple
ways that, through conquest and colonization, the female body and
female subject have been racialized and gendered and dislocated in

the service of other kinds of power. Analyzing the ideological constructions of the maligned, distorted, and manipulated indigenous woman, brings into view, as Alarcon puts it, "a most sobering reference point": The overwhelming majority of the workers in the *maquilas* are mestizas who have been "forcefully subjected" to multiple forces, some of which have been identified, many of which "await disentanglement."[52] Often single, often with children, these women are without the hegemonic patriarchal "protections" that legitimize their existence and ensure they are "civilized" in sexual and racial terms.[53]

To take responsibility for the world "as it is" on the border and in the *maquilas*, the social studies teacher must seek to see the world from the vantage point of the mostly women workers. To do so, he needs the absolutely novel engagements with the past undertaken in this emergent Chicana feminist scholarship. Yet this scholarship was itself made possible by the Chicano Power Movement, and its own aims are self-consciously partisan in that they concern identifying the relationships among racial, sexual, national, and ethnic systems of power in the service of giving birth to the female speaking subject. It is undertaken by partisan Chicanas who struggle for understandings that will aid in putting an end to Chicana/Mexicana subjugation, including the invisibility they suffer as laborers, members of families, and young students with extraordinarily high dropout rates in our nation's schools, as I mentioned earlier. For the elemental truths of their lives to *appear*, such partisanship is essential.

I developed the foregoing in order to argue that to take responsibility for the world in the sense that Arendt enjoined requires of the educator both a scrupulous impartiality *and* a close, sympathetic, even partisan stake in empowering and giving voice to the subjugated. Educators must both celebrate and resist (facets of) the politics involved in multicultural education; they are certainly profoundly parasitic in their practice upon such politics. Their work requires deep and ongoing understanding of the relation between power and knowledge. Yet, if educators aim too single-mindedly and in too partisan a fashion at empowerment, they will not fulfill their basic obligation to the young: to introduce them to *our world*. Hence,

Arendt's categorical distinction between education and politics cannot be sustained. Nor, however, can we do without the tension it places on the urge to politicize education.

In this chapter, I have tried to illuminate, but not resolve, this tension for educators. Indeed, it is this complex tension that must drive advocates of multicultural education to history. As I have argued, the deepest impulse with which multiculturalists turn to history is the impulse to tell *their* stories so as, in a Baldwinian sense, to make our *collective* ability to face not myth but our reality more fully, more deeply. Such histories can help us break up the ossification in human thought and relations and institutions by which forms of power and domination reproduce themselves. In the way these new stories illuminate the present differently, they may cause "tears of remembrance," remembrance of injuries forgotten, suffering smoothed over, injustices rationalized—complicities in human misery.[54] These tears allow us to see a world with greater depth and dimension, such seeing making possible a kind of reconciliation with the always more terrible but also more beautiful world to which we belong.

Although by no means unproblematic, Arendt's conservatism enables us to identify the way multiculturalism widens and makes more complex our sense of who "we" are, the way it "conserves" our *common* world. And to this conservative essence of education, most radical educators' theorizing does not sufficiently speak. This is not to ignore or deny the extent to which multicultural education entails, in the words of radical educator Henry Giroux, "rupturing practices," the way, as a postcolonial discourse, it "interrogates who narrates, for what audience, in what setting and for what purpose."[55] Rather, it is to redescribe and reclaim educational practices as practices that knit our common world together in more complex patterns. And this is the case, not because multicultural education leads to a better definite identity, but because of the way it illuminates and gives voice to the lives and perspectives of the formerly unseen and disregarded. Its driving questions are: Who is present? Who are *we*? It seeks to make the story to which we, as a people, belong less a mythological or ideological conception of the common world.

Notes

1. Hannah Arendt, *Between Past and Future* (Middlesex, England: Penguin Books, 1954), p. 51.

2. For Arendt's full account of world alienation, see *The Human Condition* (Chicago: University of Chicago Press, 1958). The phenomenon she describes coincides with what she calls the "rise of the social," with bureaucracy and the processes of rationalization in an increasingly administered world. Her analysis overlaps with the work of Max Weber, Michel Foucault, and Jürgen Habermas, among others.

3. See "The Crisis in Education," in *Between Past and Future*, pp. 173–196.

4. Ibid., p. 191.

5. Ibid., p. 195.

6. Ibid., p. 192.

7. The reader should bear in mind that Arendt considered education, in contrast to learning, to end upon graduation from high school.

8. See, for example, arguments made by Stanley Aronowitz and Henry A. Giroux in *Education Still Under Siege*, 2nd ed. (Westport, CT: Bergin & Garvey, 1993), p. 210.

9. See Peggy Orenstein, *School Girls: Young Women, Self-Esteem, and the Confidence Gap* (New York: Doubleday, 1994), p. 310. Note also that the overall poverty rate for Latinos is 40 percent. Two-thirds of the Latino population is Mexican American, a fact that will be relevant later in this chapter.

10. See James W. Loewen, *Lies My Teachers Told Me* (New York: New Press, 1995), p. 1.

11. I distinguish political multiculturalism from what Stanley Fish calls "boutique multiculturalism." Boutique multiculturalists celebrate cultural diversity while erasing from view the conditions of domination and inequality within and through which cultural diversity is articulated. For Fish's discussion, see "Boutique Multiculturalism," in *Multiculturalism and American Democracy*, ed. Arthur M. Melzer, Jerry Weinberger, and M. Richard Zinman (Lawrence: University of Kansas Press, 1998), pp. 69–88.

12. See Arthur Schlessinger Jr., *The Disuniting of America: The Disuniting of a Multicultural Society* (New York: Whittle Communications, 1991), pp. 137–138. See also C. Vann Woodward, "Meanings for Multiculturalism," in *Multiculturalism and American Democracy*, ed. Melzer et al.

13. These arguments can be found in many places. Two of the most well known are Allan Bloom's *The Closing of the American Mind* (New York: Simon & Schuster, 1987) and Dinesh D'Souza's *Illiberal Education: The Politics of Race and Sex on Campus* (New York: Free Press, 1991).

14. Advocates of political multiculturalism are quick to point to the disingenuousness of those who argue against the politicization of education while simultaneously voiding their own account of the past and of our intellectual heritage of any contestation. Naturalizing their object in this way is, ironically, a quintessentially "political" move. I should add that both Irving Kristol and Norman Podhoretz stand out on the right as more honest because they acknowledge the entwinement of politics and education—which they embrace. For their pronouncements to that

effect, see Neil Jumonville, *Contemporary Crossings: The New York Intellectuals in Postwar America* (Berkeley: University of California Press, 1991), pp. 231–232.

15. For the invasion of capital into the nation's schools, see Steven Manning, "Students for Sale: How Corporations Are Buying Their Way into America's Classrooms," *The Nation,* September, 27, 1999, pp. 11–18. For the effect on literacy of unequal distribution of financial resources, see Gerald Coles, *Reading Lessons: The Debate over Literacy* (New York: Hill & Wang, 1998), pp. 136–159.

16. Arendt, "Crisis in Education," p. 192.

17. Ibid.

18. See George Kateb's very perceptive discussion in *Hannah Arendt: Politics, Conscience, Evil* (Totowa, NJ: Rowman & Allenheld, 1984), pp. 163–178.

19. Arendt, "Crisis in Education," p. 195.

20. Ibid., p. 191.

21. For Arendt's beautifully argued essay on freedom, see "What Is Freedom?" in *Between Past and Future.*

22. Arendt, "Crisis in Education," pp. 192–193.

23. The well-known educational bullying of James Mill is a case in point, for in overseeing the education of John Stuart, the elder Mill tried to create the perfect utilitarian. What he created instead was a soul sorely out of touch with himself, a condition that, of course, precipitated mental breakdown.

24. "Crisis in Education," p. 192.

25. For sustained reflections on this central Arendtian theme, see "Ideology and Terror," in *The Origins of Totalitarianism* (New York: Harcourt, Brace & World, 1951), pp. 460–479; "Lying in Politics," in *Crises of the Republic* (New York: Harcourt Brace Jovanovich, 1969); and "Truth and Politics," in *Between Past and Future.*

26. "Truth and Politics," p. 231.

27. Ibid., p. 236.

28. Ibid., p. 229.

29. Ibid., p. 264.

30. Among truth-tellers, Arendt includes the historian, the reporter, the artist, the philosopher, the scientist, and the fact-finder. See "Truth and Politics," p. 260.

31. See Lucia Stanton, *Slavery at Monticello* (Thomas Jefferson Memorial Foundation, 1996), p. 41.

32. Ibid.

33. Ibid.

34. Arendt, "Crisis in Education," p. 195.

35. Hannah Arendt, "Preface: The Gap Between Past and Future," in *Between Past and Future,* p. 5.

36. I argue this in detail in *Our Sense of the Real: Aesthetic Experience and Arendtian Politics* (Ithaca: Cornell University Press, 1999).

37. This is a repeated Arendtian argument. See especially *The Human Condition.* See also my discussion in *Our Sense of the Real,* especially chap. 2.

38. This is how Arendt describes the condition of the past after the end of tradition in the West. See her introduction to Walter Benjamin's *Illuminations* (New York: Schocken Books, 1969).

39. I do not mean to preclude the importance of instruction in other ages or ways of living, of dwelling in those times and exploring the power of their achievements.

My point is that the educator's *authority* cannot lie in passing this down as an unambiguous inheritance from the past.

40. See Carlos Munoz, *Youth, Identity, Power: The Chicano Movement* (New York: Verso, 1989); and Ramon Gutierrez, "Community, Patriarchy, and Individualism: The Politics of Chicano History and the Dream of Equality," *American Quarterly*, vol. 45, no. 1 (March 1993): 44–72.

41. By contrast, the liberal assimilationist League of United Latin American Citizens promoted the image of Mexican Americans as a white ethnic group.

42. The term "Chicano" itself originated in Mexican American working-class communities.

43. See *El Plan de Santa Barbara*, the master plan of action for Mexican Americans in higher education that emerged from the three-day conference held in Santa Barbara in 1969. *El Plan* is reproduced in full as an appendix in Munoz, *Youth, Identity, Power*; see also pp. 127–169 of the same book.

44. The most important works of the 1970s were: Rodolfo Acuna, *Occupied America: The Chicano's Struggle Toward Liberation* (San Francisco: Canfield Press, 1972); Richard Griswold del Castillo, *The Los Angelos Barrio, 1850–1890: A Social History* (Berkeley: University of California Press, 1979); and Albert Camarillo, *Chicanos in a Changing Society: From Mexican Pueblos to American Barrios in Santa Barbara and Southern California, 1848–1930* (Cambridge, MA: Harvard University Press, 1979).

45. In the second edition of his book (1981), Rodolfo Acuna revised his position, arguing that the colonial model was best limited to the nineteenth century.

46. See, for example, Tomas Almaguer, "Ideological Distortions in Recent Chicano Historiography: The Internal Model and Chicano Historical Interpretation," *Aztlan*, vol. 18, no. 1 (1989): 7–28. See also Alex Saragosa, "The Significance of Recent Chicano-Related Historical Writings: An Appraisal," *Ethnic Affairs*, vol. 1 (Fall 1987): 27–42.

47. For example, males could legally vote, serve on juries, testify in a court of law, and serve in local and state legislative bodies. See Almaguer, "Ideological Distortions," p. 15.

48. James Loewen's study of the content of U.S. junior high and high school history textbooks is an excellent source for revealing the ideological nature of public knowledge being passed on in our nation's history classrooms.

49. For a disturbing perspective into the town of Juárez and its U.S. neighbor, El Paso, see Charles Bowdon, "While You Were Sleeping," *Harpers*, December 1995, pp. 44–52. See also the photographs collected in *Juarez: Laboratory of the Future*, ed. Charles Bowdon, Eduardo Galeano, and Noam Chomsky (New York: Aperture, 1998). Bowdon reports that when he goes from Juárez to El Paso, "no one ever mentions this place [Juárez]; days can pass without a single news story about Juarez in the El Paso newspapers." This is the case even though there were 520 murders in Juárez during 1995, among other possible newsworthy events (Bowden, "While You Were Sleeping," p. 52).

50. The work being done by Chicanas and some Mexicanas is by now extensive. For a discussion and analysis of some of the most important works, see Norma Alarcon, "Traddutora, Traditora: A Paradigmatic Figure of Chicana Feminism," in *Cultural Critique* (Fall 1989). Two of the more well-known works are Gloria An-

zaldúa's *Borderland / La Frontera: The New Mestiza* (San Francisco: Spinsters/Aunt Lute Books, 1987) and Cherrie Moraga's *Loving in the War Years: Lo que nunca paso por sus labios* (Boston: South End Press, 1983).

51. Norma Alarcon, "Chicana Feminism: In the Tracks of 'the' Native Woman," in *Between Woman and Nation: Nationalisms, Transnational Feminisms, and the State,* ed. Caren Kaplan, Norma Alarcon, and Minoo Moallem (Durham, NC: Duke University Press, 1999), p. 68.

52. I paraphrase from Alarcon, ibid., pp. 68–69.

53. The most brutal manifestation of their vulnerability without such protections is the high incidence of violence they suffer, including violent death. See Bowden, "While You Were Sleeping."

54. This phrase is Arendt's; see "On Humanity in Dark Times: Thoughts on Lessing," in *Men in Dark Times* (New York: Harcourt Brace Jovanovich, 1955).

55. See Giroux, "Multiculturalism Under Siege in the Reagan/Bush Era," in *Education Still Under Siege,* p. 197.

6

Is Hannah Arendt a Multiculturalist?

ANN LANE

Forty to 50 percent of the students in the American Studies Department at the University of California at Santa Cruz, where I teach, are people of color. I need hardly mention what the current demographics of California look like, and soon much of the rest of the United States will resemble the population of our program. Many of our students are activists, engaged in community organizing, environmental justice, Native American treaty rights, cultural renewal, inner-city reconstruction, prison reform, sustainable agriculture, alternative media and cultural productions, and issues of immigration, affirmative action, community health, antiracism, and renewable resources.

The attendees of my recent seminar titled "Hannah Arendt and American Political Culture" included, among others, a Central American male refugee now living in an inner city, where many of his friends have been imprisoned or killed; an African American male from Compton, California, who refuses to trade his street language for academese in order to maintain contact with "at-risk" youth; a Japanese-Irish American male committed to amplifying the cross-cultural relevance of the Japanese-American reparations movement; a young white woman who had been a gang member in Los Angeles; a Japanese American woman working in the international feminists of color network; an older Jewish American male committed to gay movements; a younger white male also active on gay issues; a Cuban American woman from an extremely conservative political background; a Central American immigrant woman working on educational opportunities for poor children; a Jewish American woman in her late forties who had been a Hollywood television scriptwriter; and a white woman in her late fifties from the Christian Coalition. Their financial situations ran the gamut from being supported by a trust fund to barely making it.

It was both exhausting and exhilarating to teach these students. There were constant tensions among them in the classroom because, for most of the students, there was much politically at stake in every discussion. Part of the seminar entailed collectively determining what counts as "political," what "democratic citizenship" means in a multicultural, migratory setting, and what kind of education is needed in such a setting, given our rapidly shifting global economy and interlinked technologies. Even had I thought it my job to politicize them (which I do not), there was no need; I also did not worry about encouraging them to take differing positions on a variety of issues that were raised—they were quite ready to argue with one another on their own, usually verbally but at the least indicating objections by an uneasy silence. Therefore, the points they tended to agree upon were all the more striking, which I will discuss below.

Arendt may appear to be an unlikely focus for a class on multicultural politics in a program that self-consciously attends to gender, class, race, and sexuality in its analyses. After all, many of Arendt's writings (particularly the works I emphasize in the seminar: *The Jew as Pariah, The Origins of Totalitarianism,* and *Eichmann in Jerusalem*)[1] deal mainly with Europe, not Asia or Latin America. Her critique is of anti-Semitism rather than racism per se. She generally ignores the axes of gender and sexuality in her theorizing. Then, too, there are passages in her work that critics have marked as anti-Semitic, racist, classist, sexist, and heterosexist.[2] Not only does she fail to meet "politically correct" standards, she has also been variously cited as an unhistorical historian and an unphilosophical philosopher. Ideologically, as well as professionally, she appears to be uncategorizable—depicted alternately as democratic, elitist, proto-communitarian, civic republican, modernist, antimodernist, postmodernist, liberal, antiliberal, Marxist, or anti-Marxist.

Given such apparent liabilities, what makes Arendt so compelling in my multicultural classroom? Why do my students learn so much from her about the very issues she would appear to be inadequate to address, about regions of the world in which she appears to have no interest, and about peoples she is said to have denigrated? How has Arendtian theory managed to travel so well and to communicate across the deepest divides with such diverse students?

Let me begin to suggest some answers to these questions by focusing for a moment on one of my students.[3] Everything about Maria's life puts her on edge: She perpetually needs money for rent and food; her family is sharply divided between those who want her to "get ahead" in life and those who encourage her political commitments; she was a high school dropout who attended junior college and now finds university work extremely difficult; many of her friends have been literally scarred by their journey across the border from Mexico into the United States; she worries continually about the safety of the indigenous people with whom she spent months in Chiapas, Mexico; and the European invasion of the Americas continually informs her experience of the world, for she is a Taino Indian, a descendant of the first contacts, who in some ways exists in the present tense with Columbus.

Maria lives preternaturally. The social and political worlds are unstable places for her and her friends, for whom the threat of deportation, statelessness, or death makes every day an emergency. She frequently spoke out of turn in class, jolting the other students with the passion of her responses to points in my lecture or our collective discussions. By all indications of background, education, temperament, and interests, Maria would seem to be the least likely of students to gravitate to Hannah Arendt. Might we not expect students with a knowledge of European history, an advanced formal education, the patience to calmly debate, and an already developed interest in political theory to be the models for such a class? Yet I found Maria to be one of the best-prepared students to comprehend Arendt in my twenty years of teaching. Paradoxically, Maria's background, education, temperament, and interests are exactly what prepared her so well to listen to what a dead, white European had to teach her.

What I mean is that there is not only an Arendt to remind us of "lost" political moments, as many current interpreters point out,[4] but also an Arendt to warn those engaged in political movement about the dangers of losing what they have initiated. Although the new wave of literature on Arendt engages her thought in refreshingly sophisticated ways, many of these commentaries view her against a backdrop of philosophical debates or in the context of an abstract struggle of ideas about political life.[5] For students like Maria, however, Arendt's troubling assertions about assimilation, chauvinism, and imperialism, along with her distinctions between the social and the political, between making and doing, seem to speak directly to their lives and struggles. Arendt's depiction of the pariah position of Jews forced to emigrate during World War II, her arguments about the dangers of refounding community on the basis of suffering, her analysis of the development of totalitarianism, and her contentions about the co-responsibility of "victims" for reconstructing a just world all carry significant meaning for these students.

My course on Arendt is divided into four sections: the concept of the "conscious pariah," highlighting her essays in *The Jew as Pariah;* the concept of "Eichmannism," dealing with the (in)famous "banality of evil" and the co-responsibility of "victims" in *Eichmann in Jerusalem;* the concept of "superfluousness" in the three parts of *The Origins of Totalitarianism,* exploring Arendt's analysis of how totalitarianism differentially "crystallized" in Nazi Germany and Stalinist Russia; and Arendt's notions of political freedom and political power, particularly as laid out in *On Revolution* and *The Human Condition.* Although I do not recommend secondary literature (apart from important biographical essays by Jeffrey Isaac and Ron Feldman)[6] until students select topics for their final papers, I utilize comparative works by U.S. authors throughout the course to provide a third point of contact for the Arendt readings (i.e., her texts; the students' own political experiences; and historical-critical accounts of social-political marginalization, justice and reparations efforts for crimes committed by the state, the development of U.S. imperialism, the holocaust against Native and African Americans, the rise of U.S. neo-Nazism and far right militia movements, democratic movements, and technological paradigm shifts surrounding cybernetics and nanotechnology).

As I noted, the students tended to argue throughout the ten weeks of the course. Their varied backgrounds gave them dissimilar points of entry for comparative analysis, so it was no easy task for them to explain their positions to one another. The content of Arendt's work proved, however, to be methodologically as well as substantively helpful to them. She draws the distinction between what and who a person is. The "what" entails the givens of one's life: the axes of his or her identity by location, gender, circumstances of class, ethnicity, and religion, sexuality, and private attachments to others. The "who" emerges only through one's words and deeds in concert with others.[7] In short, what one is can be sociologically ascertained and summarized in a list; who one is requires attention to his or her appearance in a political (public) realm, making judgments about that appearance, and finally telling a story about the meaning of his or her public words and deeds. Furthermore, Arendt argues that the issues of poverty, gender oppression, racism, and anti-Semitism—in other words, the very issues that arise from what a person is, his or her sociological positioning—can be successfully addressed only in a political arena in which the subjects of those debates take themselves seriously first as human, political agents, not primarily as poor people, women, blacks, or Jews. I will talk more about the substance of the students' responses to these ideas below, but here it is important to note that the students took these ideas as the principles of their interaction: They wanted to be seen and heard by one another as who they uniquely were, not what they were; and without that, their discussion of their issues could not really be understood by one another.[8]

Below I want to discuss several of those points about which, as I mentioned, this diverse group tended to agree: the concept of the conscious pariah, the distinction between the political and the social, and the notion of the council system. I have come to believe the students' collective observations on these issues are illuminating precisely because they differ markedly from the conclusions drawn by those critics who examine themes and passages in Arendt against a series of philosophical debates. Perhaps Arendt is indeed a multiculturalist but one who needs multicultural readers, engaged in political action, who can comprehend that line of force in her work.[9]

Transcending but Not Abandoning Identity Politics

Arendt believed that we are dangerously preoccupied with what today we would call "identity politics" at the expense of collective political responsibility. Awakening to the political import of her own Jewish identity, with the rise of the Nazis, Arendt not only fled Germany and assisted other Jews, particularly children, to escape to Palestine, but she committed herself to theorizing the ongoing possibilities for both the return of totalitarianism and what she believed to be its antidote: participatory democracy, lived out among a plurality of peoples.[10] Her lifelong sense of the urgency of this commitment led her to make forceful judgments about the ways in which we collude with tendencies toward totalitarianism. Arendt may be one of the most important twentieth-century theorists for comprehending both what sustains and what destroys democratic political participation, drawing self-consciously on her experience as a Jew escaping totalitarianism and witnessing the reemergence of Israel.

Arendt urges readers to look closely at what is already happening around them, to attend to movements that are already emergent. There is always resistance to injustices, imperialisms, and totalitarian tendencies, but we are not always attentive to it or apparently able to recognize it.[11] For students whose political action is not covered by the media and whose community efforts are largely invisible in the mainstream, there is no need for Arendt to tell them how to get started "doing" in the world. Instead, these students crave what she does give them: further understanding of the meaning of what they are doing and an urgent sense of how to "think" more deeply about what they are doing and how to sustain it. Kevin, for instance, while reading *Eichmann in Jerusalem*, began to comprehend his antigang work in L.A. as necessary not only for saving the lives of other African American youth, but also for constructing new identities, as it were, with them. He expressed the need to confront the predicament that they found themselves in: How could they resist their severe marginalization from the centers of economic, social, and political power without succumbing to the opposing temptations of erecting a violent counterculture or of "buying into," and thus being assimilated by, the very structures that had originally excluded them?

Eichmann in Jerusalem, Arendt's report on and discussion of the trial of Adolf Eichmann, called Israelis to account for what she saw as collusion with injustice.[12] In her assessment, the court prosecution perpetuated rigid essentialisms and ideologized identity claims: Eichmann was seen as an evil monster (rather than what Arendt noted he was: an unthinking cog in a bureaucratic machine dedicated to crimes against humanity); victims of the Holocaust were staged as pure, innocent targets (rather than respected as human agents); Israel was portrayed as a powerful nation-state (rather than trapped, as Arendt understood it to be, in the empty category of the nation-state and in need of transformation into a new regime, coalitional with Arab Palestinians).

Arendt made difficult demands on all "victims." She believed that Jews, in response to the horrors of the Holocaust, not only had to acknowledge the unprecedented character of the Nazi and Stalinist regimes, but also had to organize themselves as political actors in interdependent relations to other peoples.[13] Jews needed actively and continually to reinvent a "conscious pariah" position between the extremes of the assimilated "parvenu" without ethnicity and the isolated chauvinism of exaggerated identity. Arendt insists that the conscious pariah must perform an internal as well as an external critique; that is, one must interrogate one's own movement or polity as closely as one analyzes the outside society or polities. For many students, it is a relief to realize that their constant reassessment of whether their putative "friends" are really friends or whether their ascribed enemies may become allies does not necessarily constitute disloyalty to their own people or co-optation by the "others." Arendt imbues political positions with an intellectual edge that reassures politically active students that they need not check their minds at the door to the political arena. Indeed, Jose met with me during my office hours to describe his life and to tell me that Arendt had given him the language to name finally what he had long felt he was: a conscious pariah—always an outsider yet always committed, always on the margin, trying to indicate to others what he saw that they did not seem to notice.[14]

Many of Arendt's political questions about Jews, Zionism, and Israel derive at least in part from her reading of Bernard Lazare, as does her methodological approach to political and social issues. Lazare, in strong contrast to Theodor Herzl, conceived of Zionism in nonstatist terms. Lazare emphasized the notions of homeland and peoplehood rather than nation-state and sovereignty, seeing imperialism rather than "eternal" anti-Semitism as the chief obstacle to Zionism. He argued, moreover, that the political freedom of the Jewish people was dependent on their solidarity with others who were also oppressed. Such aspects of Lazare's thinking are explicit in the early essays of Arendt, where she asks why assimilation is suicide, why Jewish refugees are only the first wave, only the vanguard of displaced persons in Europe, why Judaism must be secularized, what the "myth" of exile means for Jewish people, why "exception" Jews are collusive with the most corrupt aspects of Western society, and why "bourgeois world citizenship" is a delusion.[15]

Arendt agreed with Lazare that it is not enough to recognize oneself as a Jew, marginalized by state and society across Europe. Theodor Herzl epitomized for her the pariah who, unthoughtful about his position, is disabled from acting on a principled basis. Herzl is both chauvinistic or isolationist in terms of a Jewish state as an appropriate end for Jewish people and assimilationist or accommodationist in terms of the means to obtain that state. Flipping between parvenu and separatist positions, Herzl, in Arendt's estimation, represents the danger of a narrow identity politics, built on an assumed unity of an "us" against a unified "them," on short-term opportunistic alliances, parading as utterly realistic but almost wholly ideological and clearly undemocratic.

Many of the students in my seminar took up the model of the conscious pariah to critically examine aspects of their own cultural-political backgrounds. Selena, for instance, utilized Arendt's framework to analyze the work of exiled modern-day Cuban artists in the United States who negotiate a position in between that of the parvenu, assimilationist Cuban Americans and the pro-Castro apologists in order to open up a new cultural and political space for democratic, transborder, transethnic action. I think the figure of Lazare, as he is invoked by Arendt and indeed imitated by her in much of her own writing, travels well across other cultures and speaks to students like Selena so profoundly because he shows them that there is always a third alternative to be discovered beyond the apparent choices of the status quo or the separatist opposition.

The Primacy of Politics

I find that the more politically experienced students are, the more readily they grasp Arendt's prioritizing of political over social-economic agendas, her prioritizing of respect and solidarity over pity, compassion, and caretaking. Perhaps this is the case since many have been subject to plans for bettering their lives by those who would help them while not seeing them as equals.[16] One of the students who audited the seminar, Rebecca, suffers from serious medical problems, cannot work, and therefore depends on welfare for her survival. After our class discussion of *On Revolution,* she spoke to me about what it was like to receive assistance from a bureaucracy—often well intentioned but always hierarchical and apparently incapable of recognizing her as a full human being with her own voice and analysis of her situation. Rebecca recounted the despair she felt in the absence of recognition and how close she had come to suicide in response to losing her human status.

Maria also concurred with Arendt's claim that the political question had to be prioritized above the social, that respect and solidarity were primary—even more important than mere life, even more vital than economic redistribution. She had come to understand that, she said, when living with the Zapatistas.[17] How is it that Maria and Rebecca could have an interpretation so widely variant from so many of Arendt's academic interpreters?

Many critics have been troubled by Arendt's insistence, especially in *The Human Condition* and *On Revolution,* that social issues or those issues entailed in the "social question"—that is, poverty, labor, welfare, and so on—do not belong in a political arena.[18] Interestingly enough, such commentators often criticize Arendt for cruel inattention to the needs of those exactly like Rebecca and Maria. Their animosity stems from Arendt's argument that the invasion of the social, the invasion of the poor as poor people, into politics destroys political freedom and can even encourage terror, as happened in the French Revolution.[19]

The French radicals undercut their revolution by substituting compassion for respect and solidarity, by introducing "the poor" as the object of concern of the state rather than allying with those very citizens who also happened to be poor. Arendt argued that the social question of poverty is always overwhelming and brings the state, no matter how "revolutionary," back to the management of people as if they were things, thereby opening up all means (including violence) to solve such problems.

Arendt urged us to see that citizens rediscover their linkage to one another and their own valuation through being seen and heard in the presence of one another. Political freedom and equality entail respect and solidarity, not the private passion of love, on the one extreme, or the social passion of pity, at the other extreme. Love and pity are inappropriate in a political space because the first demands too much of another and the second not enough. Focusing on "what" a person is—poor—displaces respect and attention to "who" that person is: a human agent competent to decide his or her future with others. Focusing on the eradication of poverty as the object of the state displaces attention from sustaining those spaces and occasions for transcending what we are. Our first principle, according to Arendt, must be the right to have rights. Unless that is always our foundation—that is, the sustenance of a political realm to which we have a right and in which we meet, discuss, and decide our collective fate—we risk worse than poverty, as she pointed out in *The Origins of Totalitarianism.*

It might therefore seem that poverty is ineradicable to Arendt and never a fit subject for political debate and action. Whereas many commentators believe that to be the case, most of my students did not. They took her point to be somewhat different; namely, that "the poor" should not invade political life on the basis of what they are any more than "the rich" should. (Arendt did not see the antidote to totalitarianism to be rule by a few hyperwealthy capitalists.) She looked to the emergence of movements of laborers, ethnics, students, and the like, to struggle for freedom by transcending "what" they were without denying the particularities of their identities and who claimed a share in political life on the basis of wide solidarity and respect for other groups. She saw healthy movements as composed of those who spoke for themselves and who demanded dignity and the right to rights for themselves as well as for others. Thus, the poor must speak and act for themselves primarily as citizens among citizens, not content to be represented by others, no matter how compassionately, or to have their lives treated as problems to be solved by the state.

I think that Arendt's perspective on the primacy of politics and citizenship appealed so strongly to my students not only for the reasons suggested above in the examples of Rebecca and Maria, but also because of the whole group's tendency—at least in their most lucid moments—to recognize that they had to respect and listen to one another rather than sympathize and speak for one another's social issues and political problems.

It is probably not accidental that it was Carol, a Japanese American recently returned from feminist work with other Asian women in the South Pacific, who most forcefully articulated why she believed it crucial to build alliances with others rather than "help" them. She had seen firsthand the striking difference between those groups that had benevolent development plans to assist women trapped in the sex trade and those groups that constructed political coalitions with such women. Carol witnessed that the interventions of the former groups paradoxically infantilized the women, treating them as objects totally without power in need of rescue. The coalitional groups, she explained, began from the assumption that these women did not need representation, but spaces in which to tell their stories, teach others, and determine what needed to be done with others. Such spaces of political equality generated much more inventive, efficacious results and allowed "victims" to hear themselves and see one another as competent agents.

The New Regime

Political arenas where people represent themselves emerge, according to Arendt, whenever people constitute them: in the late-eighteenth-century Committees of Correspondence, the Councils of the French Revolution of 1789 and 1871, the Ihud early in Israel's twentieth-century refounding, the Soviets at the beginning of the Russian Revolution, the German Spartacist Councils in the years of Rosa Luxemburg, the Hungarian Revolutionary Councils of 1956.[20] Such arenas enabled people to become "enlarged thinkers"—able to comprehend the common world from the multiple perspectives of others, to take political action across conventional boundaries—initiating alliances with formerly unlikely partners in unlikely places, and to reconceive the problematic character of empire, as well as that of the liberal nation-state.

Arendt believed that the council system in which extensive participation became the norm was being continually rediscovered and offered a viable alternative model of a political regime.[21] Neither the imperial state (whether putatively socialist or capitalist) nor the liberal nation-state, she argued, were sufficiently resistant to continually emergent tendencies toward totalitarianism. In fact, the nation-state was largely illusory: no longer able to unify or protect its citizens, subservient to oligarchic "bourgeois" interests, and thoroughly multinational and multicultural through migrations of economic and political refugees.[22]

Why do students, particularly those with political experiences in communities and movements, tend to find Arendt's endorsement of the council system realistic rather than idealistic? Why are they not riven by skepticism, as are many of Arendt's commentators, about the viability of bottom-up federations? Why are they not overcome with worries about long-term institutionalization of the council form? Perhaps the students themselves are merely idealistic about a democratic future and cynical about the despotic or bureaucratic governments under which they have lived. As some of the students have explained it, however, they find that Arendt articulates a fact in their lives that almost no one else has. As she puts it in a number of places in her writings, human beings have the capacity to initiate something new in the world, something utterly unexpected.

For people who have initiated actions that have moved themselves out of gangs, or openly declared their homosexuality, or begun to work with those who their families had declared the political enemy, there has been a paradigm shift in how they know what is possible in the world. Their problem is now sustaining and amplifying what they have started, countering the conventional wisdom that tells them how unrealistic they are. As Arendt explains, the problem with the council system is not that it cannot be sustained because of people's human nature, political forces, or the weight of history, but that those who initiate it and those who witness it do not always stop to think about and recognize the meaning of what they have (re)discovered. The council system needs to be understood, wherever it emerges, as an end in itself—a federation of public spaces—rather than merely the inadequate means to a particular political goal. Thus, in Arendt's estimation, the participatory, bottom-up structure of the council system serves not only as a set of interlocked spaces for democratic deliberation, but also as an instrument for reminding people of the meaning of their community.

Had Arendt lived long enough, she might well have recognized, along with Maria, yet another reemergence in Chiapas, Mexico, where peasants and their allies have formed a council system government in parallel to the formal Mexican state, not with the intent of violently overthrowing the latter, but with a goal of shifting the very terms in which Mexicans understand politics, citizenship, and justice. At least from some accounts of the Chiapas insurrection, it cannot be understood in conventional left/right terms.[23] The peasants have not become a "revolutionary vanguard," nor are their aspirations limited to being "fairly" represented in the state and incorporated into the Mexican middle class. They are both more and less radical than either of those positions—more because they so heavily stress direct, ongoing participatory decision-making by all members of the community (interestingly, children as well as male and female adults); less because they have no wish (at least according to observers' accounts) to abandon their *indio* identity for another partial identity, such as "workers of the world" or "the proletariat." Maria knows that Chiapas may indeed be crushed, but she also believes, because of the extraordinary democratic political form that she saw reemerge day after day among ordinary, severely oppressed, imperfect human beings, that the "Zapatistas" will be back.

That Arendt's analysis makes sense of the character and self-interpretation of the Chiapas uprising indicates that her political theorizing, her ability to maintain a "conscious pariah" perspective, grounded as it is in her own experience and analysis of being born Jewish, participating in Zionism, and critically witnessing the rebirth of Israel, speaks across ethnonational boundaries. In short, her work serves as a model of how someone coming out of a particular background need not abandon it to make contact with others, but rather can use it to grasp critical affinities among diverse groups of people.

A Plurality of Perspectives

As I have tried to indicate above, Arendt's concept of the conscious pariah, her distinction between the social and the political, and her claims about the council system were not only comprehensible, but very significant, to the lives and the political actions of many of my seminar students. As such scholars as Margaret Canovan and Richard Bernstein have argued, putting Arendt's confrontation with totalitarianism at the center of her writings assists interpreters to more fully grasp the meaning and intent of her reflections. My students, moreover, in reading Arendt in the context of her focus on political catastrophe and the possibilities for reconstructing a shared world, tend to take her practices of racism or ethnocentrism as political problems rather than philosophical incoherencies or moral failings.

Arendt, for example, tends to move into others' perspectives without adequately marking that she is doing so.[24] It therefore becomes, at best, ambiguous whether she is explaining or fostering racist and ethnocentric positions at various points in her work. In *The Origins of Totalitarianism,* Africans are said to be without history. In some of the essays of *The Jew as Pariah,* Arabs are said to have had no physical impact on the land of Palestine. Do these depictions represent Arendt's conclusions, or do they only move inside the perspectives of the groups she is elsewhere clearly criticizing? Further, does the elision of Native Americans in her discussions of the United States follow the dominant paradigm of which she is critical, or does it represent her own failure of historical and political analysis? Then, of course, the contentious exchanges around Little Rock and the civil rights movement offer additional material for reconsideration by students.[25]

Although students cannot always uncover the line between Arendt's views and those that she temporarily mimics, they can figure out how to expand her own methods and contentions to enhance the underlying argument they know she wishes to make within the overall trajectory of her work. In the example from *Origins,* students recognize how much more politically substantive her analysis would be had she looked for a Lazarian position among black Africans themselves. Such a position is one that takes the role of the conscious pariah and is critical of both imperialists and one's own people's responses to that imperialism, just as Bernard Lazare criticizes anti-Semitic as well as Jewish responses.

In other words, the students found Arendt a rich enough source to provide the methods by which to critique and reconstruct her analysis to fulfill her commitment to plurality. Perhaps more important, they taught themselves, through their critical reading of Arendt, to look for such Lazarian voices in their own comparative political work. Kevin, whom I mentioned above, found it imperative to look for counterparts to Lazare among African Americans and Korean Americans in L.A. to better comprehend the complex relations between those groups within his home and to avoid the clichéd, simplistic oppositions by which their relations are often depicted.

Arendt's insistence on plurality of perspectives—even if sometimes perversely executed in her writing—is a major contribution to our reconsideration of multiculturalism, in the classroom as well as in the polity. In contrast to much liberal theorizing, Arendt believes that we are born, not as single individuals, but into communities;

that "who" we are can emerge only in relation to the words and deeds of others; that we can think and judge rightly only from hearing, thinking through, and imagining the perspectives of multiple others; that democratic deliberation requires plurality of perspectives, in stark opposition to the drive of totalitarianism to reduce all viewpoints to one.[26] Especially for students from non-Western traditions that privilege family and community connections rather than individualism, Arendt's concept of plurality gives them an alternative point of departure for comprehending Eurocentric politics and history. Further, Arendt's argument that there is no democracy without sustained and articulated diversity—not mere "celebration" of the existence of multiple cultures[27]—dramatically widens the students' perception of a multicultural political agenda in the United States. Some, for the first time, realize how vital they and their work may be to a much broader population. Arendt gives them a way of understanding their own movements as part of a larger democratic revitalization project.

Students working in cross-polity coalitions of environmental justice groups and of feminist groups concerned with the traffic in women recognize, through Arendt and her interpreters,[28] what is at stake in the spaces of freedom that they are initiating. Canovan is worth quoting at length on this point:

> Recent events around the world have drawn our attention back to the kind of quintessentially political phenomena that Arendt was trying to articulate and reflect upon. On the one hand, in dramatic events, ranging from military invasions to the destruction of communism in Eastern Europe, human beings have demonstrated their capacity to do the thoroughly unexpected, to smash established institutions (including states) and upset all certainties (including borders). On the other hand, in the multifarious negotiations that are attempting to find political settlements to violent and apparently insoluble disputes, we can see the other side of political action, the ability to bridge over abysses that laws do not span, and, by binding enemies into political agreements, to create new public spaces where disputes can be talked about instead of being fought over.[29]

There are many such intersections between Arendtian analysis and multiculturalism that have been vital for my students. One more in particular, however, needs to be noted before closing these reflections. Douglas Kellner has rightfully raised the imperative of "a critical theory of technology" for democratic education in our multicultural society. He points out the prevalence of "technophilic" and "technophobic" discourses surrounding emergent technologies.[30] Their narrowly focused, unthoughtful claims do little to assist students to critically engage the very technologies that may be driving their families' migration, or absorbing their free time, or shaping their future careers, or modifying their identities. Arendt, particularly in *Origins* and *The Human Condition,* though also in *Between Past and Future,* raises questions about the meaning of contemporary technologies that are fundamental to the critical pedagogy that Kellner seeks.

Arendt argues that contemporary technologies require careful assessment for their potential to destroy plurality, at the macrolevel of instruments like nuclear weaponry, but also at the microlevel of practices such as genetic manipulation. She traces these dangers for the human condition of diversity to the methodological context in which technologies are created and deployed.

> For whatever we do today in physics—whether we release energy processes that ordinarily go on only in the sun, or attempt to initiate in a test tube the processes of cosmic evolution, or penetrate with the help of telescopes the cosmic space to a limit of two and even six billion light years, or build machines for the production and control of energies unknown in the household of earthly nature, or attain speeds in atomic accelerators which approach the speed of light, or produce elements not to be found in nature, or disperse radioactive particles, created by us through the use of cosmic radiation, on the earth—we always handle nature from a point in the universe outside the earth. Without actually standing where Archimedes wished to stand, . . . still bound to the earth through the human condition, we have found a way to act on the earth and within terrestrial nature as though we dispose of it from outside, from the Archimedean point. And even at the

risk of endangering the natural life process we expose the earth to universal, cosmic forces alien to nature's household.[31]

Arendt believes that central to the meaning of the Archimedean principle (i.e., the greater the distance, the greater the capacity to survey, to measure, to have mastery over things) is the loss of humanly scaled and shared space and time.[32] Ungrounded action, earth alienation, is necessarily thoughtless in Arendt's sense; humans can initiate actions off earth, in the universe, but they cannot carry the conditions for thinking into the universe. Arendt argues throughout much of her work that we need the plurality of worldly, literally grounded human communities in order to sustain political freedom and make thoughtful assessments of what we need to do in outer space. Paradoxically, awe-inspiring achievements in technology may generate conditions for the crystallization of new totalitarianisms, which indeed, as Arendt warned, would not look like Nazism or Stalinism.

Cybernetics and nanotechnologies, for instance, which promise the molecular reconstruction of human bodies (even suggesting the supposed end of racism by means of phenotypically changing bodies to whatever form is desired) and the cheap transformation of any physical object into another (suggesting the supposed end to hunger and poverty), valorize a wholly synthetic world that makes actual what virtual reality can only simulate.[33] As my student Rose argued in her seminar paper for my class, the question is not whether the new technological paradigm can really fulfill its promises. Prior technologies have, after all, always failed at those same promises. Rather, the question Arendt raises, Rose explained, is whether the new production technologies can unwittingly, indeed unthinkingly, succeed where Nazism could not in its "assumption that everything is possible"[34] and in its goal to make the world its laboratory for continual change. Those interested in participatory politics must not only become technologically "literate" and skilled, they must also comprehend that preserving new spaces for political speech and action has become even more urgent.

I do not know, in the end, whether or not Hannah Arendt is a "multiculturalist." Like my students, I cannot always fully interpret her intent. Perhaps her critics are correct about her severe historical limitations and philosophical incoherencies. What my students from such varied backgrounds have compellingly demonstrated to me, nonetheless, is that it is precisely the most difficult and troubling aspects of her thought that address their deepest concerns about democratic possibilities in an increasingly multicultural world.

Notes

1. Hannah Arendt, *The Jew as Pariah*, ed. Ron H. Feldman (New York: Grove Press, 1978); *The Origins of Totalitarianism* (New York: Harcourt Brace Jovanovich, 1973); *Eichmann in Jerusalem* (New York: Penguin Books, 1963). I agree with those commentators such as Margaret Canovan and Richard Bernstein who believe that *The Origins of Totalitarianism* is the central text for comprehending Arendt's corpus and that her "confrontation with the Jewish question was the catalytic agent for crystallizing her thinking" (Bernstein, *Hannah Arendt and the Jewish Question* [Cambridge, MA: MIT Press, 1996], p. 9). "The most common reason why Arendt is misunderstood is that readers tend to start in the wrong place when trying to interpret her thought.... Not only is *The Human Condition* itself much more closely related to the *Origins* . . . than it appears to be, but virtually the entire agenda of Arendt's political thought was set by her reflections on the political catastrophes of mid-century" (Canovan, *Hannah Arendt: A Reinterpretation of Her Political Thought* [Cambridge: Cambridge University Press, 1992], p. 7).

2. For example, Anne Norton, "Heart of Darkness: Africa and African Americans in the Writings of Hannah Arendt," in *Feminist Interpretations of Hannah Arendt,* ed. Bonnie Honig (University Park: Pennsylvania State University Press, 1995); Adrienne Rich, *On Lies, Secrets, and Silence* (New York: W. W. Norton, 1979); Mary O'Brien, *The Politics of Reproduction* (London: Routledge & Kegan Paul, 1981); Elzbieta Ettinger, *Hannah Arendt/Martin Heidegger* (New Haven: Yale University Press, 1995); Richard Wolin, "Hannah Arendt and the Magician," *New Republic,* October 9, 1995; Shiraz Dossa, "Human Status and Politics: Hannah Arendt on the Holocaust," *Canadian Journal of Political Science,* vol. 13, no. 2 (June 1980); Norma Claire Moruzzi, "Re-Placing the Margin: (Non)Representations of Colonialism in Hannah Arendt's *The Origins of Totalitarianism,*" *Tulsa Studies in Women's Literature,* vol. 10, no. 1 (Spring 1991); George Kateb, *Hannah Arendt: Politics, Conscience, Evil* (Totowa, NJ: Rowman & Allenheld, 1984).

3. I have changed the students' names to protect their privacy.

4. See Maurizio Passerin d'Entreves, *The Political Philosophy of Hannah Arendt* (London: Routledge, 1994), p. 97; and Michael G. Gottsegen, *The Political Thought of Hannah Arendt* (Albany: State University of New York Press, 1994), p. 234.

5. See, for example, Seyla Benhabib, *The Reluctant Modernism of Hannah Arendt* (Newbury Park, CA: Sage Publications, 1996); d'Entreves, *Political Philoso-*

phy; Craig Calhoun and John McGowan, eds., *Hannah Arendt and the Meaning of Politics* (Minneapolis: University of Minnesota Press, 1997); Larry May and Jerome Kohn, eds., *Hannah Arendt: Twenty Years Later* (Cambridge, MA: MIT Press, 1996); and Lewis P. Hinchman and Sandra K. Hinchman, eds., *Hannah Arendt: Critical Essays* (Albany: State University of New York Press, 1994). See also my review essay "Hannah Arendt: Theorist of Distinction(s)," *Political Theory,* vol. 25, no. 1 (February 1997). For some interesting exceptions to this practice, see Bernstein, *Hannah Arendt and the Jewish Question;* Honig, ed., *Feminist Interpretations;* and Lisa Jane Disch, *Hannah Arendt and the Limits of Philosophy* (Ithaca: Cornell University Press, 1994).

6. Jeffrey Isaac, "At the Margins: Jewish Identity and Politics in the Thought of Hannah Arendt," *Tikkun,* vol. 5, no. 1 (January/February 1990); Ron Feldman, "Introduction," in Arendt, *Jew as Pariah.*

7. See Hannah Arendt, *The Human Condition* (Chicago: University of Chicago Press, 1958), pp. 179–180.

8. See d'Entreves, *Political Philosophy,* p. 147.

9. Canovan, *A Reinterpretation,* p. 139; Honig, ed., *Feminist Interpretations,* p. 161; Disch, *Limits of Philosophy,* p. 142; and Phillip Hansen, *Hannah Arendt: Politics, History, and Citizenship* (Stanford: Stanford University Press, 1993), p. 240.

10. See Elisabeth Young-Bruehl, *Hannah Arendt: For Love of the World* (New Haven: Yale University Press, 1982), esp. pp. 70ff. See also Bernstein, *Hannah Arendt and the Jewish Question.*

11. *Eichmann in Jerusalem,* pp. 232–233; *Origins of Totalitarianism,* p. 482.

12. For an overview of reaction to her report on the trial, see Young-Bruehl, *For Love of the World,* chap. 8.

13. See Hannah Arendt, "Part II: Zionism and the Jewish State," in *Jew as Pariah.*

14. See Melissa Orlie's illuminating essay "Forgiving Trespasses, Promising Futures," in Honig, ed., *Feminist Interpretations.*

15. See especially Hannah Arendt, "Herzl and Lazare," in *Jew as Pariah.* Bernard Lazare (1865–1903), a French-Jewish journalist and Dreyfusard, wrote *Job's Dungheap* (New York: Schocken Books, 1948), edited by Arendt, and *Antisemitism: Its History and Causes* (Lincoln: University of Nebraska Press, 1995), introduced by Robert S. Wistrich. See also Tuija Parvikko, *The Responsibility of the Pariah: The Impact of Bernard Lazare on Arendt's Conception of Political Action and in Extreme Situations* (Jyvaskyla, Finland: SoPhi, University of Jyvaskyla, 1996). By "exception" Jews, Arendt means those who see themselves only as individuals, not as members of a people and, moreover, see themselves as better than other Jews. The "parvenu" is one who has "made" it into mainstream society and is not about to carry with him or her anything from the past; a parvenu mentality accepts unthinkingly the assumptions of the mainstream society.

16. Canovan, *A Reinterpretation,* p. 171.

17. The parallel between Maria's observations with Arendt's "exaltation of politics" is striking; see Canovan, ibid., p. 278.

18. See, for instance, Hanna Pitkin, "Conformism, Housekeeping, and the Attack of the Blob: The Origins of Hannah Arendt's Concept of the Social," in Honig, ed., *Feminist Interpretations.* See also, Gottsegen, *Political Thought,* pp. 251, 256.

19. See Hannah Arendt, *On Revolution* (London: Penguin Books, 1963), pp. 84, 101, 223–224, 249.

20. d'Entreves, *Political Philosophy,* p. 77.

21. Canovan, *A Reinterpretation,* p. 237. See also John Sitton's informative assessment of Arendt's arguments for council democracy ("Hannah Arendt's Argument for Council Democracy," *Polity,* vol. 20, no. 1 [1987]: 80–100), as well as her critics in Hinchman and Hinchman, eds., *Critical Essays.*

22. See her discussions in "Zionism Reconsidered," in *Jew as Pariah,* ed. Feldman. Also, on this issue, see the overall argument in "Part II: Imperialism," in *Origins of Totalitarianism,* esp. pp. 124, 161; and Gottsegen, *Political Thought,* pp. 256, 260, 269.

23. On the Chiapas rebellion, see, for example, the review essay by Alma Guillermoprieta, "The Shadow War," *New York Review of Books,* March 2, 1995, pp. 34–43. See also Harry Cleaver, "Nature, Neoliberalism, and Sustainable Development: Between Charybdis and Scylla" (April 1997), available on the Internet at http://www.eco.utexas.edu/faculty/Cleaver/port.html.

24. See Seyla Benhabib's chapter in *Critical Essays,* ed. Hinchman and Hinchman, p. 122.

25. See Martin Jay's afterword to *Meaning of Politics,* ed. Calhoun and McGowan, p. 350; James Bohman, "The Moral Costs of Political Pluralism: The Dilemmas of Difference and Equality in Arendt's 'Reflections on Little Rock,'" in *Twenty Years Later,* ed. May and Kohn, p. 55.

26. Canovan, *A Reinterpretation,* p. 205. See also Disch's illuminating chapter "Training the Imagination to Go Visiting," in her *Limits of Philosophy.*

27. Disch, ibid., p. 205.

28. This is especially true for those with international and transnational analyses of ongoing political activism. See, for example, Gyan Prakash, "Who's Afraid of Postcoloniality," *Social Text,* vol. 14, no. 4 (Winter 1996).

29. Canovan, *A Reinterpretation,* pp. 277–278.

30. Douglas Kellner, "Multiple Literacies and Critical Pedagogy in a Multicultural Society," in *The Promise of Multiculturalism,* ed. George Katsiaficas and Teodoros Kiros (New York: Routledge, 1998), p. 234.

31. Arendt, *The Human Condition,* p. 262.

32. See Langdon Winner, *Autonomous Technology* (Cambridge, MA: MIT Press, 1977); Jonathan Schell, *The Fate of the Earth* (New York: Avon Books, 1982); and Dana Villa, *Arendt and Heidegger* (Princeton: Princeton University Press, 1995).

33. See especially B. C. Crandall, ed., *Nanotechnology: Molecular Speculations on Global Abundance* (Cambridge, MA: MIT Press, 1996). There are numerous Web sites on nanotechnology that track its development. See also Harry Cleaver's site (http://www.eco.utexas.edu/faculty/Cleaver) for several informative articles regarding "grassroots electronic mobilization" in relation to the Zapatistas.

34. Arendt, *Origins of Totalitarianism,* p. 427.

7

Hannah Arendt on Politicizing the University and Other Clichés

PETER EUBEN

I

A favorite fusillade in the "culture wars" of the end of the twentieth century was the charge by conservative canonists and their multiculturalist critics that the other side was politicizing the university. At times, there was something almost comical in the exchange of accusations as each attempted to outyell the other: "You're politicizing the university." "No, you are." "No, you are," and so on, like little boys playing tag.

Indeed, there was something peculiar about the entire conflict, with its apocalyptic posturing and hyperbolic language of battle, war, and Armageddon. There were serious issues at stake, but these were sometimes hard to find amid a polemicism that seemed both an extension of the Cold War and an anticipation of the fevered visions that flourished with the approaching millennium. In case you think I am exaggerating, let me give you a flavor of the language. Dinesh

D'souza warned that "the new barbarians have captured the humanities, law and social sciences departments"; that an unholy alliance of multiculturalists, feminists, radicals, poststructuralists, new historians, and other varieties of leftists had breached the gates and was standing triumphant in the citadel; and that "resistance on campus is outgunned and sorely needs outside reinforcements."[1] Alan Kors, a philosopher and organizer of the National Association of Scholars, assured his colleagues that though the barbarians were in our midst, if you showed them you were not afraid, they'd crumble; but he then went on to urge the formation of monasteries to preserve reason and civilization against the barbarian ravages of the countryside and towns of academe.[2] George Will called Lynne Chaney, then director of the National Endowment for the Humanities, "the secretary of domestic defense." "The foreigners her husband Dick [then secretary of defense] must keep at bay," he goes on, "are less dangerous . . . than the domestic forces with which she must deal."[3]

Things have calmed down somewhat, though the same old charges packaged as pathology are continually recycled, as readers of *The Chronicle of Higher Education* can attest. Apparently, we are lost in moral drift and relativism; have destroyed family values, reason, academic standards, civility, respect for privacy, reticence, decency, the Puritan ethic, and authority; are corrupted by sexual promiscuity, uncloseted gays, and popular culture; and can reestablish what is best and highest in us only by retrieving what we can of the 1950s, when things were "right" and the university wasn't politicized.[4]

I have no desire to perpetuate the polemicism of the culture wars and am perfectly willing to admit that multiculturalists had their own clichés about victimization, dead white males, and oppression and that there was more than enough self-righteousness to go around. In fact, I want to lower the temperature of the conflict for at least two reasons. The first reason has to do with the way the humanities and some social sciences have been relegated to an academic backwater by technological imperatives, presentism, vocationalism, an aggressive corporativist mentality of governing boards, and increasing privatization of public universities, which leaves them vulnerable to the educational visions of the largest funders. Unless the antagonists in the culture wars recognize that the conditions that give meaning to their struggle are being jeopardized, they will wind up fiddling, or rather posturing, while Rome, Athens, and Jerusalem burn. The second reason is that only if we get past the polemicism, clichés, and ritual character of the charges and countercharges can we get to the issues all three efface.

Nor can I offer anything like a history of the culture wars, though I would, again, offer two related points about its origins. One is that conservative canonists are right to point to the 1960s as a watershed in fostering what the Trilateral Commission called an "adversary culture" that inhibited the governance by "responsible elites." But at least at Berkeley, where I was a graduate student, it mattered that the free speech, civil rights, and antiwar movements coincided with revelations that the CIA was, through the Congress for Cultural Freedom, underwriting academic research and serious journals even as the social scientists, some of whom were in its employ, proclaimed the virtues of scientific objectivity.[5] You can understand how this generated considerable skepticism about the claims of reason and proclamations of political neutrality in the classroom.

The other point is that the Cold War provided the rhetoric, impetus, and even themes for the culture wars. The sudden end of the former left us to face the elementary problems of politics without the moral and political compass provided by a bipolar world. Perhaps we had become so comfortable with the divisions between friends and enemies—remember that neutralism, nonalignment, and the third way were dismissed as proto-communist—that importing them to the domestic battle over culture was preferable to living in a world that demanded dealing with unfamiliar moral and political complexities.

In the process, our understanding of culture, great books, and politics became straitjacketed by partisan agendas both inside and outside the university. It was forgotten that culture is a way of life, a rich and time-worn grammar of human activity, a set of diverse and often conflicting narratives whereby communal understandings or misunderstandings, roles and responsibilities, are negotiated. In these terms, culture is a living, breathing system for the distribution and enactment of agency, power, and privilege among its members and beyond.[6] And it is almost never the case that a culture speaks with one voice or that it exists without fissures and contradictions. For example, take the Marxist view that culture is false consciousness because it is a constellation of unexamined assumptions, attitudes, and institutions that has the power to suppress one's awareness of one's true condition. This view is fundamental for culture being understood as a force that can limit the imagination as well as enlarge it. But it is a view that itself radically rearranges elements, religious as well as secular, derived from the culture it challenges. Or consider the way Martin Luther King Jr.'s "Letter from a Birmingham Jail" brilliantly rearranges the voices of Judaism, Christianity, the American founding, and the Western intellectual tradition as embodied in Socrates to provide a more inclusive idea of culture and politics than that advocated by those who claim to speak for that culture.

Given such a truncated view of culture, it is not surprising that a number of conservative defenders and multiculturalist critics of so-called Western culture misread the origins of that culture or read out the contesting voices it contains. Consider the debate over great books. Some conservative canonists regard such books as didactic compendia of moral prescriptions that, like pills or castor oil, can produce health when ingested in measured doses. But this ignores the question of how exactly books shape character, or if they do at all, since it is not obvious that the most literate among us are also the most virtuous.[7] It may be that the readings of certain books can make people of college age the kinds of persons canonists or multiculturalists want them to be. But there is a considerable gap between the classroom and the world outside, between what we think we are teaching and what is learned.

Indeed, it may well be that what gives certain texts the resiliency to speak to different generations and communities of readers is the way they politicize the fundamental categories of culture: nature, God, tradition, family, gender, and authority. By "politicize," I mean what Aristotle did when he argued that politicizing something (say, gender) means regarding it as man-made and so subject to human design rather than inscribed in a nature we can contemplate but cannot alter. It may also be that many of the controversies present in the debate over canonical texts are already inscribed in the plots, themes, arguments, and dramatic settings of those texts. If so, then conservative canonists who deplore the politicizing of higher education are ignoring the way the texts they celebrate contribute to an educational atmosphere they criticize.

Consider in this regard the case of Socrates as presented in Plato's *Apology*. You remember that he specifically targets those with political and cultural power—the politicians and poets—for questioning to see if they have actually thought about what they are saying and doing and whether they warrant the authority they claim for themselves. They are, as we might expect, angry and resentful at this challenge and fearful of the "adversary culture" it encourages among the young, just as members of the National Association of Scholars are when challenged by their multiculturalist critics.

It follows that university education cannot help but be politicized as long as one teaches great books that challenge the unthinking adherence to normal practices. There is nothing more politicizing than the Socratic injunction, challenge, and provocation that the unexamined life is not worth living. It also follows that depoliticizing higher education would mean generating textbooks like those often found in elementary and high schools, which lack humor, irony, passion, or outrage and which are full of moralizing platitudes, one-dimensional history, and intellectual pablum.

But if conservative canonists treat great books in ways that the books themselves warn against, multiculturalist critics of the canon fail to recognize the degree to which the texts they excoriate can be allies in their attempts to pluralize the master canon and democratize cultural power. If I wanted to ensure the hegemony of a dead white male canon, I would certainly not have students read Sophocles' *Antigone* or Plato's *Republic,* for example. *Antigone* is about the way those in power use reason as a political bludgeon against their opponents, about the incompatible obligations men and women have, about generational and gender conflict, and about how progress entails transgression. *The Republic* contains a radical critique of traditional hierarchies of class, wealth, and gender; has a dramatic structure that plays against its explicit argument; and insists that any regime be judged by the criteria of justice. These are provocative, even subversive, texts.

But the debate over great books is only part of what is at issue in the charge and countercharge of politicizing the university. When conservative canonists talk about such politicizing, they mean making class, gender, and sexual preference a litmus test for who should be hired and what should be taught by whom. They resent and reject the idea that membership in a so-called oppressed group confers legitimacy on whatever is said. Whether something is true or false has nothing to do with such categories, and the assumption that it must simply ignores the 2,500 years of argument that it needn't. For canonists, though not only them, the university is a citadel of reason and argument, not a representative assembly that makes political compromises over who should be admitted or what should be taught. Identity politics, demagoguery, and political correctness have no place in rational debate, making arguments, providing evidence, or offering aesthetic judgments. Institutions of higher learning must stand apart from political conflicts, not mimic them or become a staging ground for participating in them. If such distance is erased, so too will be the distinctions between knowledge and dogma, universal values and local prejudice, education and indoctrination, politics and intellectual judgments.

The multiculturalist reaction to this charge of politicization is one of disbelief. Here is Henry Louis Gates Jr.: "That people with a straight face can protest the eruption of politics into something that has always been political says something about how remarkably successful official literary histories have been in presenting themselves as natural objects, untainted by worldly interests."[8] Other multiculturalists go on to point out the ways in which canonical authors, liberal and rational men such as Kant and J. S. Mill, had regressive, if not racist, attitudes toward native peoples. The former wondered whether the fun-loving people of Tahiti who lacked moral seriousness and high ideals should exist at all, while the latter's view of barbarian peoples helped justify the British Empire.[9]

As this suggests, multiculturalists regard themselves as confronting Western hegemony, with its self-righteous presumption that "our" way represents a universally valid norm and the only rational method of organizing human life. They resent and reject as tendentious the division of all ways of life and thought into Western and non-Western, as well as the claim, expressed here by Jürgen Habermas, that "to gain distance from one's own tradition and broaden limited perspectives is the advantage of Occidental rationalism,"[10] as if those outside the Occident lack the reflective awareness that could protect them from being possessed by their mythical worldviews.

So each side sees the other as politicizing the university, by which they mean that they alone seek truth and seek to educate their students, while the other side consists of ideologues who wish to indoctrinate them. On the surface, all seem to agree about the need to eliminate politics from the university, though one side thinks it was unpolitical until recently, while the other believes that its politicalness has only recently been brought to light. Each feels beleaguered and that the contest between them is a zero-sum game.

But what can it mean to seek the purgation of politics if a principal purpose of the university is and must be the political education of democratic citizens? Can one sustain a distinction between a political and a politicized education in a way that honors this central task while avoiding the excesses each side rightly criticizes in the other?

There is one last issue implicit in the mutual recriminations about politicizing the university that must be addressed before I lay out such a distinction: the way politics has become an epithet. In the current lexicon, "politicizing" means doing something immoral, dirty, underhanded, corrosive, manipulative, and ideological. If this is what "politics" is, then who would want their child or fellow citizens to be politically educated?

Politics as an epithet is present in popular and high culture, in jokes on late-night television, and in film. Jay Leno's line that politics is show business for ugly people is the shortest jibe, but my favorite comes from a local talk show host. The host asked his listeners to rank the occupations they found least attractive for their children. The least attractive profession was prostitution, the next least attractive one was politics. But, as one caller quickly noted, there was not much difference between them.

One cannot pick up a newspaper or magazine without reading about the cynicism, apathy, and disaffection that mark U.S. attitudes toward politics. University students don't want to study it or do it, and movies like *Wag the Dog* and television shows like *The Simpsons* brilliantly satirize it. Pundits and professors bemoan the influence of money on it, the refusal of good men and women to run for or stay in office, the prominence of spin doctors and focus groups, and the loss of public civility and social capital. Those Americans who do engage in activities outside home and work experiment with loose ad hoc associations, such as short-term volunteer projects or support groups, all of which are intensely focused on personal concerns.[11] None of these generate the more generalized sense of trust, mutuality, and capacity for sustained collective action Alexis de Tocqueville thought a necessary antidote for a society of equal individuals deeply suspicious of authority but dangerously susceptible to the quiet despotism of the administrative state.

Sources for the contempt for politics evident in the charges of politicizing the university are many, various, and of long standing, which is why E. J. Dionne's argument that Americans hate politics because of poor politics is not wrong but is not enough.[12] To locate these sources, one could go back to Plato's *Republic,* which likens the political world to a cave and portrays politics as a threat to moral integrity and philosophical knowledge; to Christianity's view of earthly authority as a corrective for sinfulness and loss of innocence in a world that lacks ultimate meaning; to strands of liberalism in which politics is a second-order, largely defensive activity in contrast to private life, where people can choose how to live and escape the corrupting influence of power; and to those readings of Marx in which politics is an appendage to more basic economic forces, an instrument of domination and subject to the logic of history, which will eventually make it wither away. Closer to home, one could point to the distrust of politics in *The Federalist Papers,* though such distrust was part of a nationalist faith that the Constitution could, through checks and balances, provide an institutional virtue to compensate for the far too fragile existence of individual virtue. Closer still, one could analyze the corrosive dialectic in the 1960s between young people skeptical of political authority and political authorities acting in ways that justified their skepticism, and one could also look at our current politics of antipolitics, where consummate politicians jockey for positions as political outsiders.

Whatever the cause, the results are a self-consuming, self-perpetuating political cynicism in which proposals to alleviate cynicism are viewed cynically and gestures by political leaders are eventually seen as that: only gestures.[13] Clearly, the pervasiveness of political cynicism and the denigration of politics, of which it is both symptom and cause, present an obstacle to any effort to redeem politics and represent a crisis of democracy. And since there is an intimate relationship between political identity and education in the United States, the crisis here is necessarily one of education as well as politics. But crises present opportunities in addition to dangers, opportunities, for instance, to purge outworn pieties and reliance on traditions that have lost their hold and authority. "The disappearance of such prejudices," Hannah Arendt writes, "simply means that we have lost the answers on which we ordinarily rely without even realizing they were originally answers to questions."[14] Pushed back to the questions themselves, we are forced to think about them instead of indulging in polemical hyperbole or endorsing preformed judgments.

In this case, the question itself was put by the founder of the University of Virginia. "I know of no safe repository for the ultimate powers of society," Thomas Jefferson wrote in 1820, "than the people themselves; and if we think them not enlightened enough to exercise their control with a wholesome discretion, the remedy is not to take it from them but to inform their discretion."[15] Of course, there are questions about who is to enlighten the people, about how and what counts as wholesome discretion, and even about who exactly the people are. But Jefferson's challenge is clear: How can one politically educate a democratic citizenry?

II

In the remainder of this essay, I want to respond to Jefferson's challenge with the help of Hannah Arendt and Socrates. I choose Arendt and Socrates for many of the same reasons. (Indeed, I "use" him in many of the ways she does, and "my" Socrates is often hers.) Alone and together, they help us refocus the terms of the culture wars in ways that dislodge the reigning clichés and help establish a distinction between a political and a politicized education. Alone and together, they also indicate what is right and what is exaggerated in the polemical complaints of both combatants, provide a criterion for making curricular choices, and encourage a more nuanced view of "great books," as well as the culture from which they emerge and to which they speak. Finally, I choose them because each is in his or her own way an exemplary political educator.[16]

More specifically, I choose to think with Arendt because her suspicion of the idea and practice of "political education" expresses an unease about the relationship between politics and education that is more productive than that offered by the participants in the culture wars. I choose her, too, because it is so difficult to fit her into fashionable intellectual and political categories. Is she conservative, liberal, or radical, a philosopher or political thinker, a defender of the republican tradition or a democrat, an exponent of agonal or deliberative politics? The answers are easy only if you have not read her. Finally, I choose her as an interlocutor because her own reading of "great books," however problematic (as with Marx and Plato), is generative rather than didactic.

I choose Socrates because he is a canonical figure who confounds the polarities that circumscribe the culture wars and because I believe that he believed that the living of an examined life is a necessary feature in the political education of democratic citizens, though he is far more leery of politics and greatness than is Arendt. Of course, the fact that one reason Socrates was killed was for living such a life makes my argument seem ludicrously implausible. Yet it may seem less so given the fact that he lived so long; that the vote for conviction was so close, despite his repeated provocations; that he says that given a whole day, he could have convinced the jurors of his innocence; and that, as I will suggest, the examined life he advocated was an extrapolation from Athenian democratic practices.[17]

Hannah Arendt believes that "political education" is a dangerous confounding of categories, sensibilities, and activities. Whereas politics involves joining with one's equals in assuming the effort of persuasion and running the risk of failure, education presumes a "dictatorial intervention, based upon the absolute superiority of the adult"

(CE, 176). Since education can play no role in politics, where we "always have to deal with those who are already educated," anyone who seeks to educate adults "really wants to act as their guardian and *prevent* them from political activity" (CE, 177).

It turns out that Arendt's critique is focused on two specific targets. The first comprises those in the tradition of political thought, most notably Plato, who regard the authority of parents over children and teachers over pupils as the model by which to understand political authority. For Arendt, this is a category mistake that confounds the realm of politics and equality with that of education and authority. That is because political equality is not a natural condition that precedes the constitution of the public realm, but is rather an attribute of citizenship that individuals acquire upon entering that realm.

The second target is American education. Where Plato inappropriately imported analogies based on permanent inequalities into the political realm, Americans improperly bring their commitment to equality into the classroom, thereby erasing differences of young and old, the gifted and ungifted, children and adults, and, most significant, pupils and teachers. This refusal to exercise adult authority has at least two consequences: It insulates the child's world by creating a separate sphere that allows the tyranny of peers to replace the authority of adults; and it represents an abdication of responsibility by adults to prepare the young for adulthood.

Children themselves present what Arendt calls a "double aspect to an educator." Like the young of all species, a child is in a process of becoming a human being in the same sense a kitten is becoming a cat. But human parents have not only summoned their children into life, they have "simultaneously introduced them into a world" (CE, 185). That is why education is not just a function of training in the practice of living that all adult animals assume for their young, but also involves assuming the responsibility for the continuance of a world that existed before the birth of the child and will exist after its death. Since the child represents both a threat to that world and its source of renewal, education must move in two directions at once. It must protect that child against the world and protect the world from being "overrun and destroyed by the onslaught of the new of each generation" (CE, 186). Thus, adults, including teachers, must be conservative in the sense of assuming responsibility for a world they did not create and of which they may not even approve. But the authority of and the attitude toward the past that are appropriate to education have no validity in the world of politics and grown-ups.

This means that the conservatism appropriate to education must not extend to the public realm, where we act among adults and equals. Politically speaking, an attitude that accepts and strives only to preserve the world is disastrous, since the world is "irrevocably delivered up to the ruin of time unless we intervene to alter and create what is new" (CE, 192). Only if we allow the young, the new, the never before seen to actually appear in the light of day can the world be preserved against the mortality that continually threatens to overrun it. The conclusion, paradoxical as it seems, is that we must be conservative in education so we can be radical in politics and radical in politics so we can keep our common world alive and have something to conserve.

Institutions of higher learning have a peculiar, even contradictory, role in this process. They are both the end point of education and the beginning of politics. Our students are also our fellow citizens, who vote, are asked to defend their country, can sign binding contracts, and are tried as adults. (I am ignoring the increasing numbers of nontraditional students.) As citizens of a democracy, they must recognize that there is no political analogue to the educational authority they have experienced until now.

What are the implications of Arendt's argument for the culture wars? First, she agrees with canonists that education is necessarily conservative in the sense of encouraging an appreciation of what we share as a nation and a people. In a land of immigrants, education provides a common language so that the differences among us can become mutually intelligible.[18]

Second, she would insist that multiculturalist critics take responsibility for a world that they may well regard as unjust and oppressive. Certainly, taking responsibility for a common world does not preclude criticism; indeed, I shall argue later on that it requires it, especially when that world is democratic. But it may initially require what William Galston calls "moralizing historical narratives" that establish a pantheon of heroes who confer legitimacy on the central institutions and practices of society.[19] It certainly requires that the young not be treated as equals, that they be provided with a sense of security and mastery, with some moral and social maps to guide their thoughts, and that they have adulthood presented to them as an honorable status and task.[20]

Third, Arendt would also insist that conservative canonists not impose their cultural power on the young in ways that preclude them from "undertaking something new and unforeseen." They must prepare students for the task of renewing our common world by sharing their authority with those eighteen- to twenty-two-year-olds who are both their students and their fellow citizens. This does not mean relinquishing the authority superior knowledge confers. It does mean sharing responsibility for sustaining a shared life that has up until now been the prerogative and task of adults. It also means an increasing emphasis on reciprocity, on becoming students of our students as well as teachers of them, and on initiating dialogues with them that are more than asking questions until they get the right answers. Indeed, at this stage, questions become as frequent as answers, moralizing narratives yield to analyses and critique, and challenges to what constitutes the canon should be respected or even encouraged rather than dismissed as effrontery.

Fourth, by inference and example, Arendt offers a way of reading canonical authors such as Plato, Kant, and Kafka that is at once learned and generative. Unlike the antagonists of the culture wars, she is appreciative of their sense of craft and aesthetic brilliance, which, despite the undoubted influence of cultural power, makes their texts "great" while respecting, even fostering, their subversive potential. Glossing Arendt, one recent commentator has argued that "the most important and difficult problem in education is how to preserve the new and revolutionary in the child while simultaneously conserving the world as a permanent home for human beings."[21] I am suggesting that Arendt solves an analogous problem in her readings of canonical texts.

Last, insofar as conservative canonists are tempted by nativism, Arendt warns them that space and opportunity must be provided not just for the young, but for the new who are not young: immigrants. Although it is true that education helps these newcomers become Americans, it is also true that they are resources for national renewal and a "guarantee" of our national identity as a new order. What is "magnificent" and "utopian" about America is its refusal to shut itself off from the outside world (CE, 175–176).

But what about the issue of politicizing the university? How does Arendt help us here? Her insistence that trying to educate adults is a form of indoctrination and treating the young as equals is foolish are helpful observations, but they do not take us very far. What does is the way she challenges the reduction of politics to an epithet. Her way of talking about politics will no doubt sound odd, but that is the point.

III

There is one place in which Arendt would agree that education involves reciprocity between equals rather than illicit hierarchy: the public realm itself, especially a radically democratic one. The point is implicit in *The Apology,* where Socrates argues that no one in his right mind would corrupt those among whom he lives, thereby diminishing the quality of his own life. After all, if the journey and the destination were the same, it would make no sense to spoil the conveyance in which one is riding.[22] It is explicit in Aristotle's definition of a polis as a community in which political activity changes the character of the participant: "If the spirit of their participation and the nature of their interaction is the same after they have come together as it was before they left their separate spheres, their community would not be a polis."[23] This does not mean that everyone comes to the same view and shares one opinion—that, according to Aristotle, was Plato's mistake—but that people modify their opinions in the course of political debate and deliberation. In these terms, "representative democracy" is a contradiction in terms. For if the point of participation is to refine one's opinions while learning how to think like a citizen, no one can do that for me any more than someone can work out for me.

Arendt has a similar view. Like Tocqueville and Mill, she is troubled by the tyranny of majority opinion, going so far as to condemn the very idea of "public opinion" as stifling the formation of individual opinions.[24] For her, politics requires the frank speech of others who view things differently, since it is only in the exchange of opinions that we reframe and enlarge our own and, in the process, learn how to think of ourselves as citizens. To think as a citizen means asking, not "What do I want?" which leads to bargaining with others who want something different, but "What do we need?" which encourages debate in terms of the "we" that must act now and remain capable of acting in the future.

For Arendt, a "political" community requires the contentiousness of strong-willed individuals who appreciate how the world they share makes their individualism possible. "Human plurality," she writes in *The Human Condition,* "the basic condition of speech, has the two-fold character of equality and distinction."[25] If men were not equal, they could not understand one another and there could be no community. But if they were not different, if they did not bring their distinctive perspectives to bear on the world they share and continually reenact through speech and deed, there would be no need to speak and so no need for politics. And politics itself is less about accomplishing some objective, such as passing a piece of legislation, protecting one's interests, increasing one's wealth, or assuring one's security, than about being seen by others. Acting in public gives us a sense of being alive and powerful. It provides an opportunity to communicate who we are, to manifest that style of action and traits of character that make us distinctive, to announce ourselves so that others must take note and notice us.

Arendt's point of reference in her effort to resuscitate politics is the Greek polis. Her purpose is to retrieve the dignity of politics against the combined weight of the philosophical tradition since Plato, the liberal tradition since Hobbes and Locke, and the Marxist tradition that celebrates economic and social life at the expense of politics. More specifically, she goes "back once more to antiquity, i.e., to its political ... traditions, certainly not for the sake of erudition and not even because of the continuity of our tradition, but merely because a freedom experienced in the process of acting and nothing else—though of course mankind never lost this experience altogether—had never again been articulated with the same classical clarity."[26] Because Arendt's polis is less the city-state in its particular geographical, institutional, or historical configuration than "the organization of the people as it arises out of acting and speaking together . . . no matter where they happen to be," the space for direct participation (and so of political education) finds "its proper location in almost any time and anywhere" (*HC,* 198). Because we have not wholly lost the experience of political freedom—indeed, the "of course" in the quote implies we cannot lose it—the point of returning to the Greeks is not to lament a world that has passed irrevocably, but to undertake the task of providing richer meanings to words like "freedom," "power," "action," and especially "politics" while recognizing the presence of analogous experiences that exist in our own time.

Arendt's view of political participation as a form of political education reminds us of two things. The first is that many important aspects of political education occur outside of schooling; indeed, political education of democratic citizens is only one task higher education performs. It also suggests that one way universities can fulfill their role in such education is by teaching epochs and cultures whose understanding of politics, though not wholly alien from our own, is nonetheless radically different. The Socratic point is to unfreeze what seems natural and given or, more paradoxically, to politicize the idea of politics.

IV

There are other ways in which a university education can be a political one, even as it performs more specifically intellectual tasks. That way is also suggested by Arendt in her reflections on Adolf Eichmann's trial and in her book on it. What astonished, perplexed, and provoked Arendt when she wrote her book was that Eichmann lacked the evil motives one would expect from someone committing such monstrous deeds. He was not an ideologue or even anti-Semitic. Except for being preoccupied with his personal advancement, "he had no motives at all." He simply "did not know what he was doing," despite the enormity of those doings. This was not a matter of stupidity; here again, he seemed perfectly "normal." "It was sheer thoughtlessness . . . that predisposed him to become one of the greatest criminals of that period." Such thoughtlessness, and the remoteness from reality it signifies, "wreaked more havoc than all the evil instincts taken together."[27] Looking back some fourteen years later, she is moved to ask: "Might the problem of good and evil, our faculty for telling right from wrong, be connected with our faculty for thought? . . . Could the activity of thinking as such, the habit of examining whatever happens to come to pass or to attract attention, regardless of results and specific content, could this activity be among the conditions that make men abstain from evil-doing or even actually 'condition' them against it?"[28] What matters here is not what we come to know *because* of thinking; indeed, if we know what justice or academic standards are, we may well stop thinking about them. Rather, it is thinking "as such" that matters, thinking as the impetus to push past the clichés and standardized codes of expression and conduct that have "the socially recognized function of protecting us against the reality of events and actions which have a claim on our attention simply by virtue of their existence" (TMC, 9).

I want to offer a tentative "yes" to Arendt's Socratic question. Thinking in the form of the two-in-one dialogue I have with myself is indeed among the conditions that make men and women abstain from injustice and can, under certain circumstances, contribute to the political education of democratic citizens. For Arendt, it was Socrates who discovered thinking as the actualization of the dialogue between me and myself and the fact, which follows from it, that I am not alone even when I am without company. It is to this silent partner that I owe an account of my choices and actions.[29] We have all had the experience of replaying a conversation over in our minds, wondering whether what we said was appropriate, persuasive, and wise, whether we were true to our principles without being self-righteous. In these conversations, we hold ourselves accountable and may, if we find ourselves seriously wanting, have difficulty sleeping at night.

Being accountable to this silent partner means that we must, in Socrates' words, be a friend to ourselves.[30] If I contradict myself, I will be at war with myself, and so I will be unable to act in a consistent manner. Moreover, to be a friend to oneself precludes injustice since committing an unjust act would mean spending the rest of one's life in the company of an unjust person. The situation is even worse than we imagine since a murderer, for instance, "is not only condemned to the permanent company of his own murderous self but will see all other people in the image of his own action." What is destructive here is less his specific act than the perspective on the world he comes to have because of it, which then helps constitute not only his world, but the common world of citizens in which he too must live (PP, 88; TMC 33, 35).[31]

Despite this connection between the two-in-one dialogue and the world of citizens, the dialogue between me and myself does not, in the first instance, have anything directly to do with political education. But there are certain circumstances when it does become politically relevant. What are those circumstances, and what sort of relevance does political education suddenly have in them? The circumstance Arendt has in mind is where people seem to be swept away unthinkingly, when, as in criminal regimes such as Nazi Germany, tradition, moral maxims, religious beliefs, and conscience no longer function as guides for discriminating right from wrong but are themselves complicit in evil. At such times, those who think are drawn out of hiding because their independence becomes conspicuous and thus a form of action (TMC, 36).

Such thinking can be a part of political education only in result, not in aim. If it is instrumental, it undermines both the integrity of thinking itself and its status as an emergency resource when law and morality are complicit with criminality. From this angle, thinking as an aspect of political education is present in any subject or mode of reflection that helps us live an examined life, and a great book is one that stimulates the two-in-one dialogue Socrates regarded as the actuality of thought and Arendt regards as an inhibitor of evildoing.

Though the dialogue between me and myself has worldly antecedents and consequences, it is not in the first instance based on an anticipated communication with others with whom I must finally come to some agreement. The sort of thinking that does I will call, following Arendt, "representative thinking." It is a more direct mode of political education.[32] Representative thinking consists in imaginatively representing the views of others to myself. This is not a case of empathy where I adopt the point of view of someone who stands somewhere else. It is more like being and thinking in my own identity where I am not (TP, 241). Arendt talks about training one's imagination to go visiting. You don't move in or change identities with your host, but you ask him or her, "What does the world look like from over there? How do you people see things?"

The more people's perspectives I have present to my mind while considering what to do about a particular issue, the stronger will be my capacity for representative thinking and "the more valid" will be my conclusions and my opinions (CC, 221; TP, 241). That is because thinking that occurs in the actual or projected dialogue with those who constitute the "we" who must decide makes my opinion more comprehensive. This comprehensiveness may achieve a kind of impartiality but never objectivity. Where impartiality rests on our ability to see the world from different points of view that are themselves partial in the double sense of being incomplete and self-serving, objectivity presumes that we could stand outside the world as if we were not part of it. Whereas the political knowledge generated by representative thinking is discursive, objective knowledge is not. What I mean by "representative thinking" distinguishes those men who can understand the vulnerabilities women experience in everyday life from those who cannot; the work of John Sayles, say, as opposed to that of Spike Lee, whose films I often admire for other reasons. It marks writers, filmmakers, and TV producers who can portray working-class life without romanticism or condescension though they themselves are not of the working class.

The people whose homes we visit need not be alive or real. "In the last analysis," Arendt writes, "our decisions about right and wrong will depend upon our choice of the company with whom we wish to spend our lives" *(LOM).* Such company includes the examples of persons living or dead, real and fictional, who come to mind as we face decisions and choices that constitute who we are and the lives we have chosen but are also chosen for us. The pedagogic questions and general curricular implications are clear. What ways of teaching and reading texts cultivate the political and moral imaginations of our students so they are able to see the world from other points of view? Who are our intellectual "consultants" when "the chips are down"? We need to offer our students companions who will walk with them long after their memory of a specific course or argument has faded: Toni Morrison's Sethe and Sophocles' Oedipus, Augustine and Nietzsche struggling with faith and redemption, Plato and Don DeLillo on mortality, to offer pitifully few examples.

But that memory is as much a consequence of how a text was taught as which one was selected to be taught. By this, I refer to two things: one having to do with the dangers of presentism and abstraction; the other, with the relation between text and subtext. Memorable readings often move between presenting a text as familiar and alien, drawing students to it by speaking to experiences they recognize while urging them to push beyond their experience or rearrange its parts. By how a text is taught, I also mean the character of the teacher and the way what he or she does reiterates or undermines what is being said. I used to have a colleague who thought of himself as a radical democrat yet taught in a thoroughly authoritarian manner, and I have also known many dogmatic liberals.

V

For the last way in which thinking becomes political, I turn to the Socrates of Plato's *Apology* and *Crito*. He has, of course, been my companion all along. As I mentioned, Socrates is in the streets engaging anyone who is willing in conversation. But he is especially anxious to engage his fellow citizens and even more anxious to engage the politicians and poets to see if they know what they claim to know and, more broadly, if they know what is most worth knowing. Unsurprisingly, he finds that those in power do not know what they are saying and doing, while those, such as artisans, who do have a genuine skill exaggerate its importance. He claims, with what I admit is a certain amount of disingenuousness, that he is obligated to pursue these discussions because Delphic Apollo has commanded him to do so. Asked who was the wisest man of all, the god answered Socrates. Since Socrates knows he is not wise, he goes around trying to prove the god wrong so he can find out the meaning of the response. He ultimately concludes that his wisdom lies in knowing that he does not know.

Socrates is insistent that whatever wisdom he has is merely human wisdom. His claim is an expression of ignorance about things that are beyond human wisdom, such as the nature of death. But it is also a claim that whatever he knows is available to all humans rather than being the prerogative of experts. It is also an assertion about the connection between knowing and thinking. Human knowledge is never secure or certain, and so claims to Truth and Knowledge, with a capital "T" and "K," are attempts to shut people up, to tell them there is no point in continuing to think. Of course, Socrates had doctrines: about its being better to suffer than to commit injustice or about what a good life was, and it is often said that he died for these ideas. But I think it more accurate to say that he died for thinking, which continued to be his way of life even when facing the prospect of death.

Socrates emphasizes the fact that he will talk to anyone, which suggests that thinking, in the sense of examining our lives, is not a specialized activity, but an ever-present faculty in everybody; that the inability to think Arendt found in Eichmann could just as well be found in scientists and scholars, moral philosophers and lawyers. Since such thinking is an attribute of every human life, one who does not think is not fully human but is sleepwalking through life. Socrates presents his constant harassment of his fellow citizens as an act of patriotism. It is done, he says, out of respect for them and a desire to make the city he shares with them as good as possible. For him, political education consists in having people think about and improve the opinions they hold. To improve their opinions, people must first be made aware that they have them, then be helped to articulate what they are so they see rather than see through them, and then finally to recognize in them a legitimate perspective on a common world.[33]

As this implies, all people have their own opinions, their own opening to the world. Because it is theirs and cannot be known in advance, Socrates must begin with questions and listen, not just to the specific answers, but to the view of the world implicit in them.

He must be willing to be surprised and follow the conversation wherever it leads. Now, if opinions embody how the world appears to the speaker, the response cannot be to deny that appearance but to press for details, consistency, clarity, and depth of understanding—exactly what a good teacher should do. I do not think the encounters Socrates describes are staged and didactic in the sense that he pretends not to know the answers and risks nothing while his interlocutors are ignoramuses floundering for the right answers and risking everything. The encounters are reciprocal and have the quality of common exploration. The risks of dialogue are shared because anyone, including Socrates, may be unaware of the position he holds. Insofar as these encounters are as I describe them, Socrates is an educator whose mode of education respects the equality Arendt insists is necessary in politics.

I do not pretend that a commitment to the Socratic proposition that the unexamined life is an unworthy life is politically neutral, nor do I deny that it is incompatible with ways of life guided by unquestioned authority or unswerving faith. Perhaps Galston is right to warn that building the Socratic injunction into our educational system, even at the university level, means endorsing "a conception of the human good unrelated to the functional needs of its sociopolitical institutions and at odds with the deep beliefs of many of its loyal citizens."[34] But the warning is itself unpersuasive beyond the politically suspect language of "functional needs." For one thing, Galston underestimates the thinking we are forced to do in a multicultural society, as Roger Sanjek's recent study of race and neighborhood politics in New York City indicates.[35] We must be wary about separating the philosophical "we" from the unphilosophical "them" when we remember that Socratic thinking is not the prerogative of academics or philosophers. Second, what he calls "the sociopolitical institutions" include traditions of self-awareness and self-critique sufficiently strong to indicate a particular affinity between democracy and thinking.

Still, Galston has a point. But it is a point made indirectly by Socrates himself in *The Crito*. There Socrates argues that he has an obligation to obey the law—in this case, the one under which he was tried and convicted—even though it was unjustly applied. He refers to himself as a child, even a slave, to the laws since they provided the conditions of his life and education. This implies that he owes a profound debt of gratitude to what he criticizes: that the way he thinks and his commitment to the examined life are partly the product of the democratic culture which has educated him and which he extends at the very moment that he subjects it to criticism. Debates in the Assembly and law courts, as well as the central role of drama in problematizing the cultural accommodations, leaders, and policies upon which Athens depended, provided a model and inspiration for the kind of critical philosophy in which he engaged. We know from Thucydides' *History* that the Athenians were a people who gave no rest to others and took none for themselves. They were constantly in motion, militarily, politically, and intellectually. Democracy for them was as much a form of disturbance as of governance, and the disturbance, as Arendt's characterization of the polis indicates, was an integral part of the governance. Under such conditions, Socrates was right at home.[36]

Obeying the laws also implies that, in Arendtian terms, Socrates is taking responsibility for a common world. It is precisely because he does that he can, as *The Apology* suggests, be a critic of it. Unlike the participants in the culture wars, he neither draws up the wagons nor dismisses those he regards as committing injustices. That is Arendt's way as well. In this, she, like her Socrates, has left a legacy of politically educating a democratic citizenry.

Notes

1. Dinesh D'souza, "The Visigoths in Tweed," in *Beyond PC: Towards a Politics of Understanding,* ed. Patricia Aufderheide (St. Paul, MN: Graywolf Press, 1992), p. 11.

2. Quoted by Joseph Berger in "Scholars Attack Campus Radicals," *New York Times,* November 13, 1988, p. A22; and Jacob Weisberg, "NAS: Who Are These Guys Anyway?" in *Beyond PC,* ed. Aufderheide, p. 85.

3. I have discussed these quotes at great length in *Corrupting Youth: Political Education, Democratic Culture, and Political Theory* (Princeton: Princeton University Press, 1997), chap. 1.

4. See, for instance, Gertrude Himmelfarb, *One Nation, Two Cultures: A Searching Examination of American Society in the Aftermath of Our Cultural Revolution* (New York: Knopf, 1999). Though more temperate in tone and more optimistic

(thanks to the revival of religion), the book is less a searching examination than a moderated retread of conservative clichés.

5. See Frances Stonor Saunders, *Who Paid the Piper: The CIA and the Cultural War* (London: Ganta, 1999).

6. Bonnie Honig, "My Culture Made Me Do It," in Susan Moller Okin with respondents, *Is Multiculturalism Bad for Women?* ed. Joshua Cohen, Matthew Howard, and Martha C. Nussbaum (Princeton: Princeton University Press, 1999), p. 39.

7. Katha Pollit, "Why Do We Read?" in *Debating PC: The Controversy over Political Correctness on College Campuses,* ed. Paul Berman (New York: Dell, 1992), pp. 206, 210.

8. Henry Louis Gates Jr., "Whose Canon Is It, Anyway?" in *Debating PC,* ed. Berman, p. 195.

9. Bhikhu Parekh, "A Varied Moral World," in Okin, *Is Multiculturalism Bad for Women?* p. 69.

10. Jürgen Habermas, "Remarks on Legitimation," *Philosophy and Social Criticism,* vol. 24, nos. 2–3: 162.

11. See William Chaloupka, *Everybody Knows: Cynicism in America* (Minneapolis: University of Minnesota Press, 1999).

12. E. J. Dionne, *Why Americans Hate Politics* (New York: Simon & Schuster, 1991); see also the discussion of Dionne in Chaloupka, ibid., chap. 7.

13. Chaloupka, ibid., pp. 27–28.

14. Hannah Arendt, "The Crisis in Education," in *Between Past and Future* (New York: Penguin Books, 1977), p. 174. This essay will be cited as CE in the text for all subsequent references.

15. Thomas Jefferson, letter to William Charles Jarvis, September 28, 1820, in *The Collected Works of Thomas Jefferson,* vol. 12, ed. Paul Ford (New York: Putnam, 1905), p. 1630.

16. They are even more so if we sustain the tension between them over such issues as the relationship between politics and morality or greatness and justice.

17. I have made this argument at length in *Corrupting Youth,* chap. 4.

18. But as my fourth point below suggests, this ignores the way the "us" and the "common" are themselves contested.

19. William Galston, "Civic Education in the Liberal State," in *Philosophers on Education,* ed. Amelie Oksenberg Rorty (London: Routledge, 1998).

20. Arendt strongly objects to the line between children and adults becoming a wall, as though childhood were "an autonomous state capable of living by its own laws" ("The Crisis in Education," p. 195). Since it is adults who establish this separate world of children, its very existence indicates, at the very least, an abdication of responsibility for educating children into adulthood. It may even be regarded as a statement of confusion, indifference, or contempt by adults for their world or, more disconcertingly, as an unstated desire to be children, thereby renouncing the privileges and responsibilities of the world as it exists. It is as if, Arendt writes, parents said: "In this world even we are not very securely at home; how to move about in it, what to know, what skills to master, are mysteries to us too. You must try to make out as best you can; in any case you are not entitled to call us to account. We are innocent, we wash our hands of you" (ibid., p. 191).

21. Mordechai Gordon, "Hannah Arendt on Authority," chap. 2 of this volume.

22. Jonathan Schell, "Introduction," in Adam Michnik, *Letters from Prison and Other Essays*, trans. Maya Latynski (Berkeley: University of California Press, 1985), p. xxxiii.

23. *Politics*, 1280b32.

24. Hannah Arendt, *On Revolution* (New York: Viking, 1963), pp. 227–230.

25. Hannah Arendt, *The Human Condition* (Chicago: University of Chicago Press, 1958), p. 176. This book will be cited as *HC* in the text for all subsequent references. I have discussed this at length in "Arendt's Hellenism," in *The Cambridge Companion to Hannah Arendt*, ed. Dana Villa (Cambridge: Cambridge University Press, 2000).

26. Hannah Arendt, "What Is Freedom?" in *Between Past and Future*, p. 165.

27. Hannah Arendt, *Eichmann in Jerusalem* (New York: Penguin Books, 1977), pp. 287–288.

28. Hannah Arendt, *The Life of the Mind*, vol. 1: *Thinking* (New York: Harcourt Brace Jovanovich, 1978), p. 5 (hereafter cited in the text as *LOM*); and "Thinking and Moral Considerations," *Social Research*, vol. 38, no. 3 (Autumn 1971): 9–13 (hereafter cited in the text as TMC).

29. "Thinking and Moral Considerations," p. 37, and "Philosophy and Politics," *Social Research*, vol. 57, no. 1 (Spring 1990): 101 (hereafter cited in the text as PP).

30. Plato, *The Gorgias*, 482a.

31. Yet there are aspects of Arendt's argument that suggest a far wider political scope for thinking in the modern world. She argues in "What Is Authority?" (in *Between Past and Future*) that the modern condition is defined by the loss of authority, tradition, and religion (she is certainly wrong about the latter). But if we all live with the failure of inherited wisdom and with the radical break in tradition, then we are all thrown back on our own resources, all forced, to one degree or another, to be thinkers and exercise that independent judgment that thinking promotes. Perhaps this is another thing adults tell one another but not the young.

32. Arendt's views on representative thinking can be found in "Truth and Politics" and "The Crisis in Culture," both in *Between Past and Future* (the former of which will be cited hereafter in the text as TP, and the latter of which will be cited hereafter in the text as CC), and in her *Lectures on Kant's Political Philosophy*, ed. Ronald Beiner (Chicago: University of Chicago Press, 1982).

33. See Dana Villa, *Politics, Philosophy, Terror: Essays on the Thought of Hannah Arendt* (Princeton: Princeton University Press, 1999).

34. Galston, "Civic Education," p. 478.

35. Roger Sanjek, *The Future of Us All: Race and Neighborhood Politics in New York City* (Ithaca: Cornell University Press, 1998).

36. In one of her portraits of Socrates, Arendt emphasizes how corrosive of politics and practical life Socratic philosophy is, how it interrupts and dissolves practical life in a way that threatens the existence of public life. Although Arendt surely has a point, I think she overstates the case by underestimating how parasitic Socratic philosophy was on Athenian democratic practices and the way Socrates' critique contains, at the same time, a partial confirmation of Athenian democracy. Though he would disagree with my conclusion, Dana Villa has a highly nuanced discussion of the "two" Socrates as they appear in "Thinking and Moral Considerations" and "Philosophy and Politics" in *Politics, Philosophy, Terror*.

8

The Eclipse of Thinking: An Arendtian Critique of Cooperative Learning

EDUARDO DUARTE

There are no dangerous thoughts. . . . Danger does not arise out of the Socratic conviction that the unexamined life is not worth living, but, on the contrary, out of the desire to find results that would make further thinking unnecessary. Thinking is equally dangerous to all creeds and, by itself, does not bring forth any new creed. Its most dangerous aspect from the viewpoint of common sense is that what was meaningful while you were thinking dissolves the moment you want to apply it to everyday living.

—Hannah Arendt, *The Life of the Mind*

Hannah Arendt reiterated over and over: "To the extent that I wish to think I have to withdraw from the world." Following Martin Heidegger, Arendt insisted that "thinking is always out of order," because the "sheer activity" of thinking only gets *under way* when the

so-called ordinary activities of everyday life are disrupted and interrupted. For Arendt, the life of the mind *(vita contemplativa)* is a
"solitary" yet an intradialogic experience that happens outside, or
beyond, the practical world of the everyday life *(vita activa)* one
shares with others.

Arendt's "purely" philosophical depiction of thinking is the basis
upon which this chapter offers a critique of pedagogical models
that seek to create communities of learning by advocating for peer-
mediated, group learning processes. These pedagogical models are
captured under the category of "cooperative learning." The critique
offered here is aimed at one of the fundamental assumptions of
cooperative learning: that learning is best achieved in the company
of others. This assumption, itself based upon a social constructivist
epistemology, has led to the implementation of pedagogical models
that suppress what Arendt calls the "urgent need to think" contemplatively. Because cooperative learning is structurally incompatible
with the event of *withdrawal* from the company of others, upon
which contemplation is based, the result is the eclipse of thinking.
In sum, I want to argue that cooperative learning models may be
creating conditions of "nonthinking."

Arendt insisted that the need to withdraw from the company of
others and, thereby, to "*stop* and think" is as much an integral part
of the human condition as the need to appear in the company of others, where one can be seen and see others, be heard and hear others.
As Agnes Heller writes: "Human beings labor, work and act; yet
they also withdraw from laboring, working and acting. Togetherness
and solitude comprise the 'human condition'" (1987, 282). For the
moment, cooperative learning advocates appear to be limited to a
one-dimensional perspective on the human condition.

The Foundations of Cooperative Learning

The current movement in cooperative learning was initiated in the
second half of the twentieth century by two important institutional
endeavors: the Cooperative Learning Center at the University of
Minnesota and the Center for Social Organization at Johns Hopkins

University.[1] Thus, for all intents and purposes, the current work in cooperative learning is part of a movement that began in the 1960s and culminated in the 1970s with the establishment of the Minnesota Cooperative Learning Center by David and Roger Johnson (Johnson and Johnson, 1975). Indeed, as Robert Slavin (1999) of Johns Hopkins reports:

> Cooperative learning is one of the greatest success stories in the history of educational innovation. Almost unknown in the mid-1970's, cooperative learning strategies are now so commonplace that they are often seen as a standard part of the educational practice, not as an innovation. One national survey (Puma et al., 1993) found that 79 percent of third grade teachers and 62 percent of seventh grade teachers reported making regular, sustained use of cooperative learning strategies. These numbers probably overstate the actual sustained use of cooperative learning, but they at least indicate extensive awareness of the term and positive attitudes toward it.

Advocates would concur with JoAnne Putnam when she insists that cooperative learning groups "promote high achievement and positive interpersonal outcomes, but only under certain conditions" (1993, 15). Drawing on "extensive research" (e.g., Johnson and Johnson, 1989; Slavin, 1999), cooperative learning theorists, like Putnam, argue that producing "high achievement" and other "positive outcomes" is dependent upon the creation of particular "conditions." Reflecting upon years of their own work, Johnson and Johnson have identified the five basic elements that augment these conditions of cooperative learning: positive interdependence, individual accountability, promotive interaction, appropriate use of social skills, and periodic processing of how to improve the effectiveness of the group (Johnson and Johnson, 1999). In a recent publication, the co-directors of the Minnesota project explain how the realization of these core elements is not unlike the intricate balancing act that produces an exceptional baseball team: "In baseball and in the classroom, it takes a cooperative effort. Extraordinary achievement comes from a cooperative group, not from the individualistic or competitive efforts of an isolated individual" (Johnson and Johnson, 1999, 67). However, as in baseball, the "game" of co-operative learning requires a particular "playing field." For cooperative learning advocates, *their* playing field (the educational context) is marked by the five basic elements listed above. Moreover, successful performance or "play" is dependent upon the participants "seeing" the raison d'être of the game. Within the game of cooperative learning, this means students must understand the purpose of *learning together*.

"Positive interdependence" is the essence of cooperative learning. It exemplifies the "teamwork" character of a classroom setting, where students are working together so that all are able to learn. The success or failure of cooperative learning is directly related to the commitment of "students to seek outcomes that are beneficial to all" (Johnson and Johnson, 1999, 68). Interestingly, Johnson and Johnson have discovered that students' commitment to cooperative learning is initiated by an *insight* into the purpose of learning together. Positive interdependence is inextricably linked to an initial and fundamental "perception" of human interrelatedness. Thus, in order for the "game" of cooperative learning to even begin, students must first perceive that "we are linked with others in a way that we cannot succeed unless they do. Their work benefits us and our work benefits them" (Johnson and Johnson, 1999, 70–71).

The "initial perception" premise requires that educators focus on constructing a setting that will heighten the "naturalness" of collaboration. Paradoxically, students are unable to have the initial perception, and will thereby remain uncommitted to interdependent learning, unless they have encountered an educational experience that is authentically cooperative. In other words, the commitment to enter into a mutual educational effort will come about only when students have experienced interactions that promote one another's success. For this reason, advocates of cooperative learning, like Johnson and Johnson, inevitably conclude that the initial perception must be initiated by carefully orchestrated experiences that stress the "positive" aspects of interdependence. An example of this is the New Pathways program at Harvard Medical School, where first-year medical students are placed on "teams" that are challenged to take a month and a half to solve a diagnostic problem with clinical and scientific implications (Bruffee, 1993). Other examples of programs that successfully produce the requisite initial perception have been documented by the researchers at Johns Hopkins (Slavin, 1999).

Despite "perception" being so central to the success of the model, cooperative learning theorists consistently stop short of examining, philosophically, why the perception of human interrelatedness emerges so readily and clearly. Instead, they collect ample "evidence" to demonstrate why and how increasing social interdependence among students will, necessarily, augment achievement (Slavin, 1996). Unfortunately, this research offers no philosophical descriptions of why students are so willing and able to learn together. Moreover, when "critique" is offered, it merely identifies implementation problems or the failure of educators to successfully orchestrate the cooperative learning experience. The initial perception is taken for granted, as if it were a "natural" response, and any "failures" to produce it are remedied by new implementation strategies. Such strategies will correct problems that, for example, may emerge when cooperative learning strategies reproduce inequities by not engaging students who are "low achieving" and/or "social isolates" (Cohen et al., 1999). In sum, advocates are seldom reticent about the failures that emerge when cooperative learning techniques are poorly "implemented." Yet, when offering constructive criticisms and pointing out the inevitable blind spots, they stop short of examining the more fundamental *philosophic* reasons for the "success" or "failure" of cooperative learning. Of course, it is not unusual for educational theorists who advocate on behalf of a model to stop short of exploring the ground of their model. Indeed, most embrace a set of philosophical assumptions uncritically and move forward with their "quantitative" and/or "qualitative" research. Cooperative learning advocates are no exception. They move forward from the unquestioned assumption that thinking is a socially mediated process.

All researchers rely upon a theoretical foundation that has, in the words of Thomas Kuhn (1970), established a "paradigm" of thought for them. Paradigms enable researchers to fine-tune their models, confident that the fundamental questions have been answered. In the case of cooperative learning researchers, those questions about thinking that are left unexamined have in no small way been built upon the work of Russian developmental psychologist L. S. Vygotsky (1896–1934). In his influential work *Thought and Language* (1962), Vygotsky claims that in the first years of life, human thought and speech develop as separate, parallel processes. At some point, the two processes synthesize and produce a new process: Speech and thought mutually enhance and dialectically develop each other (thought becomes verbal and speech becomes rational). Vygotsky's theory also claims that thinking, as a silent and "internal" dialogue, emerges much later in a child's development. Thus, the "inner speech" of contemplative thinking develops and evolves *from* communication, or "social speech."

Within the Vygotskyan model, social speech is considered to be primary. More than any other, it is this claim that contextualizes the assumptions and commitments of the cooperative learning theorists. For if the original source of thinking is indeed communicative action, then models like cooperative learning are, in essence, *recovering* our "original" ways of learning. This adds considerable weight to the assertions that (a) knowledge is "produced" through co-cognizing, and, therefore, (b) authentic learning *ought to be* a collaborative event, or an ongoing joint activity, where students are co-creating and co-problem-solving (Gutiérrez et al., 1999). Indeed, if Vygotsky's narrative is accepted, then the initial perception of human interrelatedness is, in some sense, a re-member-ing of the original synthesis of language and thought. Understood in this way, students readily and easily adapt to socially mediated learning because it invokes memories of their earliest learning experiences. The Vygotskyan narrative enables cooperative learning advocates to identify their model as "replaying" the event of early childhood development.

Vygotsky's developmental psychology provides the solid paradigm of support for cooperative learning researchers, practitioners, and theorists. Indeed, as Kenneth Bruffee asserts, it is Vygotsky who provides cooperative learning advocates with their ultimate epistemological foundation (Bruffee, 1993, 114). As Bruffee puts it, "we think because we can talk with one another," because "reflective thought is social conversation internalized." For theorists like Bruffee, Vygotsky is the basis upon which cooperative learning advocates can claim to have "reversed the common foundational understanding of the relationship between thought and conversation that has been eloquently stated in a recent defense of conversation as the mode of education at St. John's College: 'Conversation is the public complement to that original dialogue of the soul with itself that is called thinking'" (Bruffee, 1993, 113).

Following Vygotsky, cooperative learning theorists place priority on social speech. "Priority" is used here both in the sense of social speech being "initial," or of an earlier point in time, and in the sense of social speech having precedence and privilege. In both derivations, the implications are the same for inner speech: It is understood to be of minor importance—subordinate, auxiliary. The second-class status of contemplation within the cooperative learning paradigm is underlined in theoretic discussions like Bruffee's, which claim, with a conspicuous air of triumph, to be "reversing" the so-called traditional philosophical assumption that thinking is, first and foremost, a contemplative event or is the original dialogue of the soul *(psychê)*[2] with itself. Although it appears to go unnoticed by those working within the Vygotskyan paradigm, this reversal of the origin of thinking has problematic implications.

Arendt's Distinction
Between Thinking and Acting

In what follows, I want to use Hannah Arendt as the basis from which to contest the eclipse of thinking in cooperative learning. As I have already suggested, Arendt's discourse on "thinking" raises fundamental questions for the advocates of cooperative learning. Within the Arendtian discourse, it can be said that cooperative learning's "positive interdependence" is producing a nonphilosophical form of learning. My intention is not to contest the Vygotskyan foundations of cooperative learning by arguing that contemplation, or the inner dialogue, is prior or primary. On the contrary, it is not Vygotsky's narrative, but rather the reception of it that needs to be challenged. What needs to be challenged are those models of learning that leave no room for "inner speech" and, thus, appear to "infantilize" students by requiring them to constantly "speak their minds." I want to develop an Arendtian-inspired pedagogical discourse of thinking. This type of vocabulary might clear some discursive space for the articulation of alternative pedagogical models—namely, models seeking to "induce" a state of wonder *(thaumazein)* and produce the conditions for the possibility of doing philosophy in school. I will address these implications below after providing a reading of Arendt's discourse on thinking.

When we read Arendt within the context of a critique of cooperative learning, one that is attempting to draw attention to the model's "dismissal" of the traditional philosophical mode of thinking, we are compelled to emphasize Arendt's distinction between "thinking" and "acting." Interestingly, this distinction corresponds to the dichotomy cooperative learning theorists have made between "learning together" and "learning alone." Arendt was aware, particularly in her later work, that the distinction often implied the exile of contemplation. In fact, it is her admission of this gap in her work that led her to write profusely, at the end of her life, on the *vita contemplativa*. Throughout most of her writing, she ignored the life of the mind. This gap in her work is particularly evident in her most important text, *The Human Condition*. As she suggests in the comments below, Arendt was dissatisfied with the lack of attention she paid to the most "traditional" of philosophical topics and, in her last major work, wrote brilliantly on "thinking."

In November 1972, Hannah Arendt attended a conference in Toronto, Canada, that was organized by the Toronto Society for the Study of Social and Political Thought. "The Work of Hannah Arendt" was the conference title, and Arendt was asked to attend as the guest of honor. Arendt declined to attend as the honored guest because she preferred to attend as a participant in the debates and discussions. As Melvyn Hill writes: "In the course of numerous exchanges over the three days of the conference she spontaneously revealed aspects of her thinking and the style of her thinking in response to direct questions, or statements, or challenges, as well as in response to the papers read. Fortunately, we arranged to record the discussion with a view to later publication" (1979, 301). The edited transcript of the exchanges in Toronto indicates that many of the questions were aimed at Arendt's provocative distinction between thinking and acting. Participants protested out loud, and directly to Arendt, against her claim that the split between thinking and acting is "radical and complete" (Kohn, 1990, 124). The central concern was repeated: If thinking, as Arendt insisted over and over, is indeed a solitary activity, a silent dialogue that "I" have with "myself," where does this leave the philosopher who is focused on politics? What does this split mean for the identity of the political theorist who wants her writing and teaching to make a difference in the world of human affairs? Arendt's responses followed consistently from her distinction. An example is the exchange between Arendt and the well-known Canadian theorist of democracy C. B. Macpherson:

Macpherson: Is Miss Arendt really saying that to be a political theorist and to be engaged are incompatible? Surely not!

Arendt: No, but one is correct in saying that thinking and acting are not the same, and to the extent that I wish to think I have to withdraw from the world. I really believe that you can only act in concert and I really believe that you can only think by yourself. These are two entirely different—if you want to call it—*"existential"* positions. And to believe that there is any direct influence of theory on action insofar as theory is just a thought thing, that is, something thought out—I think that this is really not so and really will never be so. (Hill, 1979, 305)

Arendt's thinking/acting distinction was particularly provocative to the educators (professors) attending the conference. Like Macpherson, they believed that their work as teachers of political theory did not produce a performative contradiction. They rejected Arendt's distinction and insisted that their theorizing (i.e., lecturing, publications) was a form of political action that involved others (the audience/students, the reader). On this critique, Arendt appeared to stand her ground:

Macpherson: But to a political theorist and a teacher and a writer of political theory, teaching, or theorizing, *is* acting.

Arendt: Teaching is something else, and writing too. But thinking in
its purity is different—in this Aristotle was right. . . . You know, all
the modern philosophers have somewhere in their work a rather
apologetic sentence which says, "Thinking is also acting." Oh no,
it is not! And to say that is rather dishonest. I mean, let's face the
music: it is not the same! On the contrary, I have to keep back to a
large extent from participating, from commitment. (Hill, 1979,
304)

Despite the chorus of disapproval, Arendt reiterated the claim that
she had held throughout her work: Thinking is a solitary, apolitical
endeavor that happens apart from practical affairs of everyday life.
To the extent that one is thinking, one has withdrawn from the company of others. Of course, her comment that "teaching is something
else" is very pertinent to this essay, and I will return to it below, in
my concluding section, where I explore some pedagogical implications of Arendt's discourse on thinking.

Although she consistently maintained that there was a radical and
complete distinction between thinking (alone) and acting (with others), Arendt admitted to being slightly inconsistent in her treatment
of the distinction throughout her career. During the course of one of
her statements at the Toronto conference, Arendt acknowledged her
inconsistency when she expressed a revealing self-critique of her
book *The Human Condition,* the very work that spurred debate
over her thinking/acting distinction: "The main flaw and mistake of
The Human Condition is the following: I still look at what is called
in the tradition the *vita activa* from the viewpoint of the *vita contemplativa,* without ever saying anything real about the *vita contemplativa*" (Hill, 1979, 305).

This commentary demonstrates Arendt admitting that she had focused on political action to the detriment of the philosophical life of
contemplation. She reiterated this point in the preface to her *Life of
the Mind.* There Arendt locates her goals for the later text as emerging from her doubts about the thinking/acting dichotomy she had articulated in *The Human Condition.* In reflecting on the earlier text,
she writes: "I was, however, aware that one could look at this matter
[the *vita activa* versus *vita contemplativa*] from an altogether differ-

ent viewpoint, and to indicate my doubts I ended this study of active life with a curious sentence Cicero [*De Republica*, I, 17] ascribed to Cato" (Arendt, 1978, 7). Again, in Toronto, when discussing the flaw of *The Human Condition*, Arendt affirms that

> the fundamental experience of the thinking ego is in those lines of the older Cato which I quote at the end of the book [*The Human Condition*]: "When I do nothing I am most active and when I'm all by myself, I am the least alone." (It is very interesting that Cato said this!) This is an experience of sheer activity unimpeded by any physical or bodily obstacles. But the moment you begin to act, you deal with the world, and you are constantly falling over your own feet, so to speak, and then you carry your body—and, as Plato said: "The body wants to be taken care of and to hell with it!"

In the next breath, Arendt went on to say that "I am trying to write about this. And I would take off from this business of Cato. But I am not ready to tell you about it" (Hill, 1979, 305–306). Of course, she was referring to her writing of *The Life of the Mind*.

Besides providing us with some insights into the evolution of Arendt's philosophical writing, these comments are quite relevant to the criticism being raised against the model of cooperative learning. Arendt is, after all, suggesting that thinking had been ignored, and perhaps eclipsed, in her writings. If this reading of her self-critique is permitted, then Arendt's attempt to pay heed to thinking will clear the way for those models of learning that may be seeking to "induce" a state of wonder and produce the conditions for the possibility of doing philosophy in school.

In the next section, I will offer a close textual analysis—indeed, an exegesis—of important sections from Arendt's *The Life of the Mind*. In offering this close reading, I have two objectives. The first is to situate Arendt's discourse on thinking within the paradoxical statement Cicero (106–43 B.C.E.) attributed to the Roman statesman and sometimes philosopher Cato (234–139 B.C.E.). These "tantalizing ambiguous lines from Cato" (Hansen, 1993, 197) represent an important heuristic for reading Arendt's discourse on thinking and symbolize an important transition in her work.[3] Indeed, Cato's aphorism appears prominently both at the conclusion of *The Human Condition* and as an epigraph to *The Life of the Mind*. Cato's lines enable us to identify the characteristics of thinking that Arendt considered to be central. The most important of these is the depiction of thinking as a withdrawal from the world of public affairs and the everyday experiences of "political" life. In turn, by reading Arendt through Cato, my second objective is to specify the experience that is being eclipsed in most schools. I am contending that the *need* to withdraw, in order to stop and think, is being repressed or ignored by many educational theories and practices, specifically those that are emphasizing the ethico-political potential of schooling. In some sense, the theories that privilege cooperative learning and action are more consistent with the "early" Arendt. Thus, my exegesis implies reading the "later" Arendt's recovery of the *vita contemplativa* against the "early" Arendt's imbalanced attention to the *vita activa*.

Cato's Aphorism

Numquam se plus agere quam nihil cum ageret, numquam minus solum esse quam solus esset. [Never is one more active than when one does nothing; never is one less alone than when one is by oneself.]

In the first part of his aphorism, Cato inverts the Greco-Roman propensity to view activity as *praxis*. The etymological root of the English word "activity" is located in the Latin *activa*. The Latin term signifies action, as expressed in the Greek term *praxis:* making, fabricating, acting in and through a common world shared by others. However, the phonetic root of the Greek term is all that remains when *activa* is translated as "practical." The meaning of "practical," as we would use the term today, is totally foreign to the term *praxis,* or what Arendt understood, in its essential meaning, to express the ways human beings create or construct a common world. Through *praxis,* according to Arendt, we create "our" world, a world that simultaneously gathers (unifies) us together as one and separates (distinguishes) each of us as individuals. Upon first glance, pedagogical models like cooperative learning recover some of the meaning of *praxis*. Whereas the category of "positive interdependence" overemphasizes the moment of gathering, or the unifying capacity of *praxis*, the result is that the model provides a counterweight, within schools, to the general ethos of individualism that is rooted in the "ideal" of practicality.

The contemporary term "practical," a category denoting a host of values (prudence, efficiency, etc.), is a vestige of John Locke's principle of "wisdom," or an individual's ability to manage "business ably and with foresight in this world" (Locke, 1996, 60). Locke's principle applies to the individual whose private needs and concerns do not remain "at home." Under the guiding influence of wisdom, the Lockean individual takes his needs to the marketplace and satisfies them within a space inhabited by others but no longer shared as a common world. In an important sense, Locke's wisdom, as the ethical principle underlining modern individualism, represents the rupture between the contemporary notion of practical (the individual's ability to manage his affairs) and the ancient notion of *praxis* (the activity through which individuals create a common world). It seems that the model of cooperative learning is located somewhere in between the discourses that are organized, respectively, around *praxis* and practicality.

Although Cato does not tell us exactly what he is up to when he is "doing nothing," it is clear that whatever it is he is doing is happening when he is by himself. That is, it is happening when he is not with others in what his contemporaries would have called the "common world" and we would call "society." Again, a paradoxical inversion: One is least alone when one is with oneself and nobody else. How are we to grasp the significance of that "activity" that produces no-thing? Perhaps if we follow Cato's retreat, or withdrawal, from the company of others, we will see how thinking gets under way. If we take a moment, we might explore the way of Cato's retreat from the company of his peers to the company of himself—exploring his way, not in the sense of his pathway or route, but as a *manner,* that is, as an *action*. To begin with this sort of description is, consequently, to begin the process of describing thinking as a process, because the act of withdrawing is now identified as the "first" moment of thinking. However, the act does not constitute thinking itself, for in withdrawing, one is merely "on the way" toward thinking. Still, in some sense, thinking begins in the first instance of withdrawing. So perhaps one should say that thinking is "under way" from the moment we have taken leave of the political or public realm of interdependence. But how does thinking get under way? What initiates this first moment, this turning?

As a fragment of thought, the aphorism is the most poetic of all forms of philosophical expression. This means it provides the most room for interpretation, and, for many, it is the quintessential invitation for contemplation. However, if we seek detail, we must look elsewhere, and this is precisely what Arendt did when attempting to describe how thinking gets going. Ironically, she turned to one of very few philosophers about whom much has been written but who wrote nothing himself: Socrates. Socrates, of course, exemplifies many of the issues Arendt confronted. Indeed, he embodied the thinking/acting dichotomy and the tension between philosophy and politics (Arendt, 1990). For Arendt, Socrates was the exemplar; as Heller reminds us, "with the sole exception of Socrates, no philosopher adequately satisfies her criteria of 'pure thinking'" (1987, 283). Thus, it is not surprising that Arendt identified Socrates as the one who best illustrated that thinking gets under way when the so-called ordinary activities of practical life are disrupted or interrupted. She writes: "The best illustration of this may still be—as the story goes—Socrates' habit of suddenly 'turning his mind to himself,' breaking off all company, and taking up his position wherever he happened to be, 'deaf to all entreaties' to continue with whatever he had been doing before" (Arendt, 1978, 97).

From this perspective, thinking gets under way when the *vita activa* is interrupted. What causes the interruption of practical life? What leads one to be, like Socrates, suddenly turned toward oneself? There is, of course, no one answer, but the example of Socrates is helpful. By all accounts, Socrates didn't have much choice in the matter. He didn't just decide to disengage and disconnect or to willingly turn off (the crowd) and tune in (to his inner voice). On the contrary, Socrates, as we know from Plato's dialogues, appears to have been constantly interrupted by the voice of a *daimon* (spirit) that drew him away from everyday life. If one is uncomfortable with talk of spirits and demigods, one might interpret this spirit's voice as Socrates' gnawing memory of his infamous encounter with the Oracle of Delphi. For us, it is perhaps more comfortable to code the *daimon* as "the echo" of the Oracle's pronouncement that "Socrates is the wisest of all." By Socrates' own account, it was the Oracle's message from the gods, relayed to him by his friend Chaerephon (*Apology*, 21a), that spurred him on his tragic quest for (dis)confirmation. He doubted the pronouncement because he understood himself to be "ignorant," or knowing nothing, and sought to prove the Oracle mistaken by finding one person who was truly wise. Thus, Socrates, the philosopher par excellence, was put under way by the "voice" of the Oracle. It is a cruel irony that we learn the details of Socrates' encounter with this voice when he speaks in his own defense at the trial of his life. Indeed, the fact that his "disruptive nature"—being a thinker—was understood to be transgressive of the Athenian public life is relevant to my critique of cooperative learning models. For the Socratic way represents a threat to any context that favors consensus over contestation.

The withdrawal that Socrates seems to have perfected was instigated by a need or desire to experience the paradoxical solitude without loneliness. This is the meaning of the second part of Cato's maxim: *"numquam minus solum esse quam solus esset,"* never is one less alone than when one is by oneself. One is never alone when one has retreated to the place of thinking: One is *with* oneself. According to Arendt, "Socrates would have said: The self, too, is a kind of friend" (Arendt, 1978, 189). Because the solitary experience of thinking does not produce loneliness, nor the more dramatic "abandonment" or negation of consciousness that is expressed in mystical writings, one might describe the withdrawal as positive independence.

An Arendtian-Inspired Pedagogy of Contemplation

As I have suggested throughout this essay, Arendt offers us a vocabulary for developing models of teaching and learning that preserve and cultivate a space for contemplation. Arendt's discourse on thinking represents something of a "sanctuary" for the life of the mind. Here, after retracing Cato's retreat, I would like to suggest that the withdrawal, the preparation for thinking, could be translated into a pedagogy that aims to get thinking under way by orchestrating experiences of positive independence. "Positive independence" refers to experiences that privilege a student's desire and capacity to work independently and, more importantly, reflectively. Such experiences would, of course, stand in contrast to, but not necessarily conflict with, cooperative learning's teamwork pedagogy of "positive interdependence." Indeed, a pedagogy of contemplation would be counterproductive if it inspired the self-centered individualism that cooperative learning advocates rightly criticize. Nevertheless, whereas the latter seeks to have students work as a team, an Arendtian-inspired pedagogy of contemplation would challenge educators to identify ways to exhort students to stop and think by themselves.

Thinking happens, Cato indicates, when the human being withdraws from the world. Thinking, properly speaking, cannot occur when one is "in the world," immersed in the business of everyday life, or compelled to "think" through and with others. On the contrary, thinking gets under way only when everyday life is interrupted and the thinker turns away, habitually, from the "shared" space of the common world. As Heidegger says:

> Once we are so related and drawn to what withdraws, we are drawing into what withdraws, into the enigmatic and therefore mutable nearness of its appeal. Whenever man is properly drawing that way, he is thinking—even though he may still be far away from what withdraws, even though the withdrawal may remain as veiled as ever. All through his life and right into his death, Socrates did nothing else than place himself into this draft, this current, and maintain himself in it. This is why he is the purest thinker of the West. This is why he wrote nothing. (Heidegger, 1968, 17)

Perhaps if we consider the example of Socrates, we will understand withdrawal as an activity that is perfected through practice. With Socrates as our model, we see that the act of withdrawing, the first moment of thinking, is not a spontaneous reaction, but a *prac-*

ticed activity—that is, an activity that is habitually repeated. The withdrawal is something akin to an exercise, a preparation for thinking itself. The disruption, the turning away, is a rehearsal. But it is a rehearsal unfolding in re-hearing: a habit of listening to an exhortation that interrupts the business of everyday life. Understood in this way, the withdrawal could be translated into a pedagogy that is consciously engaged in getting thinking under way by orchestrating experiences of positive independence. Such a pedagogy would enable students to develop a "habit" of contemplation, of thinking *by-* and *for-oneself*. Through traditional (e.g., journal writing) and nontraditional (yoga, meditation) methods, teachers could develop ways to encourage students to enter into dialogue with themselves and thereby concentrate on being in touch with their own desires and hopes. A pedagogy of contemplation, therefore, would echo the voice of the Delphic Oracle and exhort students to "stop and think" in order to take up the most challenging yet pressing of learning assignments: Know thyself!

Arendt herself provides us with examples of how this might be done. Indeed, as she stated in one of her responses to Macpherson, "Teaching is something else, and writing too." If we look to her writings, as I have done throughout this essay, Arendt herself demonstrates how one can get thinking under way through textual analysis. The dialogue between reader and author is an example of how thinking is aroused. For Arendt, thinking is initiated, first and foremost, through a dialogue one has with a text of philosophy. As Heller tells us:

> Arendt elucidates the categories of the life of the mind by presenting and interpreting *philosophies* she regarded as *representative*. We would be misled by this way of elucidation, should we fail to pay due attention to the author's intention. In Arendt's view, it is not philosophers who practice thinking . . . in the first place: we all do so. Moreover, pure thinking, as Arendt understands it, is rather under-represented in the history of philosophy. Indeed with the sole exception of Socrates, no philosopher adequately satisfies her criteria of "pure thinking.". . . More importantly, philosophy makes us think about thinking, willing, and judging. These philosophies are arsenals of a va-

riety of ideas we should, if critically, rely on in embarking upon the discovery of the life of the mind. (1987, 283)

With regard to teaching, beyond the accounts we receive from her students, we know that Arendt identified her own teaching in Socratic terms. She tells us her goal was to produce a "kind of thought, which I try not to indoctrinate, but to rouse or to awaken in my students" (Hill, 1979, 309). This description echoes those autobiographical statements offered by Socrates in his defense when he says, "I rouse you. I persuade you. I upbraid you. I never stop lighting on each one of you, everywhere, all day long" (*Apology*, 30d–31a). What is important to understand is that, in both cases, in her writing and in her Socratic teaching, Arendt was herself constantly "on the way" to the place of thinking. She was herself aroused by the desire to think, exhorted on by the "voices" of the philosophers whose ideas, once removed from the arsenal, she "heard" like so many pyrotechnical explosions.

An Arendtian-inspired pedagogy would insist that educators take up the difficult challenge of "empowering" students to learn on their own. Models like cooperative learning, of course, have taken an important step toward redistributing power within classroom settings. With these models, the educator no longer monopolizes the processes of learning. But, as I have argued, these peer-mediated models appear to be structurally incapable of liberating students to withdraw from the company of their classmates. On the contrary, an Arendtian-inspired pedagogy would embrace Heidegger's challenge to teach in the sense of to let learn:

> True. Teaching is even more difficult than learning. We know that; but we rarely think about it. And why is teaching more difficult than learning? Not because the teacher must have a larger store of information, and have it always read. Teaching is more difficult than learning because what teaching calls for is this: to let learn. The real teacher, in fact, lets nothing else be learned than—learning. (Heidegger, 1968, 15)

From the perspective of practical life and mainstream schooling, philosophical thinking and independent learning are, indeed, out of order. When we evaluate this "doing nothing" from the economy of everyday life and locate it "nowhere," it is obvious that this activity, thinking, is out of order and not part of the regular flow of human activities that spring from the fundamental needs (sleep, shelter, clothing, food). Of course, if we reflect on Socrates' story, we will probably arrive at the conclusion, with Arendt (and Plato), that the philosophical way of life is itself an interruption of or an intrusion upon the practical life of everyday affairs. It is unwelcome and, as Arendt wrote, "always out of order." But then the tragic life of Socrates points me back to question an underlying premise of this essay: If the *vita contemplativa* is a disruption upon the life of "ordinary activities," why must school life, after all, take on the characteristics of everyday life? Should it not be that "practicality" is out of order within that context where "thinking" *must* be taught?

Because the understanding of activity as "being busy" is so dominant in contemporary life, it is nearly impossible to have access to a language that would enable one to understand doing nothing as "producing" an authentic learning experience of the highest order. And this is why Arendt's retrieval of Cato is interesting for the philosophy of education. Through Arendt's reading of Cato, we are able to reflect upon and perhaps defend the role of philosophy—that is, thinking or contemplation—within the school-life experience. Through her reading of Cato, we might begin to articulate a language by which we could name, and thereby identify as significant, the activity of noninvolvement with others that unfolds when an individual has withdrawn from the hustle and bustle of the crowd (e.g., the classroom). Of course, to claim that this experience is "significant" is not to prioritize the experience or to privilege it. As I stated above, my intention is not to contest the foundations of models like cooperative learning by arguing that contemplation, or the inner dialogue, is prior or primary. What needs to be challenged is the one-dimensionality of dialogic models of learning that leave little or no room for "inner speech." Thus, in the end, perhaps advocates and sympathetic critics of cooperative learning need to stop and think about what Socrates, according to Arendt, discovered about the reciprocity between "social" and "inner" dialogic communication:

What Socrates discovered was that we can have intercourse with ourselves, as well as with others, and that the two kinds of intercourse are somehow interrelated. Aristotle, speaking about friendship, remarked: "The friend is another self"—meaning: you can carry on the dialogue of thought with him just as well as with yourself. This is still in the Socratic tradition, except that Socrates would have said: The self, too, is a kind of friend. The guiding experience in these matters is, of course, friendship and not selfhood; I first talk with others before I talk with myself, examining whatever the joint talk may have been about, and then discover that I can conduct a dialogue not only with others but with myself as well. (Arendt, 1978, 188–189)

If thinking is indeed "sheer activity," then Cato's statement serves to challenge the belief, so foundational within the contemporary school setting, that human activity is best actualized when people are in the company of others. This belief grounds the assumption that learning "naturally" occurs in practical life activities. However, models of learning that are built upon this assumption may, unwittingly, reproduce the epistemic conditions that have traditionally dominated public schooling in the United States. Hence, when cooperative learning advocates move forward, uncritically, from the "fact" that schools are socially mediated learning contexts, their preferential model for schools appears as a mere reorganization of those contexts where a student is compelled to be with others. However, it is precisely the "givenness" of schooling as a social learning context that must be questioned, and ultimately contested, if cooperative learning advocates desire to produce the ethico-political goals they seek—namely, voice (not silence), community (not individualism), and mutual recognition (not competition).

To conclude this essay, I want to invite advocates of cooperative learning models to consider the following questions: If teaching and learning "how to think" are fundamental aims of schooling, what happens if and when we take seriously Arendt's depiction of "thinking" as a solitary activity that involves a retreat of the singular ego back into a silent dialogue with itself? Can this event of thinking be accommodated by the peer-mediated models of schooling that are currently dominating our schools? Indeed, if thinking requires withdrawal from the world, how is this possible in school, where students are thrown together with others and are constantly "learning" among a crowd of others? Finally, what are the implications if, as Arendt concluded, the activity of thinking is "among the conditions that make [people] abstain from evil-doing or even actually 'condition' them against it?" (Arendt, 1978, 5). In other words, by restraining this fundamental desire, are cooperative learning models in jeopardy of (re)producing a generation of "nonthinkers" who are incapable of making ethical judgments?

Notes

1. Within the literature on cooperative learning, a typical genealogical narrative will indicate that the progenitors of the contemporary models of cooperative teaching and learning were late-eighteenth-century English and Anglo-American educators. Such narratives will, perhaps, inform us that one Colonel Francis Parker, superintendent of public schools in Quincy, Massachusetts, in the later part of the nineteenth century, "was a strong advocate of cooperative learning." Dewey is, of course, mentioned for having "promoted" the cooperative "form" of learning throughout the first half of the twentieth century (Steiner et al., 1999). In addition to providing "thin" genealogies, the literature on cooperative learning consistently limits the "origins" of the current paradigm within the parameters of Anglo-American school history and, thus, fails to explore how indigenous (i.e., pre-Columbian) educational models may have directly or indirectly influenced the development of cooperative learning models in the United States. Such omissions are problematic and, perhaps, conflict with some of the ethico-political norms of cooperative learning, for example, "openness," "pluralism," and "dialogue." At minimum, exploratory work is required to demonstrate the analogies between indigenous and colonial cooperative learning models and recognition (cf. Churchill, 1982; Deloria, 1982; and O'Meara and West, 1996).

2. When writing within the Arendtian discourse, one needs to be careful when describing thinking as an event of the soul. The "soul" that is being described in the St. John's College quotation does not necessarily correspond to Arendt's understanding of "soul." As Agnes Heller reminds us, Arendt "accepts the traditional division of the human self into *mind, soul,* and *body* while relegating emotions to the soul and the aforementioned three faculties [thinking, willing, judging] to the mind" (Heller, 1987, 282).

3. Although I do not have the space to develop the argument here, I would contend that Arendt's later work represents an attempt to recover the philosophical discourse she had experienced as a student in Heidegger's seminars. See Arendt's essay "Martin Heidegger at Eighty," *New York Review of Books,* October 1971. Margaret Canovan (1990) offers an excellent essay that is germane to this issue.

References

Arendt, Hannah. 1973. *The Human Condition*. Chicago: University of Chicago Press.

_____. 1978. *The Life of the Mind*. San Diego: HBJ Books.

_____. 1990. "Philosophy and Politics." *Social Research*, vol. 57, no. 1 (Spring): 73–104.

Bishop, Donald H., ed. 1995. *Mysticism and the Mystical Experience East and West*. Selinsgrove, PA: Susquehanna University Press.

Bruffee, Kenneth A. 1993. *Collaborative Learning: Higher Education, Interdependence, and the Authority of Knowledge*. Baltimore: Johns Hopkins University Press.

Canovan, Margaret. 1990. "Socrates or Heidegger? Hannah Arendt's Reflections on Philosophy and Politics." *Social Research*, vol. 57, no. 1 (Spring): 135–166.

Caputo, John D. 1982. *Heidegger and Aquinas: An Essay on Overcoming Metaphysics*. New York: Fordham University Press.

Cohen, Elizabeth, Rachel A. Lotan, Beth A. Scarloss, and Adele R. Arellano. 1999. "Complex Instruction: Equity in Cooperative Learning Classrooms." *Theory into Practice*, vol. 38, no. 2 (Spring): 80–86.

Churchill, Ward. 1982. "White Studies: The Intellectual Imperialism of Contemporary U.S. Education." *Integateducation*, vol. 19, nos. 1–2.

Deloria, Vine, Jr. 1982. "Education and Imperialism." *Integateducation*, vol. 19, nos. 1–2.

Gutiérrez, Kris, Patricia Baquendo-López, Héctor H. Alvarez, and Ming Ming Chiu. 1999. "Building a Culture of Collaboration Through Hybrid Language Practices." *Theory into Practice*, vol. 38, no. 2 (Spring): 87–93.

Hansen, Phillip. 1993. *Hannah Arendt: Politics, History, Citizenship*. Stanford: Stanford University Press.

Heidegger, Martin. 1968. *What Is Called Thinking?* trans. J. Glenn Gray and F. Wieck. New York: Harper & Row.

Heller, Agnes. 1987. "Hannah Arendt on the 'Vita Contemplativa.'" *Philosophy and Social Criticism* (Fall): 282–296.

Hill, Melvyn A. 1979. *Hannah Arendt: The Recovery of the Public World*. New York: St. Martin's Press.

Johnson, D. W., and R. T. Johnson. 1975. *Learning Together and Alone: Cooperation, Competition, and Individualization*. Englewood Cliffs, NJ: Prentice-Hall.

_____. 1989. *Cooperation and Competition: Theory and Research*. Edina, MN: Interaction Book Co.

_____. 1994. *Leading the Cooperative School*. 2nd ed. Edina, MN: Interaction Book Co.

_____. 1998a. *Advanced Cooperative Learning.* 3rd ed. Edina, MN: Interaction Book Co.

_____. 1998b. *Cooperation in the Classroom.* 7th ed. Edina, MN: Interaction Book Co.

_____. 1999. "Making Cooperative Learning Work." *Theory into Practice,* vol. 38, no. 2 (Spring).

Kohn, Jerome. 1990. "Thinking/Acting." *Social Research,* vol. 57, no. 1 (Spring): 105–134.

Kuhn, Thomas. 1970. *The Structures of Scientific Revolutions.* Chicago: University of Chicago Press.

Locke, John. 1996. "Some Thoughts Concerning Education" (excerpt). In Ronald F. Reed and Tony W. Johnson, *Philosophical Documents in Education.* New York: Longman.

O'Meara, Sylvia, and Douglas West. 1996. *From Our Eyes: Learning from Indigenous Peoples.* Toronto: Garamond Press.

Puma, M. J., C. C. Jones, D. Rock, and R. Fernandez. 1993. *Prospects: The Congressionally Mandated Study of Educational Growth and Opportunity* (interim report). Bethesda, MD: Abt Associates.

Putnam, JoAnne W. 1993. "The Process of Cooperative Learning." *Cooperative Learning and Strategies for Inclusion: Celebrating Diversity in the Classroom,* ed. JoAnne W. Putnam. Baltimore: Paul H. Brookes Publishing, pp. 15–40.

Slavin, Robert E. 1996. "Research on Cooperative Learning and Achievement: What We Know and What We Need to Know." *Contemporary Educational Psychology,* vol. 21: 43–69.

_____. 1999. "Comprehensive Approaches to Cooperative Learning." *Theory into Practice,* vol. 38, no. 2 (Spring).

Steiner, Sue, Layne K. Stromwall, Karen Gerdes, and Stephanie Brzuzy. 1999. "Using Cooperative Learning Strategies in Social Work Education." *Journal of Social Work Education,* vol. 35, no. 2: 253–264.

Vlastos, Gregory. 1995. *Studies in Greek Philosophy II: Socrates and Plato and Their Tradition.* Princeton: Princeton University Press.

Vygotsky, L. S. 1962. *Thought and Language.* Cambridge, MA: MIT Press.

_____. 1978. *Mind in Society: The Development of Higher Psychological Processes.* Cambridge, MA: Harvard University Press.

9

What and How We Learned from Hannah Arendt: An Exchange of Letters

ELISABETH YOUNG-BRUEHL
AND JEROME KOHN

8.23.99
Dear Jerry,
I am delighted that you want to take up Professor Gordon's proposal that we write an essay for his anthology on Hannah Arendt and education. And delighted, too, that you like the idea of an epistolary essay, an essay by mail, a contribution constructed long distance but with this miraculous conversation-like quick back-and-forth. For the thirty years we have known each other, we have had to depend on our abilities to get to the same place to talk about Hannah Arendt and her ideas and about the way in which she educated us, both when we were her students and after her death, while I wrote her biography and then you edited her papers, while we read and reread her books. This epistolary exchange is a completely startling possibility, and I wouldn't be surprised if it has an effect on how we talk.

And I think this new communication possibility should be one part of what we talk about, too.

But we can come back to this. Let me start us off by stating in a capsule form the topic we agreed to consider. Is there, so we put it, a kind of education that is particularly suited to prepare people for understanding politics? Hannah Arendt's essay "Understanding and Politics" presents her vision of how understanding and politics are—or can be—related; we want to ask about how a person can be educated for "understanding," in the sense she gave to that rich word.

Our topic is the relation—or relations—between education and politics. But we should, I think, acknowledge right away that Hannah Arendt thought about education, which, for her, was certainly not the same thing as teaching or instructing in skills, from two fundamentally different angles. First, she considered the education of children, and in those passages, she always stressed that the human condition that is crucially involved is natality, the fact that children are born as "new beginnings," born to rejuvenate and renew the world. Their education must foster them in this essential function. She insisted, then, that children should be educated conservatively, in the sense that they are introduced to the past that is conserved for them, as their legacy; it orients and grounds them as their education takes them from the shelter of their private, familial lives into the public world. Being educated is being protected by responsible adults who have the authority to shape the child's transitional growth into the world.

Adult education is altogether different. The human condition crucially involved in it is worldliness. Adults educate one another to be in the world, which, in varying historical circumstances, may mean to be at home in the world, or to be alienated from it, or some mixture of these modes. In the modern world, adults do not conservatively give one another a shared tradition, they have to make a common world. In the wreckage of shared traditions, they read traditional authors, for example, "as though nobody had read them before."

This adult education, which is the education that adults can offer one another, can be a preparation for political understand-

ing if it promotes what Hannah Arendt, following Kant, called "enlarged mentality." You learn to put yourself in another's place and see the world—through your own eyes—from there. That Arendt considered this the key education for political understanding was apparent in the first course we took with her, back in 1969. It was called "Politics in the Twentieth Century," and it was designed with readings that allowed you to follow the life of a "representative man" from his birth around 1900 up through the sixties. A man of her generation—like her husband, Heinrich Bluecher, who had been a worker, a member of the Sparticist Bund, a refugee and stateless person, a wartime correspondent, a college teacher.

As I recall this seminar, it seems to me that what we were doing was focusing on this "representative man" as an exemplary man. He was experiencing the twentieth century as a century of crises; and each crisis revealed to him an essential human condition in a new context. All the essays in Between Past and Future *are like this, too: Each one identifies a crisis—like "The Crisis in Education," "The Crisis in Culture." Each essay then delves down into the crisis, making distinctions right and left, to get to one or more of the human conditions Arendt had identified in* The Human Condition—*life, earth, world, natality, mortality, plurality—and the activities relevant to those conditions: action, work, labor. She then studies how the conditions have changed in relation to one another, as the crisis makes clear. "The Crisis in Education" that she analyzes shows not only that Johnny cannot read, but how adults have—she thinks—given over their responsibilities for educating children, which means for responding to children as "new beginnings," for responding to children's natality. The crisis of education turns out to be a crisis of natality, and one would understand this if one were able to put oneself in the place of a contemporary child.*

The education Arendt practiced, I'm suggesting, was designed to show one how to imagine an exemplary figure as a kind of crossroads where one can see elementary human conditions in flux, reconfiguring. These exemplary lives, then, are like parables. I think Hannah Arendt operated this way from the first book she wrote, where Rahel Varnahagen exemplifies a vast shift in relations between the private realm and the public realm—the emergence of society as an intermediary realm. She plays an exemplary role, again, in The Origins of Totalitarianism, *which is a book replete with exemplary figures—Disraeli, Proust, Cecil Rhodes—each of whom allows you to see down into the historical depths, the places where political processes are brewing. Many social scientists, of course, look down their noses at Arendt's method as anecdotal. But she, I think, thought that the well-chosen anecdote was worth a thousand statistics or citations or evidences.*

Let's see what this preliminary set of remarks provokes in you, and we'll go from there, my dear,

Elisabeth

June 11, 2000
Dear Elisabeth,

When you wrote to me at the end of August last year, I was, as you know, just starting up the Hannah Arendt Center at New School University. That work was and continues to be exhilarating, but it also proved so demanding that I kept putting off answering you. At the same time, I was well aware that I should respond. Part of the purpose of the center is educational, and I thought our correspondence might help elucidate that. But in addition, I felt a real sense of chagrin, due to the fact that of all the contributors to this volume, only you and I had actually studied with Arendt. That experience was formative for both of us, no doubt in distinct ways, which in itself, I thought, might be of interest to readers. Subsequently, we have both had occasion to work formally with Arendt's thought—and in your case, with the story of her life as well—but what seemed most important to me is the fact that we have continuously talked about her during all the many years of our friendship. We have done that because we wanted to, such conversations affording us a real and rare pleasure. That pleasure has something to do with the way Arendt educated us and something to do with politics, and

I thought that in our correspondence, those "somethings" might become clear, just as they have achieved a measure of clarity in our talk itself. The attempt to communicate the pleasure of having studied with Arendt, of having known her, and of still encountering her, so to speak, between us as a presence in our ongoing conversation seems to me something that ought not to be left out of this volume. It has been our experience, and if further justification were needed, one might cite Arendt's conviction that thought not only arises from experience, but that "the ground of experience," as she once put it, is what keeps thought from becoming lost in "all kinds of theories." It is likely that most of the essays in this volume will assume, quite naturally, that Arendt had a theory of education. Hence my chagrin.

Forgive me if I approach this matter indirectly, but you are used to that! I want to ask you if you think Arendt had or held to a theory of anything—of totalitarianism or politics, or of action or revolution, or of society or culture or education, or of authority or religion or history, or of human freedom, or of the distinct temporal dimensions of the activities of the human mind? Those are certainly among the topics that engaged her, but did she formulate anything that could be called a "theory" of them, either individually or cumulatively? That she theorized them is obvious, but the distinction between theorizing, "thinking," and a theory that can be stated as its outcome seems to me to have been crucial for her. In fact, the blurring of that distinction is among the shibboleths of modern thought that Arendt increasingly came to question, precisely because a finely tuned appreciation of common, communicable experience, the experience of a common world, tends to vanish in that blurring.

To give a single example of what I am driving at—one of Arendt's own examples—Karl Marx resolved the old and vexed matter of the relation of theory to practice in terms of his own dialectical theory of the laws of economic development. He achieved this at the cost, according to Arendt, of ignoring the spontaneity of action in his conception of human praxis. Although Marx's theory did not cause totalitarianism, the ideological use made of it was a significant element in Stalin's determi-

nation to destroy human spontaneity—that is, human free-dom—the only guarantee of a common world. Part of Arendt's attempt to comprehend and reveal Stalin's crimes for what they were lies in theorizing the activities of acting and thinking, but she rejects any attempt to solve the riddle of their relation by uniting them in a theory different from Marx's. There are many indications that, in her own way, she intended to deal with that relation in the book on Judging that she did not live to write. How that might have turned out we cannot know; but we do know that, for Arendt, judging is an activity different from either acting or thinking, and we can be pretty certain that she would have theorized it without fitting it into a theory. The potential danger to human freedom implicit in the finality of any theory, however well or even nobly intentioned it may be, is, I believe, what she assiduously avoided.

That last statement stands in need of explication, but for now, let me just cite another of Arendt's own examples. To formulate a coherent theory of justice would seem to be a worthwhile philosophical endeavor, one with Platonic roots but also current today, and at worst a harmless one. Would it not be worthwhile to know the truth of what we are talking about when we talk about justice? Would not such knowledge instruct us how to deal with injustice when it occurs, even if it does little to prevent injustice from occurring? But Arendt suggests something quite different. If we knew what justice was, then theoretically we could construct a great grid to lay over all possible human actions, informing us whether they are just or not. A certain amount of calculation might still be necessary, but we would no longer have to think about the meaning of justice. Insofar as philosophers from Plato to John Rawls make us think, well and good, but if the outcome of such thought were to be taken as knowledge and institutionalized, then not totalitarianism but what Arendt calls a "tyranny of reason," which would also be a denial of freedom, would result. Is not the point of justice to be just ("What I do is me . . . the just man justices," as Gerard Manly Hopkins wrote)? Arendt is convinced that it is not knowing what justice is, but rather thinking about justice, culminat-

ing in the individual act of judgment, that lets justice appear in the world. For her, this is what Socrates, the purest of thinkers, taught others by his own example: His discussions not only of justice but of all human excellences ended not in theories but in perplexity (aporia), *so that he had to go on thinking about them, becoming ever more just, more courageous, more self-controlled—in short, more himself than he was before. I think that one reason Arendt continues to fascinate us is that she was, if ever there was one, a teacher who embodied the spirit of Socrates. Like him, she never forgot that she was a human being among a plurality of human beings who share a common world, all of whom are potentially free, even from the coercion of truth. To use an old-fashioned word, this constituted her "dignity," and it goes almost without saying that she tried to foster that same freedom from coercion, of being coerced or exercising coercion, in her students.*

At this point, I am tempted to consider the controversiality of Arendt's thought, not because, as has been alleged, she held eccentric opinions and marshaled or even manipulated evidence in support of them, but because in considering the opinions of others, she proceeded to argue, with them and with herself, in order to form her own distinct opinions and convictions. That was of the utmost importance to her as a political thinker and an educator, the condition sine qua non of political responsibility. Apart from conviction, political action is futile and meaningless, giving rise to a version of what Kant saw as the "haphazard melancholy" of human affairs in which the sense of a common world comes undone. But I don't want this letter, the main purpose of which has been to provide a sense of the pleasure that thinking about Arendt has afforded us, to turn into a little essay! As we continue this correspondence, I promise to respond to what you wrote about the importance today of recovering a common world and about the roles played by an "enlarged mentality" and "exemplarity" in doing what the tradition, the handing down of the past from generation to generation, conspicuously failed to do in the twentieth century. There is certainly much more to say about the experience of studying with

Arendt, especially about that experience as a transition from private to public life, about becoming willing and fit to take one's place in a common world. My hope is that our letters will show that adults continue to learn from one another, as you and I in fact have done. But it may not be prudent to call that "adult education," for as Arendt remarks in "The Crisis in Education": "Education can play no part in politics. . . . Whoever wants to educate adults really wants to act as their guardian and prevent them from political activity."

There is only one minor quibble I have with what you wrote in regard to the first course we took with her, which you called "Politics in the Twentieth Century." It was, I think, called "Political Experience in the Twentieth Century," and that has some significance because, in it, if you remember, we read poetry, fiction, memoirs, and biographies but not a single work of political theory. Here again, it is a question of what political "experience" means to Arendt, a question of what she called the "underlying phenomenal reality" of freedom and justice, which, in terms of theories that deal with a reality underlying appearances, is virtually a contradiction in terms. I will close by simply noting that, for me, the primary benefit of having studied with Arendt is what I would like to call, at least for now, "the peculiar pleasure of particularity."

Do you think we can recapture in this correspondence the quality of our conversations, which have been so very meaningful to me?

With love,
Jerry

6.27.00
Dear Jerry
Your letter of June 11 has provoked a cluster of ideas in me, and I'm going to spin some of them out here. But first I want to say two things about this letter-writing. The first is funny: You and I may find ourselves able to carry on our conversation in writing, but it is important to acknowledge that the meeting we

had last weekend to talk over the letter-writing—not to mention three or four hours of other things—before I went off to catch a train to Philadelphia saying, "I'll write to you soon," is part of the letter-writing. Our friendship is so much about presence and talking; we always have—it can be said in retrospect—several guiding themes or questions in our conversations, but the manner is free associational and depends, I think, so much on being there. This letter, like my first one, is a precipitant of a talk.

While we are experimenting with having our conversation in writing, I think we should also acknowledge that this alteration in mode comes after a long period in which the conversation changed for other reasons. I have been thinking historically about it and considering how this history shows the education our conversation has been for us.

After we got to know each other in Hannah Arendt's last seminars, our conversation was all about her and her work. A kind of ongoing memorial service, I think, as we both felt so bereft when she died, so without our compass. I was so impressed that you could express this publicly, at the official memorial, with such composure and dignity, because I could only talk privately and write—to this day, I cannot speak about her publicly without finding myself right back in tearful, raw mourning. Then, while I was writing the biography, remember, we talked often about different periods and phases in her lifework, exploring the parts of it that had been unknown to us while she was alive. I recall long conversations about her relationship with Heidegger, personally—after Hans Jonas told me about her youthful affair—and philosophically; about her doctoral dissertation and St. Augustine; about her correspondence with Jaspers. That was when we first became aware that there was an extraordinary trove of uncollected short publications and unpublished things—all the things that you are now editing. Interspersed throughout those conversations of vie et oeuvre were those about how she might have viewed this or that political event as the years went on.

Of all those conversations, the one that went on longest—it was three or four years in the early 1980s—and was the most challenging to us had to do with the "what might have been" of the unfinished Judgment *manuscript, which Mary McCarthy then edited. The piece I wrote about* The Life of the Mind *(Political Theory, 1982) was really worked out in the early stages of that conversation—and then we both found that approach too schematic and systematic. I have always been more of a theorizer than you; or, to put that the other way around, you have always been more Socratic than I am. Thus, it is hard for you to write, to come to rest in a statement, whereas it is hard for me to resist making order and formulation out of disparate strands and paths of thinking.*

We hit this difference between us right out of the gate in this letter-writing—and on the territory of Judging, *too. You had trouble responding to my opening letter because it was too formulated. It felt to you like I was on my way to delineating Hannah Arendt's theory of education and that I was concerned with her method of theory-making. In fact, I agree with you completely that she had no such thing as a theory of education and that she did not really make theories of anything. There is no Arendtian theory or any Arendtism. But she did have characteristic ways of thinking, which involved concepts or distinctions she had clarified and historical elements and existentials that she had identified as fundamental; and she had characteristic ways of judging. These make it possible to imagine what she might have thought of something or how she might have judged something—the kind of imagining we did at length over the unfinished* Judging *volume. It was characteristic of her ways of thinking that she disparaged theory and had no interest in the deductive judging of science.*

I have always felt that the difference in our thinking styles is crucial to how our conversation has been educational to us. I don't remember that we have ever—in thirty-two years!—had a conversation about Hannah Arendt or her work end in a disagreement, although we have often (as in the case of your reaction to my letter) had to work our way carefully through the differences produced by our differences until the common understanding emerged. But, on the other hand, it is the case that after about 1985, when I first went into psychoanalytic training in New Haven and started work on my biography of Anna Freud, our conversation shifted. It is almost as though we became a threesome: you, me of the old days, and me of this new way of thinking, with whom you did not feel very comfortable. The new me was speaking a different language—and, further, a language that we both knew Hannah Arendt had viewed with the utmost distrust. However, I have never felt at odds with myself or split internally. As for me, the ways of thinking we encountered in Hannah Arendt, which were Hannah Arendt and which we each—each in our own way—took into our ways of thinking, were not so different from those of the psychoanalysts I have learned most from, starting with Freud. But it has taken quite a time for this internal conversation of mine to be in our conversation familiarly.

One of the things that Arendt and Freud had most deeply in common—and this I want to note to speak right to your "peculiar pleasure of particularity"—was their attitude, starting in their youths, toward theory. Freud had had to overcome his bent toward theory and speculation—something he did not accomplish to the full but something he accomplished to a rare degree. He was very fond of telling about how, when he was in his late twenties and visiting in Charcot's Paris clinic, the young visitors from abroad, all trained in German academic physiology, kept questioning Charcot about his clinical work because it contradicted the theories that they took for granted. Charcot, not fazed, unfurled an aphorism that stunned Freud: La theorie c'est bon, mais cela n'empeche pas d'exister—Theory is fine, but it doesn't prevent what exists. As Freud noted, astutely, Charcot was not just insisting that clinical facts should come first and theory (or revision of theory) follow, although he believed this and was masterful at clinical description and fact-collecting. He was a phenomenologist, in the best sense of the word. But, much more radically, Charcot had said that there was something that could not be denied by theory. What exists will, like a secret, come out, helped by means other than theory—by observation, intuition, experiencing fully, receptively. (And, I would add, by human caring about what exists.) That is what Arendt believed, too, and she was a superb observer, taking pleasure in the particulars.

Hannah Arendt never made any study of Freud, so she could speak about him and psychoanalysis in charming ignorance— sometimes sad ignorance, it seemed to me, as she was, I think, quite frightened of mental illness, as is not surprising in some- one whose father died when she was a child of paretic syphilis—that is, he died quite insane. But her distrust was also of a piece with her most characteristic way of thinking about the distinction between the private realm and the public realm—which, although it does not constitute a theory, is cer- tainly a key distinction. As we were saying when we met in New York last weekend, she was a sexual conservative, in a very specific sense: not conservative morally, not puritanical, but conservative in her opinion that sexual matters should exist entirely in the private sphere. What she most deeply held against psychoanalysis, I think, and I think we agree about this, was that people who practiced it or submitted to it became self- preoccupied to the point of losing their sense of public things, and, worse, psychoanalysts took it for granted that discussion of private matters—of sexuality, of fantasy—in public was a good thing, a liberating thing. She felt just the opposite: that making the private public destroyed the private as a place and a mode of refuge, restoration, re-creation. It contributed to that awful realm she called "the social," which she saw as taking over the globe like a weed.

I can very well imagine that had I reached adulthood in a to- talitarian state in which privacy had disappeared, in which there was not an inch of it to protect you from, not "the state," but "the movement," the antistate (or antipolitical, antipublic) as well as antiprivacy forces of "everything is possible," I might be much more sympathetic to the way Hannah Arendt drew her distinction. But I do find this the most troubling feature of her work. It is like a defense mechanism that has great value except when it ceases to be a defense mechanism and becomes an of- fense mechanism. Maybe it is too close to being a theory or an ingredient of ideology, an Arendtism.

Well, I could go on, but let me stop here and send this to you. More would be too much, as though we had forgotten to get up from a conversation and take a walk, have a drink, fix dinner.

Love,
Elisabeth

July 7, 2000
Dear Elisabeth,
    Your fine letter of June 27 brings up a number of topics to which I want to respond, as well as some questions that I want to ask. One of the things it makes most clear is the distinction between conversing and letter-writing. As I read your letter, I wanted to stop and say something to you, to interject an opinion here or ask a question there. But as you say, that depends on the presence of the other. Our effort to approximate our ongoing conversation in writing, therefore, will necessarily be less immediate and more reflective, holding the other present in imagination, to be sure, and thinking with the other but following a train of thought without the give-and-take of actual talk. That also sheds light on what Arendt meant by thinking as an "internal dialogue" and on what she found so right about Aristotle's definition of the true friend as "another self," a "conscience," as we might say today, or something like that.
    Your letter, because of the holiday, arrived only after July 4. The television showed a few splendid pictures of tall ships (replicas of old ships) in New York harbor, but each one lasted barely a second and was followed by an endless commentary, summed up in "umbrella" remarks from the president, all woefully inadequate and insubstantial compared to the photographs themselves. Today, public speech lacks not only profundity, for which only rarely in history has it shown much need, but pungency and even significance. Publicly expressed convictions change so rapidly that they can hardly be called "convictions," and a public realm all but devoid of conviction brings to mind Yeats's lines from "The Second Coming":

The best lack all conviction, while the worst
Are full of passionate intensity.

*On the other hand, it was of the twentieth century, now past,
that it might be said, "The blood-dimmed tide is loosed" and
"The ceremony of innocence is drowned," as Yeats wrote in the
same poem. I suppose we should be grateful that even among
"the worst," the "intensity" of public discourse seems largely
feigned today. Nevertheless, the present apathy of the people toward what concerns them in common is worrisome, and I wonder if education can—or to what extent it can—do anything
about it. Ever more elaborate, essentially democratic public
spectacles are produced but for eyes that have ceased to be con-
duits to the mind. They seem to come with a warning: "Don't
think about this!" And except on a strictly private, critical level,
we do not. It is not the case that spectacles are needed as a sop
to distract an already acquiescent mass society, but rather that
they seem, even from their producers' point of view, to be nothing but entertainment, lacking any common meaning at all. I
know that the education we received from Arendt has prompted
this train of thought, and I would like to think that it could still
awaken others.*

*The aphorism you quote from Charcot—"Theory is fine, but
it doesn't impede existence"—resonates in more ways than one.
I have no doubt that the process of psychoanalysis, perhaps especially with your own distinctively articulated contribution of
"caring" added to observation and intuition, may bring forth
what is hidden or repressed in individuals undergoing it and that
that liberating effect somehow adjusts those individuals to the
world and enables them to live more satisfying lives. Perhaps
private "adjustment" is not exactly what Arendt had in mind
when she spoke of public "orientation" to the world, but I don't
suppose that she had any such doubt either, however much she
may have inveighed against the "language" of psychoanalysis.
When we were her students, I believe we felt that Arendt both
exemplified and spelled out the conditions of a decent world,
and later we wondered why so many people resist, really seem*

not to want such a world. The first question I want to ask you is: Has that anything to do with your interest in psychoanalysis? You are quite right that I am not "comfortable" with psychoanalytic thought (I'm sure you have a psychological explanation for that!), yet increasingly, perhaps especially, since your last letter, I feel that, for you, psychoanalysis may be a form of action, especially in America, which seems, to put it mildly, disillusioned with almost all forms of political action. But as for the "language" of psychoanalysis, I would place a somewhat different emphasis from yours on Arendt's reasons for believing that sexual matters, and the entire realm of the intimate, are unfit *to appear in public. Which is to say that I think her insistence on the preservation of privacy as a realm of human existence, without which existence would not be human, along with its relation to education—all of which you recognize—may warrant further questioning.*

How is privacy to be preserved? First of all, for Arendt, in the institution of private property, but the past three centuries have constituted an age of increasing expropriation. If our bodies are our last inviolable "property," where does one draw the line? Arendt was a woman and was glad to appear as one but not as a feminist. That is very different from responding as a Jew when being attacked as a Jew, which Arendt of course did do, but the two have been confused. Her point, I think, is that publicly, every one of us appears as a unique and equally free person, whether male or female, rich or poor, Jew or Gentile, gay or straight, black or white, but never as a specimen *of gender, class, religion, sexual orientation, or, perhaps most challenging because most visible, race. Politics does not deny but transcends what each one of us is in private. In other words, the private and the public are distinct but interdependent realms of human plurality, and that is a frequently overlooked sense in which plurality is the essential condition of political life as Arendt conceives it. As you suggest at the end of your letter, that interdependence is precisely what totalitarianism destroyed, by* destroying both realms. *If, to a great extent, world alienation, the opposite of belonging to a world held in common, arises from private otherness, and if politics begins where world alienation ends, what can education, as an intermediate process, do to provide an introduction into the world? That's my second question.*

But to revert to Charcot's epigram: In a public sense, the human catastrophes of the twentieth century demonstrate that theory in the guise of ideology can and did impede tout court the existence of countless men, women, and children. That threat, as a threat to the entire world, is now diminished. But the growing numbers of uprooted, homeless, and stateless people throughout the world, to which the Nazi ideology of naturally determined inferior races and the Stalinist ideology of historically determined dying classes supplied "answers," remain today as a political problem of the first order. Would you agree that the psychoanalytic process is unlikely to resolve that problem, not only because of the vast numbers involved, but also because politics, in Arendt's sense, first and foremost, is not about caring for people but for the world? That is an important distinction for her: The failure of the French Revolution as a social rather than a political phenomenon lay precisely in its "care" for les malheureux, who had no public voice, and resulted in transforming them into les enragés, enraged at the world, thereby not alleviating but increasing their misery. That's a political consideration, and it is a recurrent theme throughout Arendt's work. Of course, it does not detract from the individual benefits of psychoanalysis, but on the other hand, how exactly did Arendt as a teacher prepare the ground for the political resolution of the problem of "superfluous" peoples?*

Her basic teaching, the source of everything that followed, was (and I think we agree on this) the unprecedented event of totalitarianism. Its essential phenomena, the "laboratories" of slave labor and extermination camps, succeeded in rendering even free human beings superfluous by reducing them to the status of conditioned animals. The dynamism of totalitarian movements would have, if those movements had not been stopped, laid waste incalculable portions of the world. This is a huge topic, and it is not necessary here, to you of all people, to go into it in *more detail*. What I want to stress is that Arendt tried to make clear to her students (and this was, I think, what motivated every course she gave, whether "Philosophy and Politics," "Ancient Political Thought," "Modern Political Thought," "Kant's Critique of Judgment," and so on) that totalitarianism occurred right in the heart of Western civilization, that it was not imported into it from the outside, "not from the moon," as she used to say, or from anywhere else. Above all, she wanted her students to realize that the occurrence of totalitarianism in the twentieth century exploded the categories of traditional political thought, a tradition that began with Plato, who, in an effort to cope with the crisis of Athenian politics following the Peloponnesian War, introduced the category of "making," of constructing a polity according to a preconceived pattern. Free action, the power generated by a plurality of human beings acting "in concert" and out of conviction, whose source lies not in any theory but in pretheoretical political experience, was thereafter displaced, fatefully, from political thought. By definition, old categories are not and never can be equipped to deal with something entirely new, and in a sense, that is borne out in the history of political thought. Hobbes's, Locke's, and Rousseau's variations on the category of "the state of nature," for instance, or the changes Marx rang on the Hegelian category of "world history," account for genuine political changes occurring in their worlds. But something much more radical was in question for Arendt: There was no longer the possibility of redefining traditional categories, as if she were dealing with an emergency and at the same time was intent on maintaining, in a modified fashion, the traditional structure of political thought. On the contrary, it was the advent of totalitarianism that sent Arendt back to free action, the source of political experience; for although totalitarianism did not succeed in destroying the world, it made clear that our entire tradition, not only of political but of moral and legal thought as well, of religion and authority in general, had come to an end. There may be a faint echo of this insight in postmodern thought, but for Arendt, this was not an academic but a factual matter, a matter, as she said, of "the history of our world."

Reflecting later on the moment in 1943 when she first learned about Auschwitz, Arendt said: "This ought not to have happened." *That is no purely moral "ought," I think, but rather as strong a statement as possible that there was something wrong with the* world *in which Auschwitz could and did happen. And yet, and this is where things get a bit complicated, Arendt's attempt to understand totalitarianism seeks reconciliation, not, certainly, to totalitarian crimes, but to the world in which they came to pass. She went about this by telling her students a strange and terrible story the significance of which lies entirely in the* present, *and she was fully aware that her "method," a matter she was always loath to discuss, went against the grain not only of political and social scientists, but also (and this was far more important to her) of those reporters, historians, and poets who, in their own distinct ways, seek to preserve in or out of time what they record and imagine. Even before she wrote* The Origins of Totalitarianism, *Arendt spoke of the desperate need to tell the "real story of the Nazi-constructed hell"*: *"Not only because these facts have changed and poisoned the very air we breathe, not only because they now inhabit our dreams at night and permeate our thoughts during the day—but also because they have become the basic experience and the basic misery of our times. Only from this foundation, on which a new knowledge of man will rest, can our new insights, our new memories, our new deeds, take their point of departure." That says, I think, all that can be said about becoming reconciled, not to totalitarianism, but to the world that gave birth to it, a world made by human beings and that only human beings can change. But in that there is much more at stake than our victory in World War II.*

And this brings me to my last question, for this has gone on long enough, although it also seems scarcely to have begun. Faced with useless categories of understanding, Arendt began anew by making distinctions, by the time-honored distinguo, *which, since Aristotle, has been the hallmark of many great thinkers who have set out to understand what previously had not been understood. A is not B, totalitarianism is not tyranny, force is not power, action is not work, work is not labor, the pri-*

vate is not public, the social is neither private nor public; think-ing is not willing, willing is not judging, sympathy is not com-passion, and compassion is not empathy ("I" am not "Thou"). These and many other of her distinctions, although obvious to her, are difficult to grasp by anyone, including, of course, most of her students, who are accustomed to a way of thinking that tends to blur distinctions, especially unusual ones. I am con-vinced that Arendt intended her teaching to be practical. Was it?

Love,
Jerry

July 22, 2000
Dear Jerry,
   The letter you started on July 7 came in with the same post that took out to DU magazine in Switzerland that piece on Han-nah Arendt's place in American intellectual life, which we dis-cussed the last time I saw you in New York. It contains this paragraph:

> In *The Origins of Totalitarianism*, Arendt first articulated her most fundamental thought—as an alarm, a dire warning. She claimed that politics—the speaking and acting of citizens in a public space, variously secured by different forms of govern-ment and law—only appears under certain historical condi-tions, and can disappear. Further, a form of government can come about that has the unprecedented and hideously contra-dictory consequence of making politics disappear *completely*. Totalitarianism, a novelty, neither a tyranny nor a one-party dictatorship, is the radical elimination of politics brought about by methodically eliminating the very humanity of, first, selected groups and eventually any group, by making humans superflu-ous as human beings.

This is, as you so rightly said, the core content of her teaching; this is what she wanted her students, us—and her readers—to grasp. And she wanted to show the consequence for thinking of finding out not only that the European intellectual tradition has no concepts for this novelty, but that the tradition was implicated in this novelty, which grew up on the very ground of the tradition.

The consequence for thinking is that the tradition is at an end and any new thinking must go forward without it. It must go forward, first, by going back historically to understand how the tradition's concepts came to be so useless for our world and how the tradition itself became implicated in horrors. So every one of her essays and books begins with a historical tour in the service of the new thinking—thus all the distinction-making that we have been remarking again and again, her educational practice. As her student, I think that the attention she gave to historical preparatories impressed me as strongly as anything; and it was here that I felt—to address the last question in your letter—that she absolutely thought she was being practical. She was like an excavator, getting the land cleared and ready, freeing thinking of customary ways, habits, rule-boundedness, uselessness.

And new thinking must go forward, second, by both envisioning and making an effort to live in what you called—and it is just the right phrase—"a decent world." Not a utopia, not a palace of ideology, not an arena for heroics, not a moral dictation, but a decent world. In Hannah Arendt's terms, I think this meant a world in which totalitarianism is not possible, in which the elements of totalitarianism—present in all modern mass societies—could never crystallize. In the preface to the first edition of Origins, she dramatically juxtaposed totalitarianism and freedom, using the "free world" rhetoric of the 1950s and long afterward, but she really meant by "a free world," I think, what you have captured with that phrase "a decent world."

Why would anyone not want a decent world? That question does propel anybody who works as a psychoanalyst, as you guessed. What we specialize in studying is the inability of people to want—and insist upon, working for it materially or spiritually—a decent world; this is the political corollary of their inability to want love and work that are satisfying and growth-promoting. Why don't they want what is in their best interests *and in the best interests of all? If the question is put the other way around, it is even more awful: Why do people want an indecent world?—for example, one in which they can order cattle car loads of people to their deaths in a camp? ... The matter comes up clearly if you consider the (totally naive) Christian instruction "Love your neighbor as you love yourself" and then ask: What about people who do not love themselves? How are they to love their neighbors? ... I think Hannah Arendt made a profound step when she rejected her first understanding, expressed in the last section of* Origins, *that evil is radical and began to think about "the banality of evil"—neither something devilish in-born in people nor something psychopathological in the psychiatric sense, but something banal, nonradical, in people. She set such a challenge to think about this—and that, of course, is one reason why it is so sad not to have her own reflections from the unfinished* Judging.

Speaking in the psychoanalytic language makes me want to respond to another part of your letter—and come back to the topic of education. You suggested that the way I practice psychoanalysis may be a form of action in today's world, in a world that "seems, to put it mildly, disillusioned with almost all forms of political action." (Disillusionment with action, which is, thank God, not the same as embracing a form of government that makes action impossible, relieves you of even considering it for yourself or others.) Yes, and psychoanalysis is (or can be) a practice concerned precisely with disillusionment, which is another way of describing self-hatred or lack of self-love. But more, I think of my practice as a form of education, and I think of myself as an educator who moved out of a classroom and into a consulting room. Of course, most psychoanalysts, hearing that, would distrust my clinical qualifications, assuming that I had not learned the basic lesson that psychoanalysis is not supposed to be, as they say, "didactic." You do not educate your patients. But this injunction usually reflects a very narrow concept of education as an imparting of information (scientific education) or prescription and prohibition (moral education). When I think of psychoanalysis as educational, I am thinking of the analyst/patient relationship in terms of the root of "education." That is, I reflect in the way Hannah Arendt taught me, looking into the words, "unfreezing the concepts," as she put it. E-ducere is to draw out. I draw my patients out (and they draw me out).

But since I always stumble after the first step in Latin, because I did not have one of those amazing Gymnasium formal educations, I go to Greek, which I could share with Hannah Arendt so pleasurably, for thinking further about "education" and what it has meant and means and could mean. As you know, there are two basic word clusters in Greek for "education": the one around the noun paideia, *which focuses on the child* (pais) *who is educated or encultured; and the older one around the verb* trepho, *which focuses on raising, rearing, tending, cherishing, often analogizing children and plants and animals. The Greek noun for "education" that is derived from the verb* trepho *is trophe, and this has all kinds of associations to feeding and nursing. In both the word clusters, but particularly in the second, older one (woven all through the agricultural metaphors in the Homeric epics), the idea is to help children grow, to garden them, not to put knowledge in them or tell them what to do. But, of course, part of helping them grow is helping them become at home in the world, enter into the common world. In the Platonic dialogues, you find the wonderful compound* koinotrophike *for a system of public education—it literally means education in common (which also means into what is held in common—like "common sense").*

I draw out of my patients what they know about themselves and then, much more slowly, what they do not know about themselves, what resides in their unconscious minds. The process releases them for growth, for getting past whatever held up or stopped their growth, for maturing. (The Greek verb for healing, therapeuein, *is related to* trepho.) *The technique is less active than Socratic questioning, but the goal is similar. The goal as I understand it is to help the patient realize that he or she has had experiences, now represented in conscious stories and unconscious stories, of disappointed love and that these pro-*

foundly shape present experience and the capacity to love and be loved—and thence to work, to labor, or to act, to think, to will, or to judge, all of the human activities. Most importantly and intimately, the patient's caretaking loved ones have disappointed the expectation to be loved. Experiences of fulfillment of the expectation to be loved or of disappointment set the foundations in people for their later feelings of being at home in the world or being alienated from and in the world—feelings that develop around events in the world.

Another way to describe the worldless self-hating I was writing about before is to say it is "educating" yourself in grievance, tending to and nourishing only your disappointment in people and the world. Educators have to counter, to cultivate, this kind of self-education—this perversion of education; so they have to love well, give the student a relationship to be in, a connection to the world. There is no such person as a self-hating educator; it's a contradiction in emotions. (Recently, I read an article that contained a statement of Goethe's to the effect that it was not the most brilliant teachers who had had the greatest influence on him, but those who loved him the most. But imagine the power of the teacher who is both brilliant and loving!)

To me, the connection between the elemental human experiences of fulfillment or disappointment in love and the lesson that Hannah Arendt set out to teach, which we agree was the core of her teaching, is in her judgment about Auschwitz: "This ought not to have happened." There is something wrong with the world in which Auschwitz could and did happen. A person deeply disturbed in the capacity to love, self-hating, does not feel: "This ought not to have happened." At an extreme, in the present historical moment, a self-hating person will announce: "Those who say this did happen are lying, they are in a conspiracy to blame the German people," etc. etc.—the Holocaust deniers. At less of an extreme: "So what? Who cares? It was a long time ago." That is disillusionment and indifference.

Funny, having written along on this all evening, and being now quite tired, I feel this enormous desire to talk with you!

That's in part because when we talk, it doesn't matter whether I have been particularly coherent or put things in a way I want to stand by and not amend in the next conversation, refine, rework. I don't want to wake up tomorrow and read this through and find myself thinking, Oh, for heaven's sake, that is so superficial, or such a repetition of things you've said before, or whatever. In our conversations, I don't ever criticize myself. So it's safer, and I am more drawn out, educated, than when I am alone and only imagining you, or being aware that this is WRITING, *which has a whole burden of public meaning to it.*

Well, enough. It is quite remarkable, isn't it, that thirty years later, we are still thinking through the things Hannah Arendt challenged us to think about. She was quite a force—like the force of the Taoist sages, doing nothing to keep their followers except set an example of great constancy. Decency.

Love,
Elisabeth

August 1, 2000
Dear Elisabeth,
When your letter of July 22 arrived, I was finishing another article, so a few days have passed before finding time to respond. But while working on that other piece, I was thinking about what you had written, and I believe we may want to retain some of that for future conversations. For instance, to pursue here a discussion of what you wrote about the tradition being "implicated" in the advent of totalitarianism, which seems to me an important but extremely complex question, would, I think, take us too far afield. Also, what you said about self-hatred being an element in the rise of totalitarian movements—well, doesn't that diminish the distinctness of the world in which those movements arose, the actual conditions in Germany and Russia between the wars? In the latter case, our difference hinges on the introduction of general psychological principles into contingent political matters, a difference that will surprise neither of us! But I think both of these questions would

be better thrashed out viva voce, and perhaps we will do that when you come here in ten days' time. As always, I greatly look forward to your visit! I have also been thinking more generally about the letters we have exchanged to date, and perhaps a good way to begin this one would be to comment on what seem to me some of their salient points.

The first thing I want to say is that I feel torn between talking about the substance of what we learned from Arendt and how she imparted it, both of which are relevant to our contribution to a book on Hannah Arendt and education. The difficulty is that when we reflect on what we learned from her, the process of how she educated us tends to become eclipsed by political considerations. Arendt never taught her own opinions, but she instilled in us the ability to form our own opinions impartially. An impartial opinion is the condition of a responsible conviction, the political importance of which I mentioned in my first letter. In that sense, the transmission of knowledge was not uppermost in her mind, at least not in graduate school, which is where we studied with her. Her own knowledge was vast and, of course, she did impart some of it, but what really mattered to her was too political, too rooted in her own experience, too "existential" to be transmitted pedagogically—all of which illustrates her point that politics is not a matter of instruction. I want to add, however, that the palpable shadow of her knowledge served to protect us, her students, from illusions, and in this singular way, she exemplified the authority of the teacher, which she found vanishing from modern theories and contemporary practices of education.

In your first letter, you mentioned almost en passant that Arendt's understanding of education "was certainly not the same thing as teaching or instructing in skills." That is true, and there is a sense in which it cuts to the heart of at least part of what we have been writing about in these letters. Education (from educare, to bring up, which itself derives from educere), and particularly primary and secondary education, was not originally conceived as a specialized "training," but rather as the development of potentialities innate in human nature. Every child has distinct potentialities, of course; and for Arendt, one of the main purposes of education is the development of the uniqueness of the person each child is in the process of "becoming." But today, millions of kids are being trained—that is, ever more elaborately prepared—to have their "aptitudes" determined, not by their development as individuals, but by the S.A.T. The measure of their success on that standardized test is viewed as the key to mastering the world in which they will live. That is one way of seeing what Arendt means by instruction "in the art of living," to which she sharply contrasts her understanding of education as teaching "children what the world is like." "The Crisis in Education," an eloquent, trenchant, but to me somewhat problematic essay, makes clear that the reason for introducing a child into the world is that he or she can come to "love the world enough to assume responsibility for it and by the same token save it from that ruin which, except for renewal, except for the coming of the new and young, would be inevitable." That essay unequivocally states the distinction between "the realm of education," in which the principles of authority and tradition are essential, and the actual "world that is neither structured by authority nor held together by tradition." In other words, what is valid in early education is no longer valid in political or adult life in general. A corollary of her distinction is that in order to develop a sense of responsibility for the world, children must, since they are newcomers to an old world, "turn toward the past." Elsewhere, Arendt says that all humanistic education deals with the past, which we know from our own experience as her students and from which follows the "historical tour" you mentioned with which she began her courses and much of her writing. Thus, although she was not a conventional historian—she once told me she didn't know "what history is"—there is a historical dimension to her thought, which is nowhere more evident than in her political and philosophical concern with the historical development of the concept of history itself.

But in your first letter, you also quoted from a different essay, "The Crisis in Culture," which is not about the education of

children. I want to cite the full quotation: "The thread of tradition is broken, and we must discover the past for ourselves—
that is, read its authors as though nobody had ever read them
before." This is still dealing with the past but differently. What
she did, and endeavored to teach us to do in graduate school,
was to retrieve the past, not as a historical whole handed down
by tradition, but rather by salvaging its "rich and strange" fragments from the destruction of time. This is not child's play or
child's work, but it nevertheless seems discordant with her emphasis on tradition and authority in primary and secondary education. It may well be that one has to know the tradition, as
Arendt did, before realizing the significance of its discontinuity,
which she herself thematized. But that is what I find problematic in the essay on the "crisis" in education, insofar as it suggests a view of tutelage that is at odds with her own experience
of the world. Be that as it may, Arendt does not go into the techniques of how children can be educated as she thinks they ought
to be, of how interest in a broken tradition can be renewed, and
certainly I am not equipped to do that. I hope other contributors to this volume, colleagues who are professionally involved
with the process of education, will deal with that matter, and I
look forward to reading what they have to say.

At this point, let me try to address the question of what we,
who were not children, learned from Arendt and of how she introduced us into the world by teaching us, largely by her own
example, to retrieve its past. The point of that was, I think, to
develop in us an ability to respond without prejudice to the
great plurality of men and women who share the world, thereby
helping to sustain the common world that totalitarianism
sought to destroy. Such responsibility, although not a matter of
knowledge, requires thought. Arendt did not stuff our heads
with knowledge but taught us to "think"; and in her sense of the
word, that was practical insofar as the habit of thinking is, as
she said, "among the conditions that make men abstain from
evil-doing." To have lost sight of a common world is one way to
speak of "world alienation" or, if you prefer, of worldlessness,
Weltlosigkeit, world loss. Arendt educated us to take part in a

possible and pleasant exercise of common sense—which she understood as the sense both of community and communication, the condition of a common world—by informing our vision through the vision of others, both living and dead. To partake of another's vision is to enlarge one's own mentality, as we've said, and I want to give an example of what that means to me.

Before me on my desk is a reproduction of Piero della Francesca's Resurrezione, *but of course the reproduction is only a reminder of the remarkably well-preserved original. The original fresco is in the Pinacoteca Comunale in Sansepolcro, where Piero was born, a small town in the center of the Italian peninsula, not far from Florence and near Arezzo. Aldous Huxley called the* Resurrezione *the "best" and "greatest" painting in the world, and so it seems to me, though not only or chiefly for the art historical reasons he offers, which are both subtle and accurate. It is unlike any other depiction of the Resurrection I know, all of which portray the risen Christ overwhelming the soldiers guarding the tomb with a spiritual, transcendent power immeasurably greater than their temporal force. Here the soldiers before the tomb are asleep, sound asleep ("the very essence of sleep," as an Italian friend once put it); one of them is supposedly a self-portrait of the painter, which is meaningful whether or not it is true. Here the power of the Christ is divorced from any relationship with force. His left leg is bent atop the tomb, as if caught at the moment of rising, but there is no sense of motion. He faces full forward, in the direct center of the painting, his eyes staring into yours. If you stare back, they transfix you, and then it may happen that they speak to you, saying, "Wake up, wake up." The longer you stand in front of this painting, the more you realize that you are or have been asleep, like any one of the soldiers in the foreground—and thus you "enter" the painting. If you remain there long enough, before but also in the world of the painting, you may begin to slough off sleep, and that for me was an experience of intense pleasure. Nor can I doubt that Piero intended to afford that pleasure, though of course I cannot prove it. This shared vision for me has nothing to do with religious authority, but it has, I believe, enlarged my mind and made me aware, even if only intermittently, of the* depth *of the common world. I never spoke to Arendt about this painting or about Piero. And although she did not "prepare" me for it, apart from having studied with her I would never have enjoyed this particular introduction into a world that I cannot and have no will to master.*

This experience is an example of what I meant earlier by "the peculiar pleasure of particularity," which now strikes me as less "peculiar," which after all is tautologous, than a difficult and profound pleasure. And I think it must be akin to what you meant when you wrote that a decent world, a world in which we know that we are guests and can become friends, is one in which totalitarianism could not occur. It is a world that is not barbarous, and the sense of belonging to it enhances life. But the hardest part of what Arendt sought to make us understand is that such a world is worth more than life.

Arendt thought that every human being is unique and born for freedom. I sometimes wonder if that is true, but I have no doubt that the main reason you and I are still eager to talk about her and think about what she said to us, after more than thirty years, is that she herself appeared to us as someone who was unique and free. And here I really do mean what she said *rather than what she wrote, for you and I were privileged to hear her speak, to listen to her voice. Today, it is not the public mask of the famous woman that is between us in our ongoing conversation, but the "naked thisness," as she put it late in her life, the "identifiable but not definable" person who continues to sound through—*personare—*the mask that is no longer visible.*

On Arendt's fiftieth birthday, Karl Jaspers wrote to his former student: "What a life you have led, a life given to you and earned by you with a steadfastness that has mastered the evil, the horror that has come from without and ground so many others down." That is beautifully said and seems almost exactly right. But to "master" that evil, Arendt had to judge for herself not only those who enacted it, but those who suffered it; and in doing so, she found that what ground them all down did not primarily come "from without." That is an instance of the diffi-

cult judgment she practiced, the other side or mental equivalent of action, neither of which can be taught and both of which are guided by examples. And examples, unlike human lives, are not infected with mortality.

We first studied with Arendt in 1968, a year of student unrest, of violent demonstrations against the war in Vietnam, and of continuous protests against the dreary and, so it seemed, deathly pallor cast over the entire political realm, especially after the King and Kennedy assassinations. In that atmosphere, Arendt was immensely popular—indeed, an inspiration—since the youth of those days found not in themselves but in The Human Condition *and* On Revolution *the possibility of a new beginning. If our initial attraction to Arendt was quixotic, there was nothing quixotic about the Arendt we came to know as a teacher. For this theorist of action, teaching itself was an unrehearsed performance, especially in the give-and-take, what she herself called the "free-for-all," of the seminar, where she asked her students real rather than rhetorical questions and responded, usually in entirely unexpected ways, to theirs. What impressed me was her nervousness, which was not irritation but agitation. It diminished when she spoke but was essentially different from the stage fright that at times afflicts a great actor before the play begins. It was more a constant state of mind, a constant impatience to get going, the result of the curious fact that she did not seem to experience inertia. Unlike most of us, who seek a starting point, a motive, a source of strength and movement in a situation, Arendt appeared as a beginning. Thus, her tangible agitation sheds considerable light on the words of St. Augustine that resonate throughout her work: "Initium ergo ut esset, creatus est homo" ("That there be a beginning, man was created"), not created to begin something with a predetermined end in view, but simply to be a beginning. That is the heart not so much of what she taught but thought about action and judgment, as well as about plurality as the sole condition of a public life in which every human individual can actualize his or her potential freedom and uniqueness. Although her attitude toward academia was critical, for the sake of this spontaneous performance, in which she exemplified the meaning that Augustine's words exemplified for her, she did not quit it, as Nietzsche had, to live in isolation and think in solitude. In her seminar, every participant was a "citizen," called upon to give his or her opinion, to insert him or herself into that miniature polis in order to make it, as she said, "a little better."*

Arendt was convinced that the need to think becomes widespread and urgent, certainly no longer the exclusive experience or sole concern of professional philosophers, in times when the security of the world, of its institutions, and especially of one's own unique place in it, is thrown into jeopardy. It was the inability of the twentieth century to sustain a common world that opened a vista leading to what Arendt saw as the original source of political life: the clearing, in the midst of a plurality of human beings living, acting, and speaking with one another, of a "public realm," which they themselves brought into existence, not for security, but for the sake of their freedom. In the world today, Arendt's conviction of the political urgency of the need to think has struck a deep, responsive chord. Although the Cold War has ended and its antagonists are mollified if not disarmed, it is not at all clear what has begun. There is plenty of evidence that the perplexities that obsessed the twentieth century have not disappeared and that men and women from virtually every corner of the earth who are turning to Arendt are still striving for release from oppression. Less immediate than our own, theirs is a more reflective but still genuinely educational experience. They cannot any longer ask her questions and listen to her answers, but they turn to her as someone they trust to animate their need to think and realize for themselves the meaning of freedom. The lasting lesson of the advent of totalitarianism in the twentieth century is that freedom is fragile and that the common world is provisional and can be destroyed. That does not necessarily mean the destruction of our planet or of our species—the one so tiny and the other so unlikely and seemingly accidental in the universe— but of those public spaces in which alone men and women can appear and be recognized in their uniqueness, which in the last analysis is their equality in freedom. From the point of view of universal nature, in which all entities are generated by automatic processes, and every alteration is either so slow as to be imperceptible or so abrupt as to seem an anomaly in need of explanation, the sensation of actual change is lacking. From that point of view, the appearance of human freedom, the capacity to spontaneously interrupt natural processes, can be regarded only as miraculous. For Arendt, that miracle constitutes human reality, *and the joy of knowing her, either immediately or reflectively, was and is the glimpse she provides into that reality.*

Looking forward to your visit with anticipation of more conversation, and with love,

Jerry

Contributors

Kimberley Curtis
is assistant professor of the practice of political science and women's studies at Duke University. She is the author of *Our Sense of the Real: Aesthetic Experience and Arendtian Politics*. She is currently at work on a book titled *Democratic Contestations: Injury, Reaction, and Resistant Identities in Second Wave Feminism*.

Eduardo Duarte
teaches at the School of Education of Hofstra University. He has published and presented widely in the areas of critical theory and cultural studies. Duarte earned his doctorate in philosophy at the New School for Social Research, where he studied and taught the work of Hannah Arendt.

Peter Euben
is professor of politics at the University of California at Santa Cruz. He is the author of *The Tragedy of Political Theory*, *Corrupting Youth*, and the forthcoming *Platonic Noise* and is the editor of *Greek Tragedy and Political Theory*.

Mordechai Gordon
is assistant professor of the foundations of education at Quinnipiac University. He has published articles on Hannah Arendt in *Educational Theory* and the *Journal of Thought*. He is currently work-

ing on a book with Joe Kincheloe titled *Civics in the Pursuit of Justice: Citizenship Education in the Twenty-first Century.*

Maxine Greene

is professor emeritus of philosophy and education at Teachers College, Columbia University. Her preferred mailing address is 1080 Fifth Avenue, New York, NY 10128. Her primary areas of scholarship are aesthetics, social philosophy, and teacher education.

Jerome Kohn

is trustee of the Hannah Arendt Bluecher Literary Trust and director of the Hannah Arendt Center and Archive at New School University. He is the editor of Arendt's unpublished and uncollected writings, the first volume of which, *Essays in Understanding, 1930–1954,* appeared in 1994. Kohn has written many articles on various aspects of Arendt's thought and, with Larry May, edited *Hannah Arendt: Twenty Years Later* (1996).

Ann Lane

teaches in the Department of American Studies at the University of California at Santa Cruz.

Natasha Levinson

is currently assistant professor of philosophy of education in the Department of Educational Foundations and Special Services at Kent State University. Her main interest right now is to think through the challenges that Arendt's conception of public life poses to moral education within and beyond schools. She is working on her first book, tentatively titled *Learning to Live Together: Hannah Arendt on the Political Foundations of Moral Life.*

Aaron Schutz

is an assistant professor in the Department of Educational Policy and Community Studies at the University of Wisconsin, Milwaukee. His research interests include Hannah Arendt, empowerment, community, democracy in education, and educational standards and assessment. He has published essays in *Teachers College Record, Re-*

view of *Educational Research,* and *American Educational Research Journal.*

Stacy Smith

is assistant professor of education at Bates College in Lewiston, Maine. Her teaching and research interests include connections between political philosophy and democratic education, the growing school choice movement, and issues of cultural pluralism as they impact educational equity. In these areas, she has recently published *Foundational Perspectives in Multicultural Education* and *The Democratic Potential of Charter Schools.*

Elisabeth Young-Bruehl

is a psychoanalyst in private practice in New York City, where she is on the faculty of the Columbia Center for Psychoanalytic Training and Research. She has published a biography of Hannah Arendt (1982), which won several literary prizes, including the Harcourt Award. Her other books include a biography of Anna Freud, *Creative Characters, The Anatomy of Prejudices,* and, most recently, *Cherishment: A Psychology of the Heart.*

Index